WITHDR....

BILINGUALISM IN DEVELOPMENT

Language, Literacy, and Cognition

Bilingualism in Development explores language and cognitive development in bilingual children, focusing on the preschool years. It begins by defining what we mean by bilingualism and what the standards are for considering children to be bilingual. Then it examines how children who learn two languages early in childhood develop both linguistic and non-linguistic cognitive skills.

The author presents her own theoretical framework for cognitive development and language processing, which she uses to interpret the differences between the performance of bilingual and monolingual children. Basing her discussion on research conducted with children of different backgrounds, the author examines the following developmental abilities: language acquisition, metalinguistic ability, literacy, and problem solving. The studies – which used various types of methodology – show that bilingualism has a significant impact on children's ability to selectively attend to relevant information. These findings are related to a number of issues regarding the education and social circumstances of bilingual children. The author considers the implications of her theory for language acquisition and cognitive development of all children.

Ellen Bialystok is Professor of Psychology at York University, Toronto, Canada. She is author of *Spatial Cognition* (with David Olson), *Language Processing in Bilingual Children, Communication Strategies,* and *In Other Words* (with Kenji Hakuta). Dr. Bialystok has received several awards and distinctions, including the Walter Gordon Research Fellowship, Language Learning Distinguished Scholar in Residence, and Pimsleur Award for Foreign Language Education.

BILINGUALISM IN DEVELOPMENT

Language, Literacy, and Cognition

Ellen Bialystok
York University

CAMBRIDGE
UNIVERSITY PRESS

404. 2 B1A
150 197

THE LIBRARY
GUILDFORD COLLEGE
of Further and Higher Education

CAMBRIDGE UNIVERSITY PRESS
Cambridge, New York, Melbourne, Madrid, Cape Town, Singapore, São Paulo

Cambridge University Press
40 West 20th Street, New York, NY 10011–4211, USA
www.cambridge.org
Information on this title:www.cambridge.org/9780521632317

© Ellen Bialystok 2001

This publication is in copyright. Subject to statutory exception
and to the provisions of relevant collective licensing agreements,
no reproduction of any part may take place without
the written permission of Cambridge University Press.

First published 2001
Reprinted 2003, 2004, 2005

Printed in the United States of America

A catalogue record for this book is available from the British Library.

Library of Congress Cataloguing in Publication Data
Bialystok, Ellen.
Bilingualism in development / Ellen Bialystok.
p.   cm.
Includes bibliographical references and index.
ISBN 0-521-63231-5 — ISBN 0-521-63507-1 (pb)
1. Bilingualism in children. 2. Language acquisition. 3. Language awareness in
children. 4. Cognition in children. I. title.
P115.2 .B5 2001
401'.93—dc21   00-045520

ISBN-13   978-0-521-63231-7 hardback
ISBN-10   0-521-63231-5 hardback

ISBN-13   978-0-521-63507-1 paperback
ISBN-10   0-521-635076-3 paperback

Cambridge University Press has no responsibility for
the persistence or accuracy of URLs for external or
third-party Internet Web sites referred to in this publication
and does not guarantee that any content on such
Web sites is, or will remain, accurate or appropriate.

The language I have learn'd these forty years,
My native English, now I must forego;
And now my tongue's use is to me no more
Than an unstringed viol or a harp.

Shakespeare. Richard II. I. iii. 159.

Materia leaned forward and cooed, "Ya Helwi. Ya albi, ya Amar. Te'berini."

"Don't do that, Materia."

"What?"

"I don't want her growing up confused. Speak English."

"Okay."

Ann-Marie MacDonald, "Fall on Your Knees"

The limits of my language means the limits of my world.

Ludwig Wittgenstein

Contents

Preface

Parents often ask me for advice about exposing their children to two languages in the home. Typically, one of the parents speaks some language other than English and they are concerned that their linguistic decisions will have consequences for the child's development. The requests come in many forms (although e-mail has become the channel of choice) and from people with obviously different levels of background knowledge, education, and experience. The motivation for their questions is usually the same – will the child learn English and will the experience of learning two languages lead to either cognitive or linguistic confusion?

These questions are interesting because of the assumptions they reveal about the folk wisdom of childhood bilingualism. First, people intuitively believe that language learning is a fragile enterprise and can be easily disrupted. Second, they assume that languages interact, and that learning one language has implications for learning another. Finally, they expect that what happens with language can impact on the rest of cognition.

All of these assumptions are empirical questions and all of them entail theoretical controversies. Moreover, they are questions for which controlled investigation is difficult, if not intractable. Ironically, it is bilingual children who also provide the most promising forum for their examination and a means of potentially resolving the theoretical disputes. What happens to children's developing knowledge of language if they are learning two languages at the same time? How do children sort out the words and meanings from the two systems and incorporate them into thought? The questions resonate to pervasive issues in the philosophy of mind, such as the relation between language and thought and the viability of an autonomous language center.

The research and ideas in this book examine the language and cognitive development of bilingual children. The discussion explores these three assumptions, demonstrating how the study of bilingual children can clarify these basic controversies. The outcomes of that inquiry have implications both for practical concerns regarding the development of bilingual children and for theoretical debates that frame our study of development. My primary interest in bilingual children, therefore, is for the story they can tell us about human cognition and development.

I was privileged to receive the Walter Gordon Fellowship from York University for the year 1999–2000, which released me from my usual responsibilities and gave me the opportunity to work intensely on this book. During the year, I spent time as a visitor in two different centers, each of which provided an indispensable environment for a particular stage of this work. First is the Max Planck Institute for Psycholinguistics in Nijmegen, where I am grateful to Wolfgang Klein for inviting me and arranging the visit. The Max Planck Institute has a perfect library and an idyllic working environment. It allowed me to spend uninterrupted stretches of time reading and offered me access to a wealth of literature that helped me prepare to write sections of this book. Second is the School of Psychology at the University of Wales in Bangor. This department, in its improbable location, has a stable full of leading scholars who are all generous with their time, personable in their interactions, and stimulating in their discussion. My time there was spent thinking through arguments and discussing ideas, and I am grateful to Nick Ellis for inviting me. The research that I describe from my own laboratory was conducted over the past fifteen years and funded continuously by the Natural Sciences and Engineering Research Council of Canada. The Council's continued support has made this work possible.

This work has been shaped by my interactions with friends, colleagues, and students over a period of about twenty years. All those encounters have influenced and clarified my positions on these issues and contributed to the form the argument takes in this book. I fear that attempting to produce the list of names will ultimately do an injustice because of the inevitable omissions. I especially thank everyone who has participated in Friday bagels as this research developed and unfolded over the years.

Writing a book is an intrusion on domestic life and my family has tolerated me uncritically. My daughters Sandra and Lauren are a constant source of inspiration. My husband Frank has undergone an extraordinary journey of his own during the several years I have spent working on this book. Despite facing life's most serious challenge, he remained selfless, optimistic, and supportive. I am grateful and indebted beyond words.

I

Faces of Bilingualism

Picture a bilingual child. What languages does this child speak? What kind of neighborhood does she live in? What are the educational arrangements that either support or demand bilingualism? Are any of the child's languages spoken in the community outside the home? What were the circumstances that led to her bilingualism? How long has the child been living in the present country? By changing even a single answer to this small sample of questions, the child being described is importantly different from one who would have elicited a different answer. Is there a common experience that unites this diversity of children? Is this common experience reflected in some deeply rooted element of their intellectual development? Does bilingualism in early childhood influence the nature of children's cognitive development?

These questions presuppose a more basic issue: How do we decide who is bilingual? We all know shreds of other languages although we would hesitate to include those imperfect systems as evidence for our bilingualism. Children's knowledge of any language is incomplete compared with that of an adult. At what point does a child have enough command of two languages to be declared bilingual? In part, the answer to that depends on how the two languages were learned and to what purposes they are put. But that does not solve the problem of deciding what is entailed by partial knowledge of one language for a child whose linguistic knowledge of *any* language is partial at best.

Experiencing Bilingualism

For adults, the idea of an "uncontaminated" monolingual is probably a fiction. At the lowest levels of knowledge and awareness, exposure to fragments of other languages is unavoidable. No language is immune to intrusion from the barrage of words and phrases that rise out of one language and through their universal appeal deposit themselves squarely into the lexicons of another. The phenomenon can reflect cultural prestige (*blasé, rendezvous*), the seat of power for commerce (*computer, Big Mac*), the lineage to intellectual tradition (*Zeitgeist, Angst*), or the fascination with a slightly exotic culture (*chutzpah, schlep*). But we would resist describing the speakers who incorporate these terms into their conversations as bilingual. Often, many of these borrowed words are not even recognized for their linguistic origins.

More language knowledge surely follows from the ubiquitous foreign language requirements that most of us were required to complete at some point in our lives. This experience may have left us with many things, but fluent command of that language is probably not one of them. English-speaking students of Spanish would hardly qualify for an educational program conducted in Spanish, and Japanese-speaking students of English struggle to formulate the most rudimentary utterances in English. Nonetheless, each of these instructional experiences leaves the student with some facility in the language, perhaps more strongly developed for one modality (reading or speaking, for example), and a level of comfort in recognizing some forms and structures. Again, these students would be unlikely to describe themselves as bilinguals.

Some people live in home environments where the language of the extended family reveals an ethnic, cultural, or national background that is different from that of the community. Here the adults can function in two languages, and children born into these families may well learn some of that heritage language through familial interaction. In some of these situations, home bilinguals are created by the deliberate decision of parents to speak to the child in a different language, usually with one parent speaking each language. In other cases, casual knowledge that the child picks up in conversation can be supplemented by extra language classes – the familiar Saturday or Sunday schools organized by various communities. Often, however, there is little opportunity for formal study of this language and little expectation that the child will learn much of it, apart from that needed for ordinary domestic routines.

In some communities, bilingualism is simply expected. In these cases, the social organization of language at home and at school gently and irrevocably places children in the position of acquiring two languages. Some of this type of bilingualism is a legacy of colonialism. Following independence, many countries maintained the colonial language (notably, English, French, Portuguese, Spanish, or Dutch) in most of their social and official functions even though it was not a first language for the majority of the population (Ellis, 1994). In Papua New Guinea, most children learn a local language and Tok Pisin, the standard vernacular, before they enter school where the language of instruction is English (Skutnabb-Kangas, 1981). In the Philippines, children may learn one of seventy languages in the home before being immersed into English and Filipino instruction at school (Galang, 1988). In Hong Kong where 99 percent of the population is Chinese-speaking, English remains prevalent (Wong, 1988). English is also the official language of Nigeria adopted from its colonial days, while for Zaire, it is French (Ellis, 1994). These situations all demand that children have high levels of proficiency in at least two languages.

Children who encounter another language in these ways experience different kinds of interactions with each language, interact in different types of social situations with each, encounter different opportunities for formal study, and may also develop different kinds of attitudes to each language. For these reasons, the various configurations that lead to bilingualism leave children with different levels of competence in each of the languages. When we think of bilingual children, we think of those who appear to function equally in two languages, move effortlessly between them, and adopt the appropriate sociocultural stance for each. Indeed, it is an impressive sight to observe a young child, perhaps four or five years old, engaged in conversation in different languages, controlling both, and not struggling at the first sign that the language needs to change to accommodate some benighted monolingual in the group. Even these children, however, may have experienced a broad range of circumstances that importantly alter the nature of their bilingualism.

Romaine (1995) describes six patterns of home language bilingualism, each one different, and each difference relevant. These patterns combine values on social and linguistic dimensions, taking account of both the minority or majority status of each language and the linguistic input received by the child. The six types are:

Type 1: one person, one language
Type 2: nondominant home language/one language, one environment
Type 3: nondominant home language without community support
Type 4: double nondominant home language without community support
Type 5: nonnative parents
Type 6: mixed languages

In each case, she identifies the relevant differences and lists the major research studies. This is a useful inventory of the circumstances children experience in bilingual language acquisition. All these children become bilingual at home, but all of them are learning their languages under different conditions that undoubtedly lead to different levels of competence in each. These differences are not pursued here but considered as variants of the experience of learning two languages in the home.

The proficiency achieved from different experiences can vary on other dimensions besides absolute competence. Dopke (1992) distinguishes between productive bilinguals and receptive bilinguals. The first is the familiar configuration of speaking two languages to some degree of competence; the second is the common but less often acknowledged arrangement in which an individual can understand or possibly even read a second language without being able to produce it.

Who Is Bilingual?

Who shall we include in the study of development in bilingual children? Is there a formal criterion for proficiency that will point to the relevant group of children? Academic speculation on this matter does not solve the dilemma. Views vary from Bloomfield's (1933) insistence that a bilingual has full fluency in two languages to the more pragmatic assertion by Grosjean (1989) that a bilingual is someone who can function in each language according to given needs. We return to this problem of defining proficiency below.

Begin with the formalities that are necessary for deciding about proficiency in a language. There is less consensual agreement about the structural formalisms of language than we might wish. For example, as speakers of English we feel confident that we understand the definitional criteria for what constitutes a *word*. Yet speakers of some other languages, notably Chinese, have little understanding of what we mean by word since that unit essentially does not exist in Chinese. When native speakers of Chinese were asked to divide a Chinese sentence into words, they first complained that the instruction made no sense and then produced a highly variable set of responses (Miller, Zhang, & Zhang, 1999). This example illustrates that we cannot take for granted the absolute and universal structure of language; our categorical and objective notions of what languages look like are not necessarily accurate.

It is not only the problem of setting identifiable limits on speaker's proficiency that blurs the boundaries of a clear notion of bilingual. Another aspect of uncertainty is introduced by examining the particular languages in the bilingual mix. We think of bilingual individuals as those people who are able to speak two (or more) languages, to some level of proficiency, but identifying what counts as a language is not a straightforward judgment. We take for granted that we know what languages are – where one stops and the next one starts. That notion, too, is illusory: the delineation of individual languages is often a matter of decree. The formal differences that divide some languages, such as Dutch and Flemish or Hindi and Urdu, are far smaller than those that divide dialects of the same language, such as versions of Chinese or Arabic (Fabbro, 1999; Spolsky, 1998). In China, it is normal for people to know both an official language and a dialect. These variants can be significantly different from each other. Some languages, such as Arabic and Malasian, are diglossic. In these cases, different styles of language are required in different settings, but the differences between the styles can be as great as the differences between acknowledged languages. In diglossia, one form of the language is used as the vernacular for informal and social purposes and another is used as the institutional form for formal, educational, or religious functions.

Children can also become bilingual by learning only one spoken language. In these cases, children might learn a spoken language (perhaps English) and a sign language (perhaps ASL), a system that is the same as a natural language in every respect (Klima & Bellugi, 1979). It is normal for hearing children of deaf parents to learn these two languages simultaneously in childhood, acquiring both in a completely natural manner from their environment. Additionally, some children learn two or more sign languages either with or without any spoken languages. Although there is little research on these situations, the data that do exist confirm that the bilingual acquisition of two languages, one signed and one spoken, by young children has precisely the same in pattern and trajectory as that for the acquisition of two spoken languages (Johnson, Watkins, & Rice, 1992).

Bilingualism also carries a psychosocial dimension that can itself profoundly affect children. The language we speak is instrumental in forming our identity, and being required to speak a language that is not completely natural may interfere with the child's construction of self. Children who are bilingual because of relocation, particularly unwanted relocation, may resent the new community language they have learned in spite of their proficiency with it. Appel and Muysken (1987) describe how some of these factors affect bilingual children by accounting for the attitudes to the language and the role of language in establishing ethnic and cultural affiliations. These factors undoubtedly have a strong causal role in determining how competent children ultimately become in each of their languages and the purposes for which they are eventually willing to use each.

The situations described above indicate some of the multidimensional aspects of bilingualism and the complexity of defining the circumstances that point uniquely and unambiguously to a set of bilingual children. All the children in those examples are bilingual, even though their lives betray very little of that common experience.

Methodological Complications

The intention of this volume is to examine how bilingualism influences the linguistic and cognitive development of children. As we have seen, however, the designation of the subjects of study, namely, bilingual children, is not straightforward. Criteria are needed, but there is a potential circularity in specifying what those criteria might be. Consider, for example, that a decision is made to include all children who have even very limited competence in a second language as bilingual, and then study their development in contrast to absolute monolinguals. Using this approach, it may emerge that bilingualism has little impact on children's intellectual growth. That conclusion, however, may be too heavily weighted by the children whose second-language competence was restricted. If the research showed that limited competence in a second-language does not lead to the same consequences as more balanced mastery, then that would be grounds to eliminate marginally bilingual children from the inquiry. The problem is that we could not know that until the data were examined. Conversely, an early decision to apply restrictive criteria to the definition may exclude some children who were nonetheless affected by their linguistic background. Using a different approach, it may be discovered that even modest control over another language adjusts the dimensions of children's development. This conclusion would have been forfeited by an overly restrictive set of criteria. The problem is that the decision about who to include as bilingual must precede the evidence for what effect bilingualism has on these children, a situation that is logically reversed.

Nevertheless, restrictions must be made. The earlier examples of situations that lead to some small measure of control over another language for children illustrate the complexity of determining the parameters for childhood bilingualism. Children become bilingual for many reasons: immigration, education, extended family, temporary residence in another country, dislocation, or simply being born in a place where it is assumed that bilingualism is normal. These precipitating conditions are often associated with a set of correlated social factors, such as education level of parents and parental expectations for children's education, degree and role of literacy in the home and the community, language proficiency in the dominant language, purposes for which the second language is used, community support for the second language, and identity with the group who speaks the second language. Children's development is affected by all of these factors. The constellation of social, economic, and political circumstances of life have a large bearing on how children will develop both linguistically and cognitively. If bilingual children differ from each other in these dimensions, as they surely do, then they will also differ in the way that their bilingualism has interacted with the highly variable dimensions of their linguistic and cognitive development. Therefore, any averaging of relevant developmental indices across the conditions for becoming bilingual will be confounded with an array of hidden factors that crucially influence development.

Another factor that complicates the equation is that languages can be used for different purposes. It is reasonable to suppose that, all else being equal, the uses for which a child must employ the second language will influence the way in which it impacts on cognitive development. Grosjean (1996) notes that this issue is partly responsible for the fact that bilinguals rarely develop equal fluency in their languages. He discusses how different causal factors, such as migration, nationalism and federalism, education, trade, and intermarriage, lead to different uses of each language in each setting. The proficiency that the child develops in each language, therefore, is a specific response to a set of needs and circumstances. Some of these specific functions become embedded as immutable aspects of language proficiency: bilingual adults routinely count and pray in the language in which they first learned these behaviors (Grosjean, 1996; Spolsky, 1998).

To understand the role of bilingualism in children's development, therefore, not only must bilingualism be defined precisely but also must it be separated from the myriad of social conditions with which it is correlated and linguistic contingencies with which it is confounded. This is not easily done. The procedure for discovering how bilingualism impacts on development is to engage in controlled research, but these definitional ambiguities mitigate against the creation of a clean empirical design.

In constructing research designs, the attempt is to identify the factors, or independent variables, that create potentially relevant groups. Sometimes the factors are included in order to dismiss their role in behavior, such as including gender in a design when it is hoped that no gender differences emerge. In a balanced design, the differences between groups lead to simple inferential conclusions. If the difference between groups is not statistically reliable, then the conclusion is that the two groups are the same. For example, a set of results indicating that a group of male and female participants who are otherwise comparable scored the same on a concept formation task would lead to an acceptance of the null hypothesis, namely, that gender (the independent variable) is irrelevant to performance. Sometimes, as in the case of gender, it is desirable to be in a position to accept the null hypothesis.

The more interesting aspect of research design is in constructing the independent variables that we wish to use as a basis for rejecting the null hypothesis. We want a difference to emerge between groups and we would like statistical evidence that the difference is reliable. Usually, this is relatively straightforward. We may believe, for example, that a significant change in performance occurs at a certain age, or in a specific instructional program, or for speakers of a particular language. The procedure is then to assign participants to levels or groups determined by these independent variables, such as age, program, or language. The reason for this is probably due more to limitations of analytic sophistication than conceptual imagination. In other words, the procedures for analyzing the data require this categorical assignment to groups, even if our conceptual notions are more graduated. Simple judgments about membership in a level of the independent variable are central to carrying out the statistical analysis, an indispensable step toward making empirical conclusions.

There are two problems when this empirical model is applied to the study of bilingual children. The first is that bilingualism is not a categorical variable. Any assignment of children to a group labeled either bilingual or monolingual is an obfuscation of the complexity of the concept of bilingualism and a diminishment of the intricacy of children's language skills. Bilingualism is not like age, or gender, or grade, or any of the usual variables we use to classify children in developmental research. At best, bilingualism is a scale, moving from virtually no awareness that other languages exist to complete fluency in two languages. At what point on this scale do we declare children to be bilingual? How do we conduct research on the impact of a variable that we struggle to define?

In the ideal research design that compares performance across groups, the two groups are exactly the same except for the single independent variable we have chosen to study. This clear divide between the groups is necessary if we are to interpret any performance differences that emerge between them. With everything else being equal and controlled, significant differences in performance that may emerge can be attributed only to the single dimension that divides the otherwise equivalent samples. It is then a straight line from examining the data to interpreting the meaning conveyed by those results.

The second problem is in the equivalency of the groups, even if categorical placements can be achieved. Bilingual children are never *exactly* the same as an otherwise comparable group of monolingual children except for the number of languages they speak. In some inevitable sense, bilingual children live different lives than their friends and neighbors who may be socially, economically, and politically similar but speak only one language. Bilingual children may have different home arrangements, perhaps being cared for by an extended family member who speaks another language. Bilingual children may travel more than monolinguals, making family visits to some other homeland. Bilingual children may spend more time than monolinguals in formal schooling, attending after school or weekend classes in their other language. Any of these differences that come with the bilingual experience may itself have an impact on aspects of language and cognitive development, aside from the bilingualism per se.

This situation presents an immense challenge to research. Controlled investigation of the impact that bilingualism might have on children's development requires that bilingual children are compared with equivalent monolinguals on specific aspects of performance. In the absence of a truly ideal control group, every effort must be made to assure that the experiences encountered by the two groups of children in the study are as comparable as possible. Additionally, it is imperative that an assessment of broad intellectual functioning take place to provide empirical confirmation that, on important developmental indices, the two groups are operating at the same cognitive level. The approach to handling this design problem is to make every effort to minimize the effect of extraneous variance by being scrupulous in designing the research studies. The only alternative would be to maintain an excessively purist attitude and refuse to participate in research that did not conform to the most rigorous definition of design control. That option, which would paralyze any scientific examination of the development of bilingual children, seems to be both unnecessary and indefensible.

Where the Research Looks

Research on bilingualism probably fails to reflect its diverse reality. The considerations that constrain research studies normally prevent many types of bilingual children from being included in scientific inquiry. An important source of evidence for how bilingual children develop language and cognitive skills comes from carefully recorded diary studies. Such accounts were among the first evidence for the nature of bilingual development, beginning with Ronjat (1913), reaching an important level with Leopold (1939–49), and proliferating greatly after that (Arnberg, 1979; Fantini, 1985; Hoffman, 1985; Saunders, 1982; Taeschner, 1983; Vihman, 1985; Volterra & Taeschner, 1978). These studies form an essential part of the database. They cover diverse languages, different home arrangements, and together include a reasonably large number of children. The majority of these accounts, however, reflect a single reality: an educated middle-class family that has made a conscious decision to raise the children with two languages. Although this does not undermine the reliability of the descriptions produced by these studies, it does leave open a question about their generalizability to other social contexts. This issue is discussed in Chapter 8.

Proficiency; or, When Is Enough *Enough?*

The problem of knowing who is bilingual conceals a more basic question: how much is enough? Who among us does not know pieces of some other language – words or phrases, perhaps a rule or two, and some social routines for greeting, toasting drinks, or asking directions? These fragments hardly count as competence in the language, but how much more is required before some implicit threshold is reached? Accepting the standard assumption that no bilingual is ever equally competent in both languages, how much language is needed before we agree that a person is bilingual?

The answer depends on how we define language proficiency. We talk about language as though it had concrete existence and could be measured by scientific instruments. We describe the acquisition of language as though we move irrevocably from a state of innocence to one of mastery along a predictable path. We identify language impairment, language delay, and language precocity without ever specifying the standard against which these cases are to be judged. We use "language" in research designs as both a dependent and an independent variable, choosing fragments to serve as stimuli but concluding truths that define the domain. But what is the norm for language competence? What do we mean by language proficiency? What are its components and what is the range of acceptable variation? Although these questions may seem to be prior to any use of language as a research instrument or conclusion about language ability in individuals, they rarely if ever are explicitly addressed.

There is an intuitive sense in which the question of judging proficiency seems trivial: we find the task of rating speakers along various dimensions, for example, for their pronunciation or grammatical correctness, to be straightforward and meaningful. These judgments, however, tend to be based on holistic impressions, the details of which elude us. What features of language are most important? Joseph Conrad obviously had masterful command of English grammar but reputedly appalling phonology. Skilled mimics can sound like a native speaker of anything while producing virtual gibberish. How can a term that has such wide application be so lacking in definitional rigor?

For a theoretician, a definition is specific to an epistemology, a set of assumptions and principles about what language is, how it is learned, and what is entailed when it is used. Different classes of linguistic theories are derived from different epistemologies and therefore lead to different conceptions of language proficiency. The two major perspectives in linguistic theory are formal and functional approaches. These theories differ in many ways, but their assumptions regarding the mechanisms for language acquisition and the nature of language proficiency are strikingly disparate. In general terms, formal theories posit endogenous mechanisms for language acquisition that lead to uniform and universally prescribed rule systems. Functional theories posit exogenous factors for acquisition based on social interactions that lead to specific linguistic forms being extracted from these encounters and building up over time into more formal linguistic rules. A more detailed comparison of these theoretical orientations is presented in Chapter 2. For the present purpose, the important point is that each perspective considers different linguistic dimensions to be essential. Therefore, for each orientation, the criteria for determining language proficiency are rooted in different domains.

Summarizing the conception that arises from each position, we have the following. For formal linguistic theories, language proficiency is the reflection of circumscribed and specialized knowledge that is an elaboration of an abstract template. This template is part of the inheritance of humans and develops with little need for social manipulation, provided children are placed in normally functioning environments where a community language is heard. It is frequently related to cognitive theories in which many such specialized modules coexist, each with their own dedicated knowledge and procedural specifications. For functional linguistic theories, language proficiency is the reflection of cognitive processes that extract regularities from the environment and record those generalities as knowledge. In this sense, linguistic knowledge is no different from other kinds of knowledge of the world – knowledge about the nature of objects and categories, for example – and becomes part of the child's knowledge. The mental representations for language are equivalent to the mental representations for any other aspect of children's knowledge of the world. Interaction is crucial for the accrual of this knowledge.

There is no doubt that these are different conceptions of language proficiency. Does one provide the correct description? For formalists, language is defined by its structure; for functionalists, it is defined by its meanings. Is there a way of measuring one or both of these aspects that will yield an objective assessment of language proficiency?

Measuring Proficiency

If language proficiency is entailed by both of these perspectives, then it may result in a concept so broad that it serves only to deposit a nightmarish disarray at the door of those whose responsibility is language testing and assessment. However, the strategy of excluding parts of the story leaves researchers in a worse situation. Should the criteria for proficiency be based on broad abstractions or concrete details? To recast the question in Chomskian terms, are the correct criteria the abstract formalisms of competence or the actual rules revealed through performance?

Part of the resolution to the measurement problem is in the difference between criterion-referenced and norm-referenced assessment. In criterion-referenced evaluations, performance is compared with a known standard having objective levels and limits. Progress is easily tracked as learners move gradually along the scale toward the objectives that signal higher levels of competence. Higher scores mean higher competence, and there is usually a level of perfection that additionally defines mastery. Using a trivial example, height can be measured on a criterion-referenced scale showing growth from childhood into adulthood, the eventual goal. The approach also has wide application in language research. The objective judgments about a language learner's mastery of the standard rules of structure, morphology, and pronunciation are part of the observable progress that signals the process of language learning.

The "nativeness" of the learner's speech is another matter and is not so easily captured by lists of features and sets of criteria. Assessments that are outside the boundaries of purely formal prescriptions cannot be conducted through consultation to a set of rules. One of the problems is that the prescriptive rules provide an incomplete and somewhat inaccurate account of what native speakers really do with language. "Performance" is not simply different from "competence"; it is systematically different. Speech communities adopt characteristic styles of speech and accept specific digressions from the rules. The only option for evaluating language learners on these grounds is to make subjective comparisons that estimate how close the learner comes to behaving as a native speaker. These judgments must be made by norm-referenced evaluation. For this, there are no absolute criteria for performance that exist outside the use of the system by a group. Norm-referenced evaluation compares an individual with the other members of a particular class, group, or community. Using height again, adults can be described by their height relative to other adults.

How do we arrive at the standards that define the norm-referenced criteria? Consider the problem of deciding about standard native-speaker English. The easiest way to do this is to construct a mental model of the prototypical native speaker and use that mold as the template for judging other speakers. But will different judges create the same template? The received pronunciation versions of English that are broadcast on the nightly news by the BBC in Britain, the CBC in Canada, NBC in the United States, and ABC in Australia, to name just a few, are identifiably different from each other. The problem becomes even more complex when we move from the acknowledged purveyors of linguistic standards, namely, news anchors, to the great unwashed territory of real people. Looking only at England, the disparity between the language spoken by the BBC broadcaster, a clerk in Yorkshire, a farmer in Devon, and a teacher in East London is undoubtedly greater than that among the international examples listed above. What is the appropriate yardstick against which we should measure learners of English as a second language? At what point would we decide that a learner's proficiency is so advanced that they have achieved native-speaker competence? These are difficult questions but neglecting to address them does not eradicate the problem.

A Process Approach

We need to make the construct of language proficiency stand still long enough to be a meaningful measure of the knowledge and skill individuals have with language. We need to establish fixed criteria that supersede the theoretical squabbles and point to critical landmarks in language mastery. These are lofty goals, but without some framework for evaluating progress it is impossible to produce meaningful descriptions of the acquisition of language, let alone its potential impact on development. The intention here is not to solve the problem but rather to simply point to approaches that may eventually provide a fruitful resolution.

Ultimately, language proficiency must include both formal structure and communicative application; it must evolve from a prepared mind and be nurtured by a supportive context; it must set clear standards of use and include disparate (but systematic) variations of the rules. We need a way of organizing this multiplicity into a coherent statement about the human potential to learn and use language. If there is no agreement about what is included in language proficiency, then any explanation that attempts to probe some of the more profound mysteries of language will be incomplete.

One way to take account of these perspectives is to adopt a process-oriented approach to language proficiency based on identifiable cognitive operations. This method would ideally set the boundaries of proficiency, acknowledge variability, but still provide some metric for gauging a learner's position, preferably on a number of dimensions.

Cognitive Dimensions of Language Proficiency

A framework proposed in earlier work for considering the relation among different uses of language and their underlying cognitive requirements may provide a starting point (e.g., Bialystok, 1991a). This framework is described more fully in Chapter 5. Two cognitive processes, analysis of representational structure and control of attention, are set out as orthogonal axes which define a Cartesian space indicating their degree of involvement in each quadrant. Language tasks, or language use situations, can be located in the Cartesian space to indicate their relative reliance on each of these cognitive processes.

The cognitive process of analysis refers to the level of explicit structure and organization that is represented with knowledge. A significant change with development is that mental representations of knowledge become more explicit and more structured. Children increasingly are able to know not only unrelated facts but also the relationship among various concepts and ideas. Other theoretical perspectives have described this development in different terms; for example, Karmiloff-Smith (1992) points to representational redescription as the fundamental cognitive change for children, and Zelazo and Frye (1997) describe cognitive complexity as the mechanism for cognitive development. Both of these perspectives describe a process similar to the role that analysis of representational structures plays in building up mental representations. Control refers to the level of attention and inhibition recruited during cognitive processing. These mechanisms of attention regulate the access to and activation of the mental representations that are involved in performing various tasks. It bears some resemblance to the notion of agency described by Russell (1996).

As a first rough measure, three broad domains of language use – oral, literate, and metalinguistic – can be positioned in terms of their cognitive demands, giving the impression of a linear development from the first to the last. Each subsequent domain roughly requires higher levels of both analysis and control. This progression is shown in Figure 1.1. The linear impression is created because the underlying cognitive processes increase equivalently with each transition. The domains are only broad categories and conceal great variability within each, so a more detailed array can be constructed for each domain.

Imagine now a closeup of the domains individually. Under a larger magnification, a single domain could be expanded to fill the space of the whole matrix, because it too consists of graduated variability along both cognitive dimensions. For example, the oral domain could be spread out with various oral language activities dispersing across the space. Oral language uses include highly skilled functions such as lecturing and more common activities such as casual conversation. This diversity is illustrated in Figure 1.2. The cognitive demands, and hence the degree and nature of language proficiency involved, are strikingly different in these two cases. Similarly, children's conversations, consisting of short utterances situated in the "here-and-now," make the lowest demands on cognitive processes, but conversations in a second language require both more formal knowledge and highly skilled attention to perform at a reasonable level of proficiency.

The same exercise can magnify and expand the variation concealed by each of the other two broad domains. For literacy tasks, reading and writing at different levels of competence (for example, beginning vs. fluent reading), for different purposes (for example, studying vs. skimming), or in different genres (for example, fiction vs. poetry) are based on different levels of these underlying cognitive processes and convey different levels of language proficiency. These are shown in Figure 1.3. Finally, metalinguistic tasks, often used as the quintessential evidence for language proficiency, also differ among themselves in these ways. Some examples of these tasks and their relative placement in this matrix are shown in Figure 1.4.

A framework still needs to be integrated with a set of formal criteria. The procedure would be to include some of the product-oriented sets of

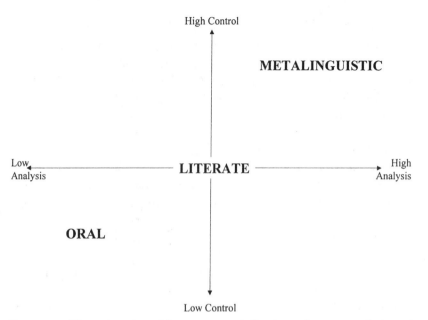

Figure 1.1. Three domains of language use indicating values on analysis and control.

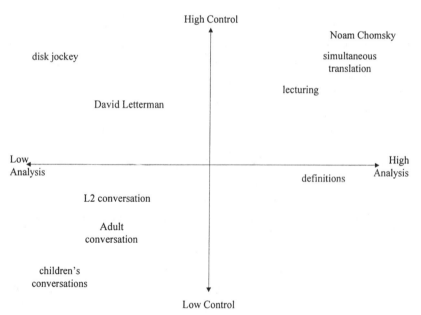

Figure 1.2. Tasks included in oral uses of language indicating their demands for analysis and control.

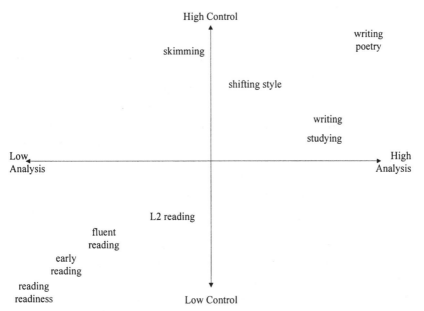

Figure 1.3. Tasks included in literate uses of language indicating their demands for anlysis and control (L2 = second language).

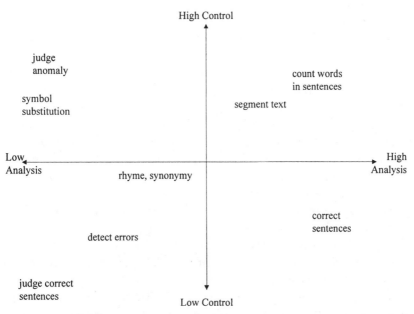

Figure 1.4. Tasks included in metalinguistic uses of language indicating their demands for analysis and control.

abstract linguistic features that define formal linguistic theories in this process-oriented account. In that way, the absolute, formal, or criterion-referenced standards would be stated separately for situations that share a functional and processing context. Research questions, then, could be made precise enough for the appropriate measures of proficiency to be constructed. For example, research that has ostensibly examined the viability of the critical period hypothesis for second-language acquisition (see discussion in Chapter 3) has usually examined only one or two aspects of language proficiency but made claims about the question at large. A more differentiated approach to explaining proficiency would allow us to say what it would mean to function like a native speaker across several domains and then to evaluate the success with which language learners approximate those performances. This approach would likely eliminate simplistic conclusions that force a choice between two opposing positions and compel us to consider a more complete set of factors in our conception of language learning. Allowing for a more nuanced explanation by removing false dichotomies and incorporating degrees of variation along specified dimensions will advance theorizing around many questions (Bialystok, 1998).

Toward a Definition

Where does this leave a definition of language proficiency? The primary consequence of this process-oriented approach is that it eliminates the possibility of constructing an overriding definition that includes the range of skills arrayed on these matrices. There can be no single statement that captures the multidimensionality conveyed in this view. Instead, the definition needs to set constraints and limits, pointing to critical areas. Language proficiency is the ability to function in a situation that is defined by specific cognitive and linguistic demands, to a level of performance indicated by either objective criteria or normative standards. The proficiency displayed by children as they learn language is just as valid as the proficiency of a highly skilled native speaker engaged in a formal debate, but the demands of each situation are different in ways that can be systematically captured.

This sets out two agendas for assessment. The first is to establish the criterion-referenced achievements that provide a guideline by which we can assess the proficiency of language learners. The second is to embed these descriptions into a context that is sensitive to the age, proficiency level of the learner, and the linguistic functions they are required to carry out. This embedded inventory is the norm-referenced protocol. These tasks are complementary, and it is difficult to think that one could be achieved independently of the other. Advances in testing sophistication, developmental psycholinguistics, and sociolinguistic frameworks are the background against which these assessments will emerge. Ultimately, the aim is to have an objective means by which we can judge the bilingual proficiency, as opposed to the monolingual proficiency, of young children.

Those pronouncements about the mandate for test developers are intended to set out a long-term project that will introduce rigor into the description of language proficiency. It would allow us to know, for example, that the reading comprehension of a ten-year-old who has been studying English in school for three years should be at a specific level, or the oral conversational fluency of an eight-year-old with a particular background in English should be at some other level. But that is a different point from the need to have formal criteria for deciding on who is to be included in the category of bilingual. Most research takes a rather casual approach to this question. In case study research that tracks the development of children's two languages, the amount of input in each and consequently the amount of language acquired in each is very different. In cross-sectional designs that compare bilinguals and monolinguals, parental report is often the only indicator of the children's language competence. More carefully designed studies include some proficiency testing in both languages, but this is not always done.

So we come full circle. Having strongly asserted that a proper definition of language proficiency is at the core of investigations of language, we have avoided confronting it in any serious way. At present, at least, there are no objective tests or accepted standards. Children cannot be subjected to a simple assessment and classified for their position on some absolute scale of bilingualism. The insurmountable problem from a methodological perspective is simply that bilingualism is not a categorical variable.

What we need to do is to constantly be aware of the issues. Research with bilingual children must minimally specify how the important variables distribute in the sample and how they have been controlled in the selection of research participants. Participants need to be comparable on the dimensions that matter – monolinguals and bilinguals must represent similar social backgrounds, and bilinguals must use their two languages in the same types of contexts. Ideally, proficiency tests that assess competence in the same type of language use that is being tested in the research should be routinely administered to participants, and the bilinguals should be assessed in both languages. Clearly, this is not always feasible.

For the most part, the studies reviewed in this volume consider that the bilingual children have functional fluency in both languages. Using formal criteria, especially the type that underlie criterion-referenced tests, this proficiency would probably not be the same for the two languages, and probably not the same as monolingual speakers of either. For example, it is normally the case that bilingual children have a larger productive vocabulary in one of their languages, and that their vocabulary in each language is less than that of a comparable monolingual speaker (see Chapter 3). Still, their functional proficiency in the two languages is equivalent – they can carry on conversations and engage in the same kinds of activities. Vague though this may be, it is an implicit acknowledgement of the myriad factors that comprise fluency. It may in fact be as close as one can come to equating underlying proficiency in two languages as a first step to evaluating the impact of that proficiency on children's development.

Finally, research on the effect of bilingualism on children's development has both a universal and unique dimension. The universal information is that which we can extrapolate to all bilingual children; the unique information follows from the individual circumstances of the children studied in the investigation. We need both, and we need a means of integrating them. The purpose of this volume, however, is to focus on the universal: how do bilingual children learn two languages and what happens to them in early development?

Starting with One Language

The pattern is familiar: cries evolve to babbles, babbles are shaped into words, and words are joined to create sentences. This sequence describes the path taken by all children as the language they hear around them is examined, internalized, and eventually developed into native-speaker competence. Although recent research has shown the immense variability in both rate and achievement for children learning their first language (Fenson et al., 1994), the process nonetheless has an enviable consistency about it, especially compared with the erratic and idiosyncratic variability of second-language acquisition. But these visible landmarks of progress in themselves reveal little of the internal complexities and mental revolutions that are propelling the child into linguistic competence. How do children learn language? We begin by trying to understand how a child learns one language in a relatively simple cognitive and social environment, so that when the stakes are raised, we have a basis for describing and interpreting a child's experience with multiple languages in complex social circumstances.

The formal study of language acquisition began with the scrupulous observation of young children learning to talk. Before there was a single hypothesis probing the nature of this process, researchers were recording the speech of their children and creating a database. The most famous of these was Leopold (1939–49) whose four-volume report remains a classic in the field. Interestingly, Leopold's daughter, the subject of the study, was being raised bilingually, although it took several decades for the study of bilingualism and second-language learning to gain a respectable position in studies of language acquisition. Beginning in the late 1950s, Roger Brown and his students carried out the first major program of research into child language acquisition that incorporated both observation and experimental manipulation. Brown's (1973) eventual report and interpretation of these investigations focused only on the earliest stages of acquisition; the intention to continue the project by reporting an equally detailed analysis of the next stage was never realized. Nonetheless, the contribution of the work carried out in Brown's lab is enormous: methodologically it provided the tools for analyzing and coding speech through constructs such as mean length of utterance (MLU); theoretically it presented hypotheses that were ultimately accepted, discarded, or revised, but always remained crucial in moving the field forward; and empirically it recorded the data, namely, the utterances of Adam, Eve, and Sarah, elevated to sage-like status that were the raw material upon which a generation of language researchers were bred. The more diverse extensions of this research into myriad areas of language and language-related studies by Brown's students are compiled by Kessel (1988). Surely, this proliferation of scholarship is testament to the wisdom of beginning at the beginning: before we can explain why things are happening the way they do, we must know what the child is doing.

In spite of agreement among researchers that normative data are essential for theory building, reliable observations based on large numbers of children have been notoriously difficult to compile. Studies of children's language acquisition tend, by necessity, to be small-scale, inferential, obtuse, and confounded. But even the prototypical example of minimalist experimentation, the case study of a single child, presents a daunting task to the researcher. Documenting children's utterances in the compilation of a language diary requires Herculean efforts, but researchers who have persisted have harvested a wealth of insights (Bowerman, 1973; Clark, 1973; Dromi, 1987; Tomasello, 1992, to name a few). The challenge of empirical studies is to create indirect means of asking questions, since we cannot ask children directly to comment upon their linguistic reflections. Further obstructing the process of collecting valid data is the possibility that children's cognitive competence, or incompetence, is masking the production and distorting the appearance of children's language abilities. We can access children's language only through the filter of their cognition, and the two may not be equally developed. It is a wonder that research in children's language acquisition is possible at all.

Two recent initiatives from which we will undoubtedly reap the benefits for years to come have provided a technical boost to the enterprise of studying children's language acquisition. The first is the Child Language Data Exchange System (CHILDES) developed by MacWhinney and Snow (MacWhinney, 1991; Sokolov & Snow, 1994). This is a computerized database of transcriptions obtained by researchers over the past twenty-five years reporting vast amounts of children's speech collected under different conditions, examining children at different ages, and including different languages. The database is accompanied by programs to carry out the transcription and analysis of the speech samples.

The second is the large-scale investigation of 1,803 children undertaken by Fenson, Bates, and others (Bates et al., 1995; Fenson et al., 1993, 1994) to provide the normative base for the MacArthur Communicative Development Inventories. The intention was to collect sufficient data on language and communicative development so that the competence of an individual child could be described with reference to this norm by means of a percentile score. The researchers assessed the language abilities of children between 8 and 30 months of age using a checklist system given to parents.

The CHILDES data base is primarily a research tool in that it provides the raw data upon which hypotheses and interpretations may be tested and played out. In contrast, the MacArthur Inventories are a more practical resource, enabling researchers and practitioners to submit the facts of language acquisition to scrutiny under existing theories and programs. These functional differences follow from an epistemological disparity between the two resources. The data in the CHILDES database are the raw, uninterpreted utterances of children engaged in actual linguistic interactions; the data in the MacArthur Inventories are the theory-biased results of a particular methodology for data collection, guided by particular hypotheses about what was worth examining. Both are useful, but each must be considered in its own terms for its unique contribution to the field.

Landmarks of Language Acquisition

Spurts, plateaus, and individual variability characterize the progress of children's language acquisition. Nonetheless, there is a common pattern and a standard progression, and the important evidence upon which an explanation can be built must derive from what is conventional. The theoretical relation between the various aspects of language, such as grammar and lexicon, is controversial, and some of the positions in this debate are described in the section outlining alternative theories of acquisition. Regardless of their theoretical status, however, the distinctions provide a useful heuristic for dividing language into manageable segments making them accessible and amenable to scrutiny. Therefore, this brief review of children's major achievements as they move into the mastery of language examines their progress individually in the areas of lexicon, syntax, phonology, and pragmatics. The purpose is not to review all that is known about language acquisition but to identify some events that are either decisive in evaluating alternative theoretical interpretations or relevant to situations involving bilingualism and second language acquisition, or both. The review is brief, and brevity invites caricature, but worse, simple analysis of single factors excludes the possibility of finding interactions, arguably the richer and more veridical level of analysis. It is not even clear that the artificial domains of language competence into which the discussion has been divided are valid. Bates and Goodman (1997) even object to the idea that vocabulary and syntax are separate parts of children's developing linguistic competence.

Lexicon

Descriptions of children's vocabulary acquisition need to delineate three aspects of development: its rate and pattern, the way words are used (or misused), and the relation between lexicon and the child's cognitive development. In the normative study for the MacArthur Inventories, Bates, Dale, and Thal (1995) report that by sixteen months of age children could reliably understand a mean of 191 words and produce a mean of 64 words. After that point, there is the legendary production spurt: by thirty months, the mean number of words in productive vocabulary is 534. This period of rapid vocabulary growth during the second year of life has been called the "vocabulary burst" (Bloom, 1973; Dromi, 1987; Nelson, 1973). More recent work has modified the description, noting that not all children follow this pattern of nonlinear spurting (Goldfield & Reznick, 1990). However, even allowing for individual variation within the pattern, the rate of vocabulary growth throughout childhood is astonishing. Anglin (1993) places this progress at about 5 words per day during the school years; Clark (1995) estimates the rate to be 10 words per day until the age of six and only slightly fewer through to the age of seventeen; Pinker (1995), in the boldest proposal of all, declares that children learn one word every two waking hours from about eighteen months old through adolescence.

A second salient aspect of children's early vocabulary is that early words are not always used correctly. Children make consistent, classifiable errors in their efforts to use their fledgling vocabularies. This issue is worth considering in some detail because it takes on new dimensions when a second language is added. Children's use of words in incorrect or inappropriate contexts not only provides a basis for understanding how children learn two languages, but also contributes to understanding how adults communicate through a language over which they have imperfect control (Bialystok, 1990).

Children typically make four types of errors using words: overextension, underextension, overlap, and mismatch (Anglin, 1977; Clark, 1973; Dromi, 1987; Tomasello, 1992), but the greatest research attention has focused on overextension. Overextensions occur when children apply words beyond their usual meaning, as in the famous example of using *doggie* to refer all four-legged animals, like squirrels. In an influential theory of semantic development, Clark (1973) argued that these commonly observed overextensions of names in children's speech indicated that children's lexicons contained incomplete entries for the semantic features. Dogs and squirrels, for example, each contained the features "small," "furry," "four-legged," but lacked more specific information that distinguished them. Since the meaning of the word was considered to be the sum of these features, these words actually meant the same thing for children; dogs and squirrels were categorically equivalent.

In subsequent research it became clear that children's comprehension of these terms showed the proper respect for categorical boundaries. Children were not suffering from a conceptual confusion about biological taxonomies but were being resourceful in extending a limited system beyond its apparent limits (e.g., Barrett, 1978; Huttenlocher, 1974). The concepts to which words had been overextended usually shared some perceptual or functional feature with the actual meaning of the word, and children were attempting to label an unknown concept with a known word on the basis of analogy. Expanding the argument, Barrett (1995) identified a large number of factors that could lead children to make these incorrect lexical choices: retrieval errors, object recognition errors, intentional error for effect, metaphorical use of words, pronunciation errors, substitution for simplification of speech. These are only some of the possible reasons that children's utterances contain word choices that adults may consider incorrect. In short, overextension is more likely evidence of strategic use of language than it is of children's semantic or conceptual incompetence.

A prevailing issue in the debate over alternative conceptualizations of language is the extent to which language functions as an intellectual module that is isolated from more general cognitive processes and autonomous in its acquisition and function. The question is controversial and emotionally charged because the decision on this matter is fundamental in characterizing competing models of language structure and language process. However, if there is any aspect of language that might be freed from this attachment to a specialized modular function, and hence from the debate itself, it is vocabulary.

What evidence is there that vocabulary development might be part, even a highly specialized part, of children's general cognitive development? For some portion of vocabulary, words are mapped onto cognitive structures that many researchers believe must be established before the word can be learned. For example, Tomasello and Farrar (1984) found that children learned movement words such as "fall down" only after they were successful in solving a task based on visible displacements. Similarly, Gopnik and Meltzoff (1986) found a relation between children's use of disappearance terms, like "all gone" and the completion of object permanence. Specific correspondences such as these are compelling evidence for the close association between children's developing conceptual skills and their linguistic competence. Bates, Dale, and Thal (1995) caution that the correspondence between cognitive and linguistic ability is restricted to measures of language comprehension, not production. This allows the possibility that children understand these terms properly before the indicated cognitive concept is complete and those terms appear appropriately in production. Although the correspondences between words and concepts do not resolve questions of causality and directionality, their yoked development is an important wedge into the otherwise intractable problem of the ontological status of language in the child's mind. These associations become more detachable and amenable to scrutiny when children are learning two languages or learning languages with different semantic structures, an issue that is discussed in Chapter 3.

Syntax

From the time children begin combining words to create compositional utterances, an achievement that begins to reveal itself at about eighteen months of age, there is an unmistakable respect for the word order demanded by the grammar of the adult language (Braine, 1976). The limitations that restrict children's speech to a fraction of the necessary units for a fully elaborated sentence seem nonetheless constrained by the rules of grammar. More impressively, infants in the first year are able to distinguish between meanings of reversible sentences using only word order as a clue. Hirsh-Pasek and Golinkoff (Golinkoff et al., 1987; Hirsh-Pasek & Golinkoff, 1991, 1996) have developed a comprehension test that demonstrates these apparently precocious abilities. Infants are seated in front of two monitors, each depicting one direction of action between two agents (cat chases dog; dog chases cat), while a tape is played that describes only one of the displayed scenes (*The cat is chasing the dog*). These infants look significantly longer at the scene that matches the description than at the one that reverses the direction of action. Still, it is not clear how strongly children's responses in this task are evidence that they are undertaking syntactic analysis. Akhtar and Tomasello (1997) insist that the use of word order to interpret reversible actions is very late to develop. Instead, they claim that children learn about the use of specific verbs in familiar contexts, making it appear that they have gained a more general understanding of syntax. Akhtar and Tomasello's claims are based on production data, a skill known to lag significantly behind comprehension, but there is still an inconsistency that must be reconciled in order to determine the state of children's knowledge of syntax. What, then, is the evidence for syntactic structure in children's language acquisition?

Two aspects of syntactic development are noteworthy for general discussions of language acquisition and relevant to the extensions of these explanations into second-language acquisition. The first is the order in which the morphological system is mastered and the second is the overextension of syntactic rules.

One of the striking discoveries in the study of language acquisition by Brown and his collaborators was that there was a relatively fixed order in which fourteen grammatical morphemes (such as plural (-*s*), progressive (-*ing*), and articles) were acquired into the productive competence of the children they studied. Documenting mastery of specific linguistic units is precarious because children's early speech is so variable. Brown's (1973) decision was to base judgments of acquisition on the criterion that children used a specific form in 90 percent of the obligatory contexts. Comparing different criteria for determining the point of acquisition, Bates, Bretherton, and Snyder (1988) confirmed the stability of the order of acquisition of seven of the original fourteen morphemes across a group of children. This regularity in the order of acquisition of grammatical markers is a crucial fact of language acquisition that needs to be addressed by any theory. The stability of the order across children who clearly experience different forms of input, different rates of learning, and different cognitive abilities points to an explanation more intrinsic to the language itself, or to some language-learning capacity, than to the capriciousness of environmental input. Moreover, impressive similarities have been noted across languages (e.g., Slobin, 1982), a point to which we return in the next chapter.

A second characteristic of children's early syntax is the existence of a period of time, usually beginning in the third year, in which they overextend grammatical rules to irregular forms. The preeminent example of this is the overuse of -*ed* to indicate past tense on irregular verbs, creating such forms as *goed* instead of *went.* Why do children universally and reliably commit such errors? The observation of this pattern has been a persistent example of data invoked to distinguish between the two major competing theoretical approaches to language acquisition, formal and functional views (discussed below). It is a telling exercise in theory building that the same observation is considered central to two completely diverse interpretive positions. Nonetheless, the phenomenon is evidence of an important productive process in children's language acquisition, and it is a lightning rod for competing theories as they recruit these descriptive facts into their predictive potential.

Phonology

Phonology is the only aspect of language that is unequivocally evident from the infant's first moments of life. The newborn baby reveals virtually nothing of the extraordinary potential that will be shaped into the ability to use structured rules of order to express intentions and concepts in socially regulated ways; the ability to vocalize these ideas, however, is manifest. Recognizable speech is, of course, "a far cry" from the infant's first vocal outbursts, but the natural reliance on this channel of communication is evident. Equally, children born without the ability to hear begin life with manual gesticulations that are structurally and functionally equivalent to the vocal babbles of hearing children (Petitto, 1997).

The evolution of the infant's first cries into comprehensible speech undergoes several important milestones: the first linguistic sounds are discriminated at about one month old; babbling begins at about seven months of age, the first word appears by approximately twelve months, and the next two or three years are spent refining the sounds and prosody to match the adult standards of the speech community. The earlier view of this development was Jakobson's (1968) claim that there was a discontinuity between the playful babbling of infants and the emergence of words. The current consensus is for continuity: speech follows naturally from babbling (e.g., Locke, 1995), although babbling may not be an essential prerequisite for speech (Kent & Miolo, 1995). Three aspects of this development are important to note. The first is the way in which speech sounds are organized into phonemic categories; the second is the sequence of sounds incorporated into babbling and ultimately into speech; and third is the nature of the errors observed in early speech production.

The seminal study in research on speech perception is the work by Eimas and others (1971) in which they reported that infants between one and four months old could reliably discriminate between computer-generated versions of the sounds *ba* and *pa*. More important, the infants could make these distinctions only for sounds that carried phonemic significance; acoustic differences of equal psychophysical magnitude that were linguistically irrelevant went unnoticed. This is a profound result: after only four weeks of life, there is evidence of a preparedness to organize heard speech into linguistic categories. Extensions of this research into the abilities of infants to distinguish between sounds for languages other than those in their environment are discussed in Chapter 3.

The second issue in children's developing phonological abilities is the pattern and sequence of sounds over which children gain mastery. Although it is reasonably straightforward to trace the course of phonological development across the major stages of cooing, babbling, and speaking, the qualitative shape of children's vocalizations at each of these stages is highly variable. The continuities are more apparent when the analysis focuses on individual children. Vihman (1992) reports that the syllables most practiced by infants during babbling are the ones most likely to appear in children's first words, lending further credence to the functional significance of babbling in language development. This link can be seen as well in the relation between the consonants that appear in babbling and those that predominate in children's early words. In both cases, the sounds are drawn from the same small subset of the possible consonant sounds of the language (Stoel-Gammon, 1985).

Third, as sounds turn into words, children consistently encounter difficulty with certain phonemes. Words take on a "baby talk" quality because they lack phonemic specification and include many homonyms. Many of these errors are systematic and reflect the application of specific rules, such as devoice final consonants, substitute stops for fricatives, or reduce consonant clusters to singleton consonants (Menn & Stoel-Gammon, 1995). The application of these rules, however, appears to be determined by a number of factors, such as the position of the sound in the word, although the same rules apply irrespective of the language that the child is learning. Even the designation of these regularities as rules may be an overstatement: Priestly (1977) studied a child who appeared to produce completely idiosyncratic forms of common words. Hence, these simplification processes are rules only in a restricted sense as their application is neither predictable nor assured. They may be better described as strategies adopted by children to solve problems at a moment in time. In this sense, they may share common ground with the strategies used by children to refer to objects and concepts beyond their lexical repertoire.

Pragmatics

Pragmatics is the study of language use, and the quintessential use of language is communication. Communication, however, includes much more than language, so any examination of the pragmatic aspects of language cannot fail to incorporate territories normally beyond the scope of standard linguistic analysis. Communication begins well before language is evident and includes interactions that are clearly outside the child's developing linguistic competence. As language evolves, the focus of pragmatic analysis shifts to the correspondence between the emergence of linguistic devices and their capacity to signal specific intentions and the sensitivity to socially determined rules of interaction. The mastery of these linguistic devices, and the nonverbal behaviors that precede them, are all central to children's development of pragmatic competence, and their emergence, like other more formal aspects of language, is systematic and orderly.

The pragmatic dimensions of language include a range of linguistic and nonlinguistic properties that contribute to the maintenance of linguistic interaction. Some are mechanical, such as the dynamics of turn-taking; some are social, such as mutual attention to an agreed topic; some are cognitive, such as the speaker's communicative intents; some are cultural, such as rules of politeness; and some are linguistic, such as the use of discourse markers to connect ideas. All these aspects of the pragmatic use of language are learned by children at the same time as they are learning the formal structure of the system.

Before children have mastered any of the formal aspects of language, however, they are capable of interacting in a conversational style and communicating their intentions. In this sense, communication begins long before language is established. How does language fit into the infant's communicative behavior? The solutions present much the same options as did the comparable question regarding babbling. One view, *continuity,* holds that language is the continuation of communication by other means. Some researchers have identified specific communicative intents in infant interactions and assigned them a causal role in the subsequent development of language as a communicative tool (Bates, Camaioni, & Volterra, 1975; Bruner, 1983; Coggins & Carpenter, 1982). As children acquire words and linguistic structures, these forms come to supplement and eventually substitute for the prelinguistic efforts made by the infant to communicate specific intentions. The opposite view, *discontinuity*, asserts that formal linguistic knowledge imposes a qualitative divide between preverbal and linguistic communication. Advocates of this view deny that infants' preverbal expressions convey intentional content or even that early words convey symbolic meaning (Barrett, 1986; McCune-Nicolich, 1981). A more moderate compromise position is proposed by Ninio and Snow (1996, p. 49): "Linguistic communication thus starts with words substituting for gestures, but the language system, once established, soon diverges from its nonverbal origins."

The question of the continuity or discontinuity of linguistic knowledge with communicative ability is central, not only for understanding the role of pragmatic competence in language acquisition, but also for determining a theory of linguistic structure and language acquisition. If language is one part of a larger communicative ability and grows naturally out of children's interactions, then the burden of explanation for language structure and acquisition must begin with infant's early interactions and experiences. Language exists for communication and must be explained in those terms. Thus the function of language – communication – is primary and must be placed at the center of explanation. Conversely, if the communication that is prior to the acquisition of linguistic structure is rudimentary, incomplete, or unsystematic, and it is only with the onset of language that intentions can be expressed reliably and systematically, then the essential aspect of language is its form, or structure. In this case, the pragmatic functions of language emanate from its formal structure, and communication is a consequence of an orderly formal system. This divide marks a major difference between formal and functional theories of language acquisition, each adopting a different position regarding the primary quality of the object of study.

Approaches to Language Acquisition

The patterns of development may be consistent, but the mechanisms responsible for that development are far from apparent. Children come to language learning as biological beings with distinctively human brains, interacting in a social context, and receiving massive linguistic input. Surely, all these features contribute to language acquisition, although identifying these as necessary ingredients does little to explain how that happens. It is incumbent upon a theory of language acquisition to identify the mechanism by which these forces combine so that language acquisition is guaranteed and linguistic competence is ultimately a part of children's cognitive repertoire.

Theories differ in their designation of the locus of this mechanism. As one moves from explanations based primarily on innate factors through to those focusing on linguistic input, the mechanisms drift outward, shifting the balance of their explanatory force from factors that are essentially endogenous, residing in the mental and cognitive predispositions of the child, to those that are primarily exogenous, encountered in the contingencies in the environment. It is simplistic to assume that any one of these approaches alone could adequately account for the monumental task of mastering an entire language, theoretical boasting notwithstanding. The dynamic that animates the debate between alternative theories is more a case of staking out territory and explaining some aspect of language structure or language use at the expense of others. Language, conveniently, is vast and multifaceted; theorists begin with a conception of language that captures their view of its most essential nature, and fashion an explanation that addresses those elements. Other facets, those that do not form part of the core conception of language, are dealt only passing reference in explanations of language structure, use, and acquisition. Hence, reconciliation among theories is often more a matter of integrating the complexity of language in all its forms, each with a different theoretical interpretation, than of choosing among competing explanations for the same phenomenon, although that happens too.

Criteria for Distinguishing among Theories

The variety of distinctive approaches to theories of linguistic structure, and, by corollary, to explanations of language acquisition, has proliferated in the past decade. The singular predominance of the generative paradigm based on Chomsky's revolutionary rethinking of the nature of linguistic structure and its relation to mind has ceded to a range of alternative conceptions that aims to address specific lacunae or weaknesses identified by the adoption of that approach. These alternative theories represent a diversity of thinking and emanate from disparate linguistic traditions, yet they share certain features that allow them to be considered together, at least for the purpose of characterizing their contrast to generative linguistics. The range of theories polarizes around a divide between formal and functional theories of language. The formal theories are most concerned with an analysis of the abstract underlying structure of language, while the functional theories are primarily concerned with understanding language in the contexts in which it is used.

Three issues in language acquisition are central to every linguistic theory and distinguish between the formal and functional approaches. First is the *independence* of language from other cognitive functions. In formal approaches, language is relatively autonomous from other cognitive domains and carries its own universal structure, but in functional conceptions, language is convergent with the rest of cognition. Second is the role of linguistic *input.* In formal generative theories, linguistic input is needed to trigger the emergence of the grammar from the universal template, but it has only a minor influence on the actual linguistic insights that result. In functional approaches, language is constructed from the input obtained through social interaction. Although there may be cognitive universals that guide the process of language acquisition, explanations for the emergence of specific language structures are sought in the linguistic (and, to some extent, conceptual) input. The third issue is the nature of *linguistic knowledge.* In formal grammars, linguistic structures are represented as abstract rules, whereas in the functional approaches, linguistic rules (where they exist) begin as specific, often contextually bound, inventories of knowledge.

In addition to the major formal and functional alternatives, there are some hybrid accounts that do not yield easily to the pressures of a forced dichotomy. An early acknowledgment of the need to approach language acquisition from both sides was submitted by Bruner (1983). He proposed that the language acquisition device (LAD), the engine of learning for generative linguistics, is accompanied by a language acquisition support system, (LASS), the social, interactive, and cognitive structures that bring the child to language, assure that appropriate interactions take place, and present the information to the child's conceptual system in ways that are clearly interpretable and conducive to learning.

A different kind of interactionist account, called a "biolinguistic" approach, has been proposed by Locke (1993). The essential feature of his explanation is that language acquisition depends on two jointly crucial components of human information processing: a grammatical analysis module (GAM) and a specialization in social cognition (SSC). His assumptions straddle both sides of the divide on the three criteria identified above: (1) regarding independence, at least some of language is modular and specialized, specifically, phonetic processing and generative morphology, but language processing includes other domains as well; (2) regarding input, the environment is needed to shape the nonmodular aspects of language, but the core, including the SSC, is universal and automatic; and (3) regarding rules, some parts of morphology are governed by abstract rules, but others, such as irregular forms, are simply associative.

Finally, some recent proposals from the perspective of evolutionary cognition have attempted to situate language ability into a conception of the phylogenetic emergence of human intelligence. Although such explanations are fairly straightforward if language is considered to be independent of other cognitive functions (e.g., Pinker, 1994, 1997), the argument requires more subtlety if we aim to avoid implanting the germ of a language module in species that precede *Homo sapiens* in evolution. A detailed proposal of this kind is the theory developed by Deacon (1997) in which he argues that language evolved from a general symbolic function that began to emerge in the prefrontal lobes about 2 million years ago. Although the theory leaves some rather large gaps concerning specific aspects of language that are not easily subsumed in a more general symbolic system, it has the appeal of embedding the innate basis of language in the human mind without requiring humans to be prewired for any *specific* knowledge about language. Further, it provides a plausible evolutionary account of how cognition came to include that ability. This theory illustrates the important point that it is simplistic to consider nativism to be a binary feature of knowledge, that is, language is innate or it is not innate. Many conceptual foundations could give the appearance of innate language ability without actually instantiating language themselves.

The three characteristics that distinguish between the major theoretical positions on first-language acquisition lead to different conjectures about the processes involved in second-language acquisition. In turn, different interpretations of second-language acquisition impact on conceptions of children's cognitive competence. Therefore, it is worth considering how each of these approaches sets out the parameters of second-language acquisition.

First, if language acquisition is governed by a dedicated module that has been designed through evolution to discover the structure of language, then the process of language acquisition, and to a large extent its outcome, will be universal. There should be little difference in the acquisition process for children who are learning one or more languages, whether they are learning them simultaneously or sequentially. Presumably, each language learning experience will be controlled by the device set out for this purpose and guided by the universal grammar that is at its core. Conversely, if language acquisition is an aspect of more general cognitive development, regulated by the generic processes that guide children through the acquisition of conceptual knowledge and skill development, then there is no reason to expect that any two language learning experiences will be the same. In sequential second-language acquisition, for example, children already know one language, and that knowledge, part of children's conceptual repertoire, is certain to influence the acquisition of another language. Thus, under functional views in which language acquisition is not specialized and autonomous, children's experiences in learning, and presumably using, multiple languages will necessarily be different from those involved in the first language.

Second, input is needed for an innate universal language structure only to activate its function. This feature of universality of linguistic structures will affect the ease with which a second grammatical system can be acquired. If all languages emanate from a universally defined set of constraints, then the implementation of these constraints in a first language should provide a template that either facilitates, in the case of similar structures, or inhibits, in the case of contrasting structures, the construction of a new grammar. In either case, the input triggers the search for structure without having much affect on which structures will be discovered. Conversely, if the source of universality is the child's developing cognitive system, then the patterns of acquisition in the two languages could be quite different from each other. Presumably, children's experiences in the two languages will provide different kinds of input, different conditions of learning, and different communicative needs. These differences would shape the emerging system in each language. Guided by the different linguistic, cognitive, and social input available in each language, the path of acquisition for each language will be different.

Third, the nature of linguistic rules will profoundly influence the process of second-language acquisition. Generative positions that consider linguistic rules to be abstract formalisms have to deal with the problem of what aspect of this intrinsically complex knowledge is actively part of the child's competence. The main evidence offered to support the idea that abstract rules are the basis for linguistic performance is the overregularization that is characteristic of children's speech (described in the section above on syntax). The alternative views do not credit children with such abstract knowledge but endow them instead with specific, contextually bound representations that can be used as a basis for abstraction of principles. This means that each new language would need to be built up from the repertoire of the specific constructions that are the basis of the rule system that is eventually constructed.

Although theoretical perspectives differ on the matter of innateness, the issue is in some sense a red herring – not much follows from either position and the issue can easily lead one away from more important distinctions. Both extreme views are untenable: to say that language is innate is not to say that knowledge of specific linguistic structures is innate, and to say language is not innate is not to say that humans have no preconditioned bias to learn language in some form. Nonetheless, strong positions are taken on the issue and it is worth considering some consequences of each alternative. One question that arises if language is assumed to have at least some innate component is whether there is a critical period for language acquisition. Although there is no logical necessity that connects the notion of a critical period to the other characteristics of the formal position (modular, universal, abstract), they are at least plausibly connected. The concept of a critical period does not easily follow from a functional view in which language is a cognitive activity, developed from social interaction, and based on specific linguistic and cognitive rules. Nonetheless, the question about the existence of a critical period that sets a maturational limit on language acquisition has significant consequences for second-language acquisition. This issue is discussed in Chapter 3.

Each theory of language is part of a rich epistemology. The purpose of this review is to outline in broad form some of the major theoretical alternatives, an exercise that will inevitably do disservice to the complexity of each. The simple heuristic of categorizing theories as examples of broader types is often in itself an act of theoretical destruction. The purpose of the exercise is to consider the implications of the major alternatives for theories of second-language acquisition and bilingualism by children.

Formal Theories

The revolution in linguistic thinking that was unleashed by Chomsky (1965) in his standard theory included radical proposals for the nature of linguistic knowledge, its relation to other forms of thought, and the manner in which children learn their native language. Most of these ideas are well known, and indeed they formed the accepted wisdom of linguistic theory for some time. Although many linguists working within the Chomskian model have modified aspects of the original proposals, such as lexical-functional theory that is based on grammatical functions like "subject" (Bresnan, 1982), or extended the theory beyond the original boundaries, such as the formal analysis of semantic structure (Jackendoff, 1990), the essential flavor of the theory and its position with respect to the three criteria described above remains recognizable. Pinker (1984, 1994) has been the most assiduous of the Chomskian scholars in working through the theory from the perspective of its implications for language acquisition. In the process, he has refined and modified some formal aspects of the theory and combined it with a more careful consideration of learning mechanism to create a model that, at least in principle, could explain how children learn language. Although Chomsky was interested in the logical problem of language acquisition, he was not concerned with the actual unfolding of language in the minds of young children. Pinker has made a major contribution in describing that process.

The essence of the human capacity for language is attributed to an evolutionary adaptation of human biology that specialized the human mind, but not the mind of other species, for language. We learn language because we are prepared to learn language. It is simply in our genes (or is, as Pinker, 1994, claims, an instinct) and the mere exposure to linguistic input is sufficient to set switches in motion and the wheels of language acquisition turning. The response to the problem of how language is acquired is to point to the language acquisition device, the hypothetical homunculus whose responsibility it is to filter through all the language input and extract from it the essential rules of the system.

For formal theories, the recourse to innate structures to assure that language will be learned is traced to the absence of convincing alternatives. The dilemma rests on the "poverty of the stimulus argument" and its companion quandary "no negative evidence" (e.g., White, 1989). How could children master the complex and abstract principles of language using only inductive reasoning when the language they hear is poorly formed, incomplete, and sparse? Moreover, how do children restrict their hypotheses about the potential nature of linguistic structure to a correct subset of those structures when adults rarely inform children that a grammatical rule has been violated? Something besides environmental language and parental prodding is necessary to guarantee that things will go well. A language acquisition device takes care of the first problem (poverty of the stimulus); universal grammar handles the second (no negative evidence).

Another feature of formal theories is their identification of abstract rules as the essence of linguistic knowledge. Wasow (1989) states that for generativists, the definition of grammar is "a finite system of rules for characterizing the membership of some language – that is, for specifying all and only the sentences of the language" (p. 163). This allows language to be infinitely productive and enables children to command the vast range of acceptable permutations of linguistic strings without ever having heard the specific instantiation.

All formal theories share these characteristics – language is specified as modular and distinct from other cognitive functions, and it develops from an innately prescribed universal grammar governed by a language acquisition device, creating a set of abstract formalisms about structure. These prescriptions, however, are still vague with respect to the problem of how language is actually learned. Here, different versions of formal theory suggest different mechanisms.

Government-Binding Theory

The development of government-binding theory (Chomsky, 1981) elevated transformational grammar to a position of broader generality than was the case for previous linguistic theories, including his own, by stating the theory in terms that were more universal and hypothetically applicable to all languages. Those features of language that were considered to be universal to all natural languages were called principles; those features that varied across languages were called parameters. Hence, parameters were an attempt to reconcile the apparent differences across languages with the claim that all natural languages reflect universal principles of structure and organization. Principles are the universal properties of all languages, such as the X-bar principle that controls the structure of phrases; parameters are optional variants on these principles, such as the pro-drop parameter that determines whether or not a particular language allows the deletion of subject pronouns. The idea was to reduce differences between languages to a limited number of these parameters and to define the parameters so they had a minimal number of possible values, preferably only two. During language acquisition, the universal principles operate to organize the heard language for the child, but the child must determine how the parameters need to be set for the specific language they are trying to learn.

Learnability Theory

Pinker (1984) is persuaded that it is logically impossible for children to learn languages on the basis of the input they are presented. Recently, some scholars have shown that a more careful analysis of verbal interactions between children and adults shows that the situation is not nearly as devoid of corrective information as previously believed (Bohannon & Stanowicz, 1988; Hirsh-Pasek, Treiman, & Schneiderman, 1984). The way in which adults respond to children's utterances, according to such measures as the frequency with which they repeat or elaborate on the child's words, corresponds to the grammaticality of the child's utterance. These contingencies in adult responding make it at least possible for children to extract the necessary feedback regarding the formal acceptability of what they have said. These corrections, however, are subtle and largely erratic and, according to Pinker (1989), inadequate to satisfy the needs of language learning. Consequently, Pinker turns to a formal learning theory, learnability, for a model of how children learn language.

Learnability theory is a computational formalism that has been applied to modeling language acquisition (Berwick, 1986; Wexler & Culicover, 1980). The approach involves the identification of four components of the model: a class of languages (one of which is the target), a learning environment (that provides the target language), a learning strategy (that maps sequences of inputs onto hypotheses about language), and a success criterion (the correspondence between the generated hypothesis and actual target language structure) (Atkinson, 1986; Pinker, 1989). These four components are constrained by their degrees of freedom: assumptions about any three of the components determines the values on the fourth.

Government-binding theory and learnability theory are not dichotomies but solutions to different aspects of the same problem. Atkinson (1986) points out that a difference between them is that learnability theory offers a significant learning procedure and an infinite set of alternatives, while government-binding theory posits a trivial learning procedure and restricted grammar. For Chomsky, in other words, language acquisition is less a problem of learning than it is a matter of explication or emergence. Learnability tries to reduce the burden on innate systems by finding some formal solution whereby children can learn at least part of the system on their own. Language learning becomes less a matter of magic and more a matter of logic.

Pinker (1984) proposes that the mechanisms by which the child builds up knowledge of grammar from the heard input implicitly organize segments of speech, or phrases, into categories that correspond to grammatical categories such as noun and verb. By combining these phrasal units with contextual meaning, children can use these phrases as a frame for building up the rest of grammar. Once words have been correctly classified for their function in the sentence, they can be used productively in new utterances. As Pinker demonstrates, this system is remarkably powerful in generating a fully functioning grammar. To accept that children are able to properly segment speech into the appropriate phrases and then to classify them according to functional criteria set out by adult grammar, however, requires a leap of faith.

A substantive contribution of Pinker's views has been in his explanation of the overgeneralization error in which children generate inappropriate past tense forms (e.g., Marcus et al., 1992; Pinker, 1994). He argues that the error indicates that two different mechanisms are involved in learning past tense forms. The first mechanism is recall from associative memory, the repository in which the irregular forms have been represented. The second is a generative rule that affixes the morphemic endings to verb stems as required. Normally, retrieval of an irregular form suppresses the generative process, but children's memory traces are too unreliable to prevent the regular formation by the rule, hence the error results. These errors decline as the child's associative memory for the irregulars is enhanced and solidified.

Minimalism

In a recent revision of the theory, Chomsky (1995) has enormously reduced the number of constraints and rules governing language structure, thereby abolishing as well the principles and parameters. In the new theory, there are only two mechanisms, called MERGE and GT, which govern the generation of all linguistic structure and produce all acceptable utterances. This greatly generalizes the theory, since there are no longer levels of symbolic representation in the analysis of linguistic structure. These are profound changes to the theory because they impinge on part of the essence of what made formal theories distinct from their functional counterparts. The radical modularity of language, for example, has yielded to a more communicative structure. Furthermore, the stage has been set for language, however isolated and modularized it may be, to interface with the conceptual structures that have always been part of general cognition and not involved in language processing. Jackendoff (1997) has taken this opening further and described an architecture in which conceptual-semantic knowledge is integral to syntactic processing.

Functional Theories

A paradigm for understanding language acquisition that does not begin with nativist assumptions about language in the mind is the broad class of functional theories. In these approaches, language emerges out of children's ordinary experience to fulfill specific cognitive, social, and communicative functions. These theories differ from each other in detail and emphasis, but share a commitment to understanding the formal structure of language through the realization of cognitive structures in interactive situations. In a sense, children "invent" language as they develop, although various degrees and types of constraints may limit the kind of language they create.

Fillmore (1988) points out that an important feature of functional theories is the status of syntax and the relation between syntax and semantics. In formal grammars, the essence and epitome of language is syntax, but functional grammars allow structures to incorporate grammatical, semantic, and pragmatic patterns. As Van Valin (1991) explains, the functionalist view is that language is a set of relations between forms and functions, conferring no special status on syntax. The variety of information that enters these relations and converges on language and language use, including nonlinguistic information, is treated as equally relevant to the formal study of language as syntax is in formal accounts.

Although functional theories differ from each other in myriad ways, they converge on their values for the three characteristics of acquisition theories identified above. The first issue is the architectural integrity of language. In functional theories, language is fully integrated with all other cognitive domains and depends entirely on them for its structure, meaning, and use. This feature is a defining characteristic of cognitive grammar: "language is neither self-contained nor describable without essential reference to cognitive processing" (Langacker, 1986, p. 1). Logically, placing language in the center of other cognitive domains influences its very nature. It no longer makes sense, for example, to consider that categories defined strictly in formal linguistic terms, such as syntax, noun, verb, phrase, have psychological reality. This creates the opportunity to redefine the essential building blocks of language and to incorporate into them materials that are not traditionally or uniquely linguistic. Language acquisition, then, becomes part of cognitive development and may be constrained by the limits of cognition as well as enhanced by its support.

The second common characteristic is the role given to linguistic input in establishing the emerging grammar. Because a universal grammar is logically precluded, language is defined through individual experiences. The mechanism for this is worked out most carefully by construction grammar and connectionism, each in its own way. The commonality is that the language heard by the child is the complete and sufficient source of linguistic data from which representations are built and patterns abstracted. Different input would set the child on a different path in constructing the language.

The importance of input in formal theories is replaced by a reliance on social interaction in functional theories. Because language is situated so centrally with other cognitive functions, social interaction, and the social context in which language occurs, are automatically part of the linguistic representation. Indeed, language can barely be separated from the surrounding context. This orientation to language makes the question of innate structures irrelevant because there is no substantial core to linguistic structure that could be presumed to exist in any form prior to children's experiences with language in the world.

Whatever the means, linguistic representations, largely redefined as cognitive representations, form the competence of native speakers. These representations have a form radically different from those that are characteristic of formal grammars. Unlike the competence that characterizes linguistic knowledge in generative (and probably other) approaches, Langacker (1986) describes linguistic knowledge as "procedural" rather than "declarative." This knowledge is comprised of a structured set of cognitive routines, called "units," each consisting of an unanalyzed pattern that can be activated when needed. The organization of these units is hierarchical but not generative; in other words, units can combine to form other higher-order units, but there is no logical or algorithmic procedure from which they can generate the acceptable grammar of a language. In construction grammar, linguistic knowledge consists of a repertoire of patterns. These proposals are discussed more fully below. In no case, however, is the representation considered to be an abstract linguistic constraint.

Cognitive Grammar

In proposing a new theory called cognitive grammar, Langacker (1986, 1987, 1991) claimed that the established linguistic theories had seriously misconstrued the nature of language. His theory is not simply a reformulation of traditional linguistic principles but is rather a novel approach to defining the major issues in linguistic inquiry.

In cognitive grammar, language is "an integral facet of overall psychological organization" (Langacker, 1988, p. 4), rather than a logically organized set of generative algorithms. The structure of language is reconceptualized away from the traditional constructs of syntax, semantics, and phonology set out by generative grammar and considered in terms of a new set of components. Langacker (1988, p. 11) posits grammar as "a structured inventory of conventional linguistic units," where "unit" seems to refer to any cognitive routine. The complexity of these units varies from single words (or possibly morphemes) to long phrases, but they are units because they function as preassembled wholes. There are three types of units: semantic, phonological, and symbolic. Symbolic is an unfortunate term for the third type of unit, and its status is actually quite different from the other two. The nature of semantic and phonological units is transparent, but a symbolic unit is defined as a relation between those two. The set of these relations is the grammar, but the grammar does not exist independently of semantics and phonology. The relation, in other words, is defined solely in terms of the units it associates.

The basis of language in cognitive grammar is the set of meanings or the conceptualization that emerges from cognitive processing in real situations. Meanings are derived from the entire social and pragmatic context in which language occurs. In generative grammars, variations of sentences such as "Bill kissed Mary" and "Mary was kissed by Bill" are considered semantically equivalent. In cognitive grammar, the different nuances, images, and circumstances evoked by these alternative formulations are part of their meaning; the two sentences do not "mean" the same thing.

The centrality of meaning and the reliance of meaning on a broad range of contextual factors, as well as complex networks of semantic relations and associations, lead equally logically to the position that meaning cannot be computed from semantic features encoded in the language. Meanings are expressed through the imagery in which a domain is construed (Langacker, 1986), and through prototypes and figurative language, where meanings diverge on a continuum of similarity and shared features (Lakoff, 1987). In this broadened conception of meaning, semantics becomes part of decisions about grammatical well-formedness, making such judgments relative rather than absolute. Judging grammaticality is a problem-solving task that incorporates information from any source that may be relevant to the nature or purpose of the utterance and evaluates it against its similarity to linguistic convention.

Cognitive grammar is a proposal that aims to correct the neglect of cognition and experience that is characteristic of formal views. By placing language in the midst of general knowledge structures and problem-solving processes, it is possible to more effectively explain the communicative and pragmatic functions of language than is so in theories that isolate language from these resources. No special status is given to linguistic structures, at least in terms of assigning psychological reality to grammatical categories. Although proponents of cognitive grammar seem untroubled by the linguistic systematicity that emerges in the representations of units, there is little explanation for their regularity. It is possible that empirical evidence alone constrains these representations so that children cannot fail to build up correct patterns that characterize the language heard around them. This explanation, though, seems too simplistic. By rejecting the inherent structure of language, it fails to account for the commonality of many aspects of structure across languages. Indeed, cognitive grammar has been applied almost exclusively to English, so broader claims about language structure and acquisition are premature. Parenthetically, Van Valin (1991) argues that it is functionalist theories and not formal theories that have developed by analyzing a wide variety of languages. It seems that this is one issue in which both sides wish to claim the moral high ground of breadth and universality.

Construction Grammar

Construction grammar is a cousin to cognitive grammar. Like cognitive grammar, language structure is built up from a set of units that includes aspects of form, meaning, and usage. Also like cognitive grammar, construction grammar encompasses a wider range of linguistic phenomena than is usually addressed by formal theories. Unlike cognitive grammar, however, construction grammar has a generative aspect to it, although it is clearly not transformational.

The basic unit of analysis in a construction approach is the linguistic or grammatical construction. Constructions can be constituted at any level in the grammatical hierarchy that is laid out in generative grammar: morpheme, phrase structure, simple sentence, complex sentence. Fillmore (1988, p. 36) defines construction as "any syntactic pattern which is assigned one or more conventional functions in a language, together with whatever is linguistically conventionalized about its contribution to the meaning or the use of structures containing it." Less obtusely, Goldberg (1995) defines construction as "form-meaning correspondences that exist independently of particular verbs. That is, it is argued that constructions themselves carry meaning, independently of the words in the sentence" (p. 1). For Tomasello and Brooks (1999), it is "a complete and coherent verbal expression associated in a relatively routinized manner with a complete and coherent communicative function." It is clear from these definitions that the motivation for deciding on grammatical units and patterns is not a formal system but a functional context. Syntax, lexicon, pragmatics, and quite possibly extralinguistic factors conspire to shape communicative outcomes, and these forces collectively determine the structural shape of the language. Grammar cannot be separated from lexicon, and form alone cannot determine function.

Construction grammar is pitched at a more circumscribed range of phenomena than seems to be the case for cognitive grammar. Cognitive grammar focuses on explaining semantics and includes all cognitive systems that contribute to the establishment of meanings in the analysis. Construction grammar incorporates all levels of linguistic description in its explanation of meaning, but discusses linguistic form in a recognizably formal sense, albeit a formalism that is entirely different from that underlying the generative approach.

The important aspect of construction grammar is in its implications for child language acquisition. Children learn the pairings between linguistic constructions and basic experiences. The linguistic associations that apply to conceptually simple and familiar experiences, corresponding to verbs such as *put, make, do,* and *get,* are the ones they learn early and universally appear across children's acquisition of different languages (Goldberg, 1998).

Tomasello and his colleagues (Tomasello, 1992; Tomasello & Brooks, 1999) have presented a well-articulated version of the constructivist approach, used it to address some central issues in language acquisition, and presented empirical evidence to assess the efficacy of the view. Children's acquisition of language is built up from their knowledge of "scenes," the familiar routines and experiences in which they participate, that are eventually lexified into linguistic constructions, and then organized into abstract structures. As the individual scenes are classified into larger groups, the linguistic commonalties among them are noted, paving the way for the emergence of abstract linguistic knowledge. In this way, children gain linguistic competence that can be defined in some traditional grammatical terms, even though the origin of that knowledge and its organization bears little resemblance to the formal categories of transformational grammar.

A feature of linguistic competence that makes the formal view so appealing is the productivity of linguistic knowledge across novel constructions. For generative grammar, this productivity is the very essence of the system: because rules are construed as abstract constraints, they enable speakers to produce, understand, and judge the acceptability of novel utterances. Tomasello (1992) accepts that this productivity is a defining feature of language and endeavors to explain how it is consistent as well with construction grammar. Tomasello et al. (1997) demonstrated that children's combinations of novel nouns into new constructions showed a limited but systematic productivity of the linguistic repertoire. Similarly, Akhtar and Tomasello (1997) were able to explain developmental differences in using verb morphology productively in terms of functional considerations such as salience, intention, and frequency of specific forms in children's experiences. In construction grammar, in other words, productivity is achieved without the presumption of any abstract or innate knowledge. Rather, productivity is built up gradually through knowledge of specific forms, applied in a limited way to semantic subsets, and eventually extended to broader, more abstract grammatical classes (Tomasello, 1992).

Tomasello and Brooks (1999) identify three sets of processes responsible for children's development of linguistic knowledge. The first process makes simple constructions more complex by combining pieces into larger constructions, copying heard utterances, and adding to existing constructions. The second makes them more abstract by extracting commonalities, possibly by assessing similarity to a "prototype" construction. Finally, the third process produces the abstract linguistic categories, such as subject, through the generalization of form and function of individual constructions. As Tomasello and Brooks (1999) point out: "The major problem for constructivist theories has always been to explain how children can begin with utterances containing only words and end up with productive grammatical constructions based on abstract lexical and relational categories" (p. 32). Their detailed discussion of these three processes has made an important contribution to resolving that problem.

The evidence presented by Tomasello and his colleagues in support of the constructivist explanation of language acquisition is a careful analysis of children's first utterances, the context from which they emerge, and the generalizations and abstractions that result from them. The logic of this argument is that if children's linguistic competence can be fully explained in terms of their cognitive and social interactions with the world, and abstract linguistic knowledge can be wholly derived from these experiences using ordinary cognitive processes, then clearly there would be no need to invoke magical notions such as innate knowledge, universal grammar, and transformation.

Connectionism

A strong alternative to traditional explanations of learning and cognition has been offered over the past decade through the approach called connectionism or parallel distributed processing. These are models of human cognitive functioning that differ from standard cognitive theories in their presumptions regarding the architectural configuration of the human mind, the role of input in learning, the mechanism by which thinking (or learning) is achieved, and the nature of knowledge and its representation. The first detailed statement of these models was presented by Rumelhart and McClelland (McClelland & Rumelhart, 1986; Rumelhart & McClelland, 1986), but enormous development of the theory and the proliferation of numerous guides and reviews of the approach have made it widely accessible. Recently, approaches that incorporate features of both connectionist systems and standard symbol manipulation systems have been developed and present an interesting alternative to both (e.g., Clark, 1989).

The mechanism responsible for learning in a connectionist system is an integrated network of associations among processing units that detects regularity in the environment. Representation is the pattern of interconnectivity among the units. The system is essentially statistical: inputs are associated with outputs on the basis of frequency patterns. This is not simple empiricism, however, because the input and output layers are mediated by complex networks of hidden units that functionally replicate the role of such cognitive constructs as working memory. As the network builds up richer and more complex associations of this sort, the system increases its power to learn and engage in problem-solving. Some connectionist models allow a clear mapping between the associative patterns and specific meanings, making a cognitive interpretation at least plausible. Clark (1989) calls these "semantically transparent," and it is the form of modeling that presents the most serious challenge to conventional symbolic theorizing.

Connectionist models have been most successfully applied to domains in which the input appears to be complex and the learning mechanism impenetrable. Language is a manifest example of such a domain. An early application of connectionist modeling developed by Rumelhart and McClelland (1986) was a simulation of the acquisition of past tense *-ed* morphology, described above. Unlike the learnability explanation in which different mechanisms are responsible for retrieved and generated results, the connectionist alternative posits only a single process. This is the fortification of associations between verbs and their past tense form through probabilities extracted from input data (e.g., Elman et al., 1996; Plunkett, 1995).

The early models aimed at simulating the past tense construction were somewhat crude and were strongly criticized. Pinker and Prince (1988), for example, argued that the phonological representation of the input was unnatural and ambiguous; the kinds of errors that were committed did not conform to errors children actually made; and the shape of learning for the simulation violated the three stages described above that characterized children's progress. The debate led to the creation of models that were more sophisticated and produced simulations that were more faithful to the patterns of input, performance, and learning known to characterize the experience of children (e.g., MacWhinney & Leinbach, 1991; Plunkett & Marchman, 1991). Current connectionist simulations provide more natural profiles of language learning and account for more of the important factors that influence children's actual acquisition (e.g., Allen & Seidenberg, 1999).

In a connectionist explanation of language acquisition, the language in the environment is the input to the system and the output is the organization of this information into something that resembles a structured grammar. There are, of course, no actual rules that correspond to the emerging structures or define the grammar. Rather, the structure inherent in the input sets the weights and associations in the network and produces responses that honor those relationships. In this sense, the output appears to be strongly determined by external factors and leaves little role for the child's active participation in the creation of language. This impression is false, however, because the connectionist network itself can be constrained in ways that imitate preconceptions and biases that the child brings to the experience of language acquisition. Nonetheless, connectionists are correct to suggest that the impetus for language acquisition is in the contingencies of the linguistic environment, and the representations that are built from interactions in the environment are networks of associations. Because the mechanism operates on the concrete instantiation of language, lexicon is the primary level of description and the key to learning. Bates and Goodman (1997) take this view further and argue that the emergence of grammar depends directly on vocabulary size. In their view, grammar is the solution that evolved naturally from the problem of mapping a multiplicity of meanings through a system (the human mind) with severe capacity limitations (Bates & Goodman, 1999). It really is just about meanings.

A specific connectionist model that has been well grounded in research is the competition model developed by Bates and MacWhinney (e.g., Bates & MacWhinney, 1989; MacWhinney, 1997). The primary mechanism that drives language acquisition is cue validity, a statistical relation between a stimulus cue and an outcome. The strength of the cue in influencing outcomes is determined by factors such as its reliability. Language learners build up response patterns based on these cues, and these patterns are the working grammar of the language. For example, word order is a reliable cue to meaning in English but not Italian, so English speakers, and children learning English, pay attention to word order but Italian speakers do not. The effects of these cues are so profound that Bates and MacWhinney (1981) reported that the cue validity relations learned for a first language continue to define the processing patterns of a second language even after an extensive length of time living and working in the second language. The essence of the "competition," then, exists among cues that potentially direct language processing. Language input into a connectionist system establishes response patterns that are the working knowledge of the language.

The notion of innate linguistic knowledge is logically incompatible with a connectionist system, since the origin of all knowledge is in the associations extracted from environmental patterns. Nonetheless, connectionists do not necessarily discount the possibility that some surrogate for nativism has a role in learning and development. One concession to innate constraints is in the structural biases that limit the way the connectionist network functions. As stated by Elman et al. (1996, p. 31), "almost all connectionist models assume innate architectural constraints, and very few assume innate representations." Another effort to confront innateness is achieved through definition. Elman et al. (1996) define "innate" in terms of interactions between genes and the environment: "innate refers to changes that arise as a result of interactions that occur within the organism itself during ontogeny. That is, interactions between the genes and their molecular and cellular environments without recourse to information from outside the organism" (p. 22). Those interactions that are between the organism and the external environment that lead to behaviors common to the species they call "primal." Thus, by distinguishing between endogenous organismic changes and interactive consequences that emerge from the environment, innate is placed back into the formula. Yet, if we accept that endogenous interactions at the cellular level create constraints that function as knowledge for the organism, would it not be simpler to describe this situation as innate knowledge? At some organic level, knowledge must be describable in cellular terms, usually stated as connections among neurons. The difference between the descriptions for what constitutes innate knowledge is tough to detect.

Out of the Dichotomy

How could one begin to choose between these vastly different contenders for the rightful explanation of language acquisition? The question is probably misformed: the domain of language is sufficiently broad and its acquisition sufficiently complex to require some contribution from several of these interpretations. Language is, in part, a formal system, and the formal theories are fine-tuned to capture that aspect. But language is also a social tool, and the functional theories exploit that feature. In short, formal approaches attempt to explain language; functional approaches attempt to explain communication. These are not mutually exclusive conceptualizations of language, so the theories that explain them need not be mutually exclusive, either.

Undoubtedly, both formal and functional theorists would reject this characterization of their positions. Formal theorists may point to the productivity of the system as evidence for its communicative effectiveness and perhaps the very reason that communication is possible. The defense, however, would rest on a rather narrow definition of communication. Functional theorists would likely insist that they do indeed account for formal structure and even for its acquisition. The formalisms they refer to, however, are difficult to separate from the cognitive and conceptual categories from which they arose. In that sense, these categories are only minimally linguistic.

Partly, the unrestricted field of proffered explanations flourishes because there is no consensus regarding a definitive set of criteria or definition for language proficiency (see discussion in Chapter 1). Although theoretical linguistics may describe the properties of language, proficiency with the system is a far more complex matter. As an aspect of human knowledge, language use includes a social context, pragmatic applications, cultural and regional variation, motivational and other individual differences, conceptual (cognitive) content, experience and history, and probably many other nonlinguistic factors. So just what is it that we wish to explain when describing children's acquisition of language?

Contributions and Limitations

Both formal and functional theories of language acquisition have, to some extent, missed this point. They are not competing explanations for the same phenomenon, yet they both suffer by not recognizing the need for the other perspective. Consider first the functional approaches. Their main failure is that they leave unsolved the mystery of coincidence: how to explain the constraints that make natural languages similar to each other and children's progress in learning them so parallel. To a great extent, functionalists must place faith in the empiricist principles that transform patterns in the environment into mental structures or knowledge. In construction grammar, for example, Tomasello (Tomasello, 1992; Tomasello & Brooks, 1999) locates children's early utterances in their knowledge of scenes and other routines. From individual concrete experiences, children extract commonalities, associate events with words, and build up structure. Similarly, in connectionist approaches (e.g., Elman et al., 1996), the concrete foundation is lexicon. After passing a vocabulary threshold, structure begins to emerge in children's knowledge of language. But how does the correct structure get built up? Linguistic principles are not inherent in the knowledge of scenes or words, yet children manage to find just the right combinations of words and sounds, and moreover, they all do it in the same basic order at about the same age.

In these functionalist explanations, ordinary social mechanisms, such as social interaction, are sufficient for children to internalize language from the environment. Moreover, proof of the sufficiency of the explanation is demonstrated through computer simulation, such as connectionist modeling. Language is in the environment, children interact with the environment, and children learn language. But what is language, why is it structured as it is, and why are all languages so similar? The functionalist approach treats language as though it were like yogurt: once some exists, it is fairly straightforward to reproduce it, but where did the first yogurt come from? And why does yogurt from different places always come out more or less the same? To make yogurt, one must start with yogurt. There is something essential about its nature. So, too, with language: once it is in the environment, there are a number of ways one can explain how individual children obtain their own copy, but how did languages develop the predictable regularities they did, especially when the same regularities are observed across highly disparate languages? And why does the path to acquisition always look so similar? The functionalist response is to deny they are dealing with yogurt: the idea of linguistic universals is a fiction and each language is as different from all others as is each child who learns it.

The formal theories are equally parochial. Although they easily explain the emergence of structure, they are too complacent about the experiences that are necessary to trigger these insights. In these explanations, it is sufficient to be exposed to heard language, presumably in an interactional setting, for the innate mechanisms to create linguistic principles. This seems implausible as an explanatory device. Even with a direct connection between the experiences the child is having, the meanings the child is considering, and the linguistic structure the child is noticing, there is no incentive for the child to learn the structure. It is also mute on any explanation of how this formal competence becomes a productive aspect of the child's own linguistic system. Language is considered an abstraction that has almost magical qualities, something unknowable except by divine intervention, and unconnected to praxis, a point criticized long ago by Bruner (1983). The formalist response is to point to the absolute certainty with which children transform themselves into native speakers, irrespective of incredible variations in intelligence, opportunity, and experience.

Divide and Conquer

The two theoretical approaches have coexisted by dividing the territory, more or less along the boundaries of linguistic domain. Formal theories are biased to focus primarily on syntax and phonology, while functional theories focus essentially (but not exclusively) on semantics and pragmatics. Dedicated proponents of each side reject this dichotomy. Lakoff (1991, p. 55), for example, states, "Generative linguistics may require only form, but functional linguistics does not require only function." Instead, he goes on to claim that functional linguistics "makes use of both function and form, by stating correlations between them." His argument does not mitigate against the central point that the focus of analysis for each of these two perspectives is starkly different. However, language proficiency quite obviously needs both of them. Still, the division of labor between these approaches reveals certain ironies in the issues and methodologies adopted by each.

First and most obvious, the definition of language within each approach corresponds to the domain of acquisition each is tailored to explain. For formalists, who are best placed to explain syntax, language is defined by its formal grammatical structure; for functionalists, who provide a compelling account of meanings, it is the communicative situation that defines language.

A second irony is evident in the methodologies chosen by each. Formal models use a biological metaphor to explain the relation between language and other cognitive functions. Language is considered a "mental organ" that contains an innate "bioprogram" to unravel the structure of heard language. Linguistic ability arose through evolutionary selection in the development of our brains. These statements place language firmly in a biological and neurological context. Research investigating these models, however, relies almost exclusively on observational behavioral data. In contrast, functionalist theories use a social-interactionalist framework for explaining language. Nonetheless, the majority of the work in neurolinguistics that seeks evidence in brain functions, cortical activity, and computer simulation is conducted by functionalists.

A methodological interregnum is in order here. It is the job of the theorist to lead us along a path from some origin to some conclusion and hope that the path itself provides an explanation for the route. The path, in this case, begins with language as an abstraction and ends with knowledge or competence in the brains (or minds) of children. The problem is to find a link between entities that are ontologically, structurally, and possibly logically different, namely, language and brains. The theoretical challenge is to define the path, or process, so that the steps of that process appear plausible. This is achieved by defining the process to be congruent with the endpoint, the conception of language proficiency. For formalists, the brain is considered to be a modular organ with specialized processors, some of which are dedicated to the discovery of linguistic structure. In this sense, brains resemble language. Language acquisition, therefore, is the process of discovery by this dedicated module of the inherent structure of language. For functionalists, the brain is a distributed system of neurons, and language is a series of associations between forms and meanings that are regulated by the context. Language acquisition, then, is the process of building up enough of these connections. Thus, the assumptions about the brain are inspired by the conception of language that each is hoping to prove and are instrumental in guiding the research that is waged in their defense.

Third, there is an irony in the attention that is drawn to the different conceptions of nativism in the two approaches. This is much less of an issue than it is made out to be. It seems unlikely that anyone would seriously argue that we could explain the child's acquisition of something as rich and complex as language in the absence of some predefined disposition, constraint, or bias. For some functionalists, it is the innate constraints of the perceptual-cognitive systems that drive language acquisition. For formalists, it is language itself that sets the constraints on our perceptual faculties. There is a trivial sense in which everything we learn we were in some way prepared to learn, and "prepared" inevitably raises the specter of "innate." The evidence from infants' early appreciation of phonological distinctions discussed earlier in this chapter is an illustration of a linguistic domain that is functioning within strictly defined constraints in the first weeks of life. Is it innate? While such examples do not warrant wholesale acceptance of an innate capacity or a prewired representational system, they do require one to reconsider the initial state of the child upon which environmental cues and experiential interactions play out their roles. Unconstrained empiricism is simply not an option.

Finally, there is an irony in the relevance each approach has to the acquisition of other languages. In studies of second-language acquisition, the predominant view is the (formal) generative approach, even though the most interesting implications for second-language acquisition and bilingualism come from the functionalist perspectives. It is in these functional theories that language learning is more tied into cognitive functioning, social context, and individual interaction, all factors known to be crucial in learning a second language (Bialystok & Hakuta, 1994). However, functionalist accounts rarely step outside the bounds of English, either in describing the structure of language or its acquisition. As Lehmann (1988) points out in a review of Langacker (1987, p. 122), cognitive grammar displays a "virtual absence of attention to languages other than English. . . . The work might well be entitled *Foundations of English Cognitive Grammar.*" Construction grammar is less vulnerable to this criticism. Tomasello and Brooks (1999) point out some specific differences between languages, but these tend to refer to rather trivial order of acquisition effects. More substantively, Slobin's (e.g., 1985) collection includes the acquisition of diverse languages, many of them interpreted within interactionist principles. Nonetheless, the impact of functional theories has not been widely accepted in the domain of second-language acquisition to the extent of that of formal theories. It would seem that these explanations have much to contribute to the study of second-language acquisition and bilingualism. These are examined in the next chapter.

The tension between the two major approaches to explaining language acquisition is reminiscent of a debate being waged over a different issue. Gould (1997) accused Dennett (1995) of being a fundamentalist who wished to attribute all evolutionary change to a single mechanism: natural selection. Such a single-factor explanation, Gould argued, results in an orthodoxy that is narrow and full of presumptions about the nature of change. Gould claims that Darwin never meant that natural selection was the only means of change, just one of several possibilities, albeit the most important. Gould describes his own view and that of his supporters as Darwinian pluralism, an acknowledgment of interactions between a variety of forces and factors, only some of which are under our control and amenable to our observations. Gould may well be unduly sanctifying the virtues of his own view, but the point is still correct and it applies equally to language. We need linguistic pluralism, not dichotomized camps.

When the complexity of language is considered, the fact that children learn it easily and rapidly seems remarkable. Children learn to interact in social situations, to focus their capacities for speech and interpretation onto a highly rule-governed system, and to extract from this experience an abstract knowledge of those rules and words. In light of this accomplishment, going through the process a second time to learn the details of a different structural system may be less daunting. But how do language learners simultaneously tackle the need to uncover the structure of two systems? It is to those situations that we now turn.

3

And Adding Another

It is immensely difficult to understand how children learn one language. The competing descriptions each explain only part of the process, so a complete understanding requires integrating pieces from different perspectives. The need to weave together a larger fabric from distinct fragments is not surprising given the complexity of the enterprise and the number of factors that impinge on children's experience in language learning. This complexity is multiplied when one considers the factors relevant to a child's experience in learning two languages.

The questions that one need ask about children learning two languages are different from those guiding the study of monolingual language acquisition but they reflect the same divide between formal and functional paradigms. For example, the difference between simultaneous and sequential acquisition of a second language matters only under certain interpretations of the process of first-language acquisition. Applying formalist assumptions, both varieties of second-language acquisition should be similar because they are guided by the mechanism of the language acquisition device and shaped by the constraints of universal grammar. Hence, any input to the child would lead to the construction of the appropriate grammar. Following functionalist assumptions, however, the sequence and timing of second-language acquisition would be different depending on whether the two languages were acquired at the same time or in sequence. In these views, social interaction and previous knowledge drive language acquisition, placing a significant divide between the experiences associated with simultaneous or sequential acquisition of a second language.

A fundamental question about children learning two languages is whether the acquisition of each language resembles the process and path experienced by a monolingual child learning only that language. However, the apparent simplicity of this question is deceptive, as it incorporates a set of assumptions about the nature of language, the process of acquisition, and the structure of mind. Again, whether or not we consider that children acquiring two languages are comparable to monolinguals is rooted in a position regarding the nature and acquisition of a first language.

A plausible but complex view of language acquisition is achieved by incorporating aspects of both the acquisition of linguistic competence explained by formal theories and the acquisition of communicative competence explained by functional theories. This synthesis of perspectives seems more imperative as a means explicating children's acquisition of two languages than it does for the usual monolingual language acquisition. As again becomes apparent in the discussion of the cognitive impact of bilingualism (Chapter 7), the study of bilingual children advances theorizing by forcing explanations onto a broader palette. Similarly, questions about children's language acquisition allow greater access to some of the central issues of mind when children are learning two languages than when they are learning just one. This point is discussed in more detail below.

The integrative view that follows from including both formal and functional perspectives appears complex – it cannot be stated in a few simple assumptions and constrained by a limited number of factors. One consequence of this complexity is that it removes the possibility of generating simple dichotomies and describing concepts categorically. Hence, the differences between first- and second-language acquisition, between simultaneous and successive acquisition, and between presence and absence of proficiency in a specific language need to be examined more analytically and described in greater detail.

The entire process of using language is different when two languages are available. A dichotomy in which mastery is assessed individually for each of the two languages fails to capture the essential nature of having two languages at one's disposal. Grosjean (1989, 1998) proposes a solution in which a scale is used to describe language competence for bilingual speakers. He postulates that bilinguals engage in a range of language functions each of which varies on a dimension from monolingual mode, mimicking the language behavior of a monolingual speaker of that language, to bilingual mode, naturally incorporating aspects of both languages into production. In a bilingual mode, for example, language mixing and switching is normal and comprehensible. Bilinguals move freely along this dimension in response to social and linguistic circumstances. He calls this the *bilingual view,* in contrast to the *monolingual view* that would ascribe two language competencies on this dimension to a bilingual, each of which corresponded to a monolingual speaker. The underlying linguistic competence that permits this movement along the dimension from bilingual to monolingual modes indicates that linguistic representation for bilinguals is importantly different from that of monolinguals. Therefore, we should not expect language acquisition in each of the bilingual child's two languages to replicate exactly the pattern experienced by a monolingual child learning only one of those languages because the representational system for both languages are different.

Another question is whether a second language must be learned by a certain age in order to achieve native-like competence. If there is one certainty that people hold about language acquisition, it is that children can learn a second language better than adults can. Indeed, there is no shortage of anecdotal and empirical evidence to support this supposition. A frequent interpretation of this prodigious talent by young people is that it is the reflection of a critical period for language acquisition in humans. The claim has serious implications because of the logical connection between first- and second-language acquisition. If it could be demonstrated unequivocally that there is a critical period for first-language acquisition (no small feat given the nature of the data required for such a proof), then it may or may not follow that humans are constrained in their ability to learn another language later in life. In other words, establishing the existence of a critical period for first-language acquisition would tell us nothing about whether or not such a constraint exists for second-language acquisition. However, if there is a maturational limit on the time period during which a second language must be learned, then it follows necessarily that any language learning by humans is so constrained. This is a powerful generalization about human cognition and has implications for issues such as how languages are learned, the status of a linguistic bioprogram, and the organization of mind to include a contained language module. These issues resonate profoundly through our conceptions of intelligence and the human potential for learning. Access to these issues, then, begins by deciding whether there is a critical period for second-language acquisition.

Mastering the System

We tend to think of children's minds in protective terms: some things are too hard for them to understand, some details are unnecessarily confusing, and some information is too burdensome. These patronizing cautions emanate from the assumption that the mind is a container – a vessel of limited capacity that must be filled with care. It follows, surely, that trying to squeeze two complex languages into such a fragile receptacle would lead to bewilderment, frustration, and failure. However, nothing we know about memory substantiates these fears. Indeed, the fact that millions of children routinely grow up with more than one language in their environment and appear to suffer no obvious trauma should allay the concerns of most parents.

Early research on the possibility of children learning two languages to an equal and acceptable level of proficiency was far less sanguine in its conclusions. Macnamara (1966) undertook a detailed review of seventy-seven studies published between 1918 and 1962, performing a sort of early "meta-analysis." These studies included numerous languages and language pairs as well as various situations and circumstances for children's bilingualism. Although he gave few methodological details for the studies, he did point out which ones were more trustworthy and in fact excluded some studies where he believed that methodological flaws undermined their conclusions. Linguistic assessments included tests of vocabulary, spelling, reading, and grammatical complexity, to name a few. Macnamara concluded that "bilinguals have a weaker grasp of language than monoglots" (p. 31), and supported this conclusion by listing a running score for the number of studies in each linguistic skill that reported each conclusion. For example, twenty-four studies investigated vocabulary, of which six reported bilinguals were equal to monolinguals and eighteen reported vocabulary superiority for monolinguals. Macnamara thus concluded that bilinguals had vocabulary deficits. Six studies investigated spelling, of which one reported a bilingual deficit and five showed no difference. Thus it was concluded that spelling is not affected by bilingualism.

Macnamara offered four reasons for his conclusion that bilingualism causes language deficits. First, linguistic contrast creates interference, especially for highly divergent languages (cf. Lado, 1957); second, cultural assimilation is crucial to language learning and is not usually present for bilingual children (cf. Whorf, 1956); third, language models are often inadequate (parents may not be native speakers) and opportunities to learn, such as school attendance, may be absent; and fourth, time available to learn each language is less for bilingual children, including as well the effects of age, ability, and incentive (cf. critical period hypothesis reviewed below). He concluded that the time factor accounts for the deficits in vocabulary, that linguistic interference and faulty models account for deficits in grammar and phonetics, but that the real explanation for the deficit would require complex interactions among all of these.

Macnamara's conclusions that bilingual children failed to learn both languages adequately have not been supported by more recent research and thinking about these issues (discussed below). Aside from methodological flaws in the research (some of which Macnamara details), there is an illogic to the argument. Consider a paradigm case in which a child learns Spanish at home as the family language and attends school in English. The community is primarily Spanish-speaking and the child has only school as an environment to develop English skills. It is not surprising that the type of competence that the child develops in each of these languages is different. In an ideal situation, we would expect the child's spoken Spanish to be equivalent to Spanish monolinguals and the child's academic English to be equivalent to English monolinguals, but social circumstances rule against that outcome. The child's oral Spanish may be compromised by such factors as dialect, family educational levels, and range of communication experiences. Similarly, academic English might be diminished by the lack of support at home for high levels of English usage. The point is that assessing children's linguistic skill requires understanding children's language experiences, and the objective outcomes of such assessments are uninterpretable without knowing about the context. Invariably, the language assessments used in these studies were formal tests administered in both languages. There is no reason to believe that children should have the same *type* of competence in both languages given these vastly different experiences with each. Romaine (1999, p. 259) makes the same point: "It does not make much sense to assess bilinguals as if they were two monolinguals since it is unlikely that a bilingual will have the same experiences in both languages." In short, these studies may tell us very much about the social context for learning language but almost nothing about the nature or impact of bilingualism on the language proficiency that children can achieve.

There is some empirical evidence that the structure of language proficiency is not the same in the two languages of a bilingual. Lemmon and Goggin (1989) tested a large number of university students who were Spanish-English bilinguals and found a complex pattern of language proficiency. Using a battery of language tests, they found variable proficiency for the different skills and different factor analysis structure for English and Spanish. The lesson is that we require more sensitive tests of language proficiency to understand a learner's competence in each language. Generalizations across types of proficiency must be made cautiously.

Recent research has been more careful in comparing abilities and attending to the contexts in which children learn different languages. Not surprisingly, the results are quite different from those using less sensitive methods. The attempt is to carry out a detailed study of linguistic skills when the monolingual and bilingual groups are known to be equivalent in other relevant factors. In this way, the process of learning each aspect of linguistic competence is traced individually for the various language skills, and each one can then be compared with the progress made by monolingual children learning the same system. These studies not only inform our knowledge of the effects of bilingualism on children's language acquisition, but also contribute to our understanding of how these individual aspects of linguistic competence develop and interact.

Two questions that are fundamental to interpretations of the nature of language and its acquisition are, first, the relation between language and the conceptual system (alternatively construed as the relation between language and thought), and, second, the possibility of an innate mental structure for language. These questions address two of the three issues that distinguished between formal and functional theories of language acquisition described in Chapter 2. The first is the problem of the autonomy of language from other cognitive processes and the second is the role of innate structure in language acquisition.

These questions are staggeringly difficult to investigate when children learn one language and have one conceptual system. Bilingual children, however, offer an opportunity to disentangle some of their important dimensions. For the first question, we can examine the way that bilingual children acquire vocabulary in their two languages; for the second, we can study the syntactic and phonological systems of young bilingual children. These examples will provide descriptive information about the language development of bilingual children and comparative possibilities to assess the generality of the acquisition by monolingual children outlined in Chapter 2, and offer a window into some of these more profound questions about the nature of language and thought. We begin by examining the progress of acquisition for children learning two languages, then consider the evidence for a critical period for language acquisition, and finally reflect on the implications of the story for these more basic issues in language and cognition.

Lexicon

How does the need to learn two vocabularies influence children's progress in language acquisition? Do bilingual children share their processing and acquisition resources across the two languages, essentially controlling half the vocabulary range in each language that would be mastered by a monolingual child? Alternatively, do processing resources expand to fill the considerable needs required to store two lexical systems? Both positions seem unlikely. Children's developing cognitive capacities surely impose limitations on the breadth of information that can be stored in accessible memory, ruling out the possibility of two complete vocabularies. At the same time, however, children indeed seem capable of learning more than the minimal range of vocabulary required for one functioning language system. Somewhere between these options, bilingual children probably function in an interlingual purgatory, less masterful than a monolingual in either language but surely more extensive in their communicative possibilities than any monolingual.

As with many aspects of language acquisition, hypotheses such as these defy empirical examination. If there is one prevailing certainty about vocabulary acquisition, it is its variability across children. In fact, the more normative data that are gathered, the more variability emerges as the predominant characteristic (see, e.g., Fenson et al., 1994). A properly controlled study of the effects of bilingualism on lexical acquisition would need to compare the vocabulary of bilingual children in terms of its size, conceptual coverage, and linguistic sophistication to the vocabulary they *would have had* in each language had they been learning only one of them. Such hypothetical speculation is quite obviously untestable, so comparisons must be waged across groups and, therefore, between individuals. The inevitable differences in ability and circumstance between any two children make these contrasts at best a weak proxy for the issue of real interest, the influence of bilingualism on vocabulary growth.

This methodological problem of comparison does not arise to the same extent for other aspects of language, such as syntax or phonology, probably because in these cases the sheer quantity of information learned is not the most significant variable. In syntactic acquisition, for example, it is sufficient to establish the progress children make in terms of utterance length, type of error, and structural sophistication. Although there is certainly individual variation in these dimensions, it is reasonable to assess progress according to age norms, and the balance between the two languages is more stable than the possibilities for enormous asynchrony that exist for vocabulary.

In addition to being a problem in its own right, the difficulty of measuring and interpreting vocabulary size in the two languages of a bilingual child also emerges simply from the complications of research into children's bilingualism. Research comparing bilinguals to monolinguals necessarily uses between-subjects designs. Such research always requires extra precaution in assuring that the variable of interest is the only relevant difference between the subjects in the two groups. For comparisons between bilinguals and monolinguals, this is not simple to arrange.

Researchers conducting these studies attempt to create groups that are comparable in all respects but their bilingualism. Partly, the assumption of equivalence is a convenient fiction because children growing up with two languages are necessarily different from children growing up with only one in ways that are not revealed by assessments of language ability (see discussion in Chapter 1). Nonetheless, such simplifying assumptions are essential if progress is to be made in understanding the nature of development for bilingual children. To this end, a test of receptive vocabulary, such as the Peabody Picture Vocabulary Test (PPVT) is sometimes used both as an indication of the degree of balance between the two languages and as an index of the comparability of the bilingual children's language abilities in each language to those of monolinguals. Ideally, it should be shown that the receptive vocabularies for the monolinguals and bilinguals in their common language are similar. It is further beneficial if the receptive vocabularies in the bilingual's two languages are comparable to each other. This would support the claim that the child is a relatively balanced bilingual, a representative of an idealized class of bilinguals.

Published research generally meets the selection criteria of guaranteeing the comparability of the monolingual and bilingual children studied; indeed, they would be deemed unworthy of publication if they did not. Nonetheless, studies frequently report differences in the PPVT scores of monolinguals and bilinguals (Ben-Zeev, 1977; Bialystok, 1988; Merriman & Kutlesic, 1993; Rosenblum & Pinker, 1983; Umbel et al., 1992). Some research has used the differences between PPVT scores in the two languages as an indication of relative dominance of the two languages and not as a problem to be solved, thus treating unbalanced bilinguals as qualitatively different from their more balanced peers (Bialystok, 1988; Cromdal, 1999; Hakuta & Diaz, 1985). This approach allows one to investigate the role of balance between the two languages in determining other language and cognitive outcomes. What is not dealt with, however, is how the results of these studies are affected by discarding children who fail to meet the criterion for PPVT competence in one or both of their languages. As long as children are selected for study based on their relative proficiency in the two languages, we may never really know the complete picture. How do minimal levels of knowledge of another language influence children's development? A more graduated approach to language proficiency would be necessary to determine the answer to such questions.

A comprehensive source of data on the vocabulary growth of bilingual children comes from two studies based on longitudinal research with Spanish-English bilingual children in Miami, Florida. In the first, Pearson, Fernández, and Oller (1993) compared the receptive and productive vocabulary acquisition of 25 bilingual children with that of 35 monolingual children, all between the ages of 8 and 30 months old. In the second, Pearson and Fernández (1994) evaluated the patterns of productive vocabulary growth in 18 bilingual children between the ages of 8 and 30 months. The main source of data is parental reports of children's receptive and productive vocabularies. Not all the children were visited with the same frequency or at the same intervals, but sufficient numbers were used so that averages at particular ages could be extracted.

Their assessment of vocabulary includes four measures: the vocabulary size in each language (therefore contributing two measures), the combined total vocabulary for both languages, and the conceptual range given by the number of unique concepts that are labeled in either language. Therefore, a concept labeled in both languages counts only once toward the conceptual score. Children are not credited with knowing the name for something in the two languages but for the breadth of concepts that are labeled by their cumulative lexical resources. The relation between total vocabulary and conceptual range reveals an interesting aspect of the child's bilingualism. If the child uses the second language to echo the dominant one, then the child would obtain a high score for total vocabulary but a diminished score for the conceptual range because the labeled concepts have already been counted in the other language. However, if the child uses the two languages in distinct contexts and for individual functions, then the child would receive a high score for total vocabulary and a high score for conceptual range. These relationships are probably strongly influenced by the sociolinguistic and pragmatic circumstances of the child's bilingual experience.

In the first study, the total production vocabulary for bilingual children was not significantly different from that of the monolingual children. Moreover, the bilingual children who were dominant in English controlled about the same productive vocabulary in English as did monolingual English children, and bilingual children dominant in Spanish were similarly comparable to Spanish monolinguals. The weaker language in each case, of course, fell below these levels. A similar pattern was found for comprehension, although in this case there was some evidence for an enhanced receptive vocabulary by the bilingual children compared with the monolingual controls.

The second study provides more detailed information because the data are reported for individual subjects and not simply group norms. Indeed, the most striking aspect of the results is the individual variability among the children. Not only are the children acquiring vocabulary at different rates and at different levels, but also are they different from each other in terms of their language environment and the balance between their developing languages. This is to be expected and probably has little to do with the children's bilingual experience. Nonetheless, it is necessary to extract some general pattern from the sample in order to address the issue of vocabulary growth in some useful way.

Pearson and Fernández (1994) compared the total vocabulary sizes to those reported by Fenson et al. (1993) for a monolingual population and concluded that they "fell within the broad range" of those data. This is true, but little is excluded in the broad range; the normative data set includes levels that range from the 10th to the 90th percentile for children's vocabulary acquisition. A more detailed analysis comes from comparing the total vocabulary with the levels reported as the median for each age in the monolingual sample. Comparing the individual data with the norms reported by Fenson et al. (1994) yields a rather different picture. The median number of words in the monolingual study is approximately 75 words at 18 months, 150 words at 20 months, 200 words at 22 months, and 300 words at 24 months. Using these standards, 10 of the 18 children in the bilingual study had total vocabularies within these ranges. The other eight children, however, were well below these levels, their total vocabulary placing them at the 10th percentile or lower for the monolingual norms.

Although the majority of the children still scored within the normal range for total vocabulary size, it is puzzling that the two studies led to such different results. The contradiction is hard to resolve because the data are reported differently in the two studies: Pearson, Fernández and Oller (1993) report group percentiles but Pearson and Fernández (1994) report individual vocabulary size. It is possible that the subjects in the first study were more advanced than those in the second or that the monolingual group in the first study was below average in its vocabulary acquisition.

Other studies that have investigated these issues usually report an overall deficit in the vocabulary of bilingual children compared with monolingual speakers of one of those languages. For example, Doyle, Champagne, and Segalowitz (1978) compared the vocabulary size of the dominant language of bilinguals with monolinguals of that language and found a quantitative advantage for monolinguals and concluded that bilinguals lagged behind monolinguals in vocabulary development. They noted, however, that the bilinguals displayed better verbal fluency than monolinguals. This is an important contribution to a conception in which competence is distributed across a number of skills, some involving formal knowledge of structure and others involving communicative uses of language. Just as aspects of language development are controlled by different mechanisms (e.g., some formal, some functional), so too bilingualism has a variable impact on specific aspects of development.

The patterns of vocabulary acquisition for the two languages, although idiosyncratic, develop systematically in response to language exposure in the environment. This in itself is not surprising, although a strong formal theory of language acquisition would assign very little importance to both the quality and quantity of heard language. On these views, children's ability to learn the ambient language is triggered by being in its presence, and the learned forms override impoverished input and poorly formed utterances. Pearson et al. (1997) showed instead that there is a correlation between language input and language acquisition if the language heard in the environment is related to the active area of language acquisition for bilingual children. Even as the dominance patterns changed for the bilingual children, the language predominantly heard by the child at that moment in time determined the child's pattern of language acquisition. These situations may provide a more sensitive test of the role of heard language in the process of language acquisition than is possible to achieve with only monolingual children. In monolingual language acquisition, the child will always learn *some* of the language, but it is impossible to know what progress the child would make were the environment to present that language in either qualitatively or quantitatively different ways. With only one heard language, those dimensions cannot be varied.

The role of input in monolingual and bilingual situations may also help to explain why the vocabulary acquisition of bilingual children can differ from that of monolinguals even though the syntactic and phonological development does not. It may be that the acquisition of syntax and phonology is adequately triggered by exposure to the language, but vocabulary needs to be learned. The triggering would have the same effect for all children exposed to that language, but vocabulary learning requires a more intentional learning effort that could not be sustained at the same level across the two languages.

Syntax

But *do* bilingual children acquire syntax in the same manner as monolinguals learning only one of the languages? There is a vast literature aimed at describing the progress made by children in learning the grammar of two languages, either simultaneously or successively in childhood. Such details exceed the purpose of the present discussion, but a number of accounts provide good reviews and documentation of these processes (e.g., collections by Meisel, 1990, 1994). The issue here is not to spell out the specific details of children's progress in learning syntax but to assess the relation between children's acquisition of syntax when they are learning two languages and when they are learning just one.

The predominant view regarding the way that children learn the structure of two languages is that it is parallel to that found by monolingual children in each language. According to Romaine (1995), "the majority of studies seem to support the conclusion that the developmental sequence for the bilingual child is the same in many respects as for the monolingual" (p. 217). She interprets this parallel development as evidence for an innate component to language acquisition.

Meisel and his colleagues (Meisel, 1990, 1993) have been involved in a large-scale investigation of children acquiring both French and German. Their position is largely derived from a formal view in which an autonomous grammatical system shapes language acquisition from the very early stages, but they allow a significant role for general cognitive mechanisms. Their data provide evidence for the assertion that children learning two languages understand the difference between the two systems and learn the structure of each in much the same way that the corresponding monolinguals do. For example, Muller (1990) showed that these children learn the gender assignments of words in both languages at about two years of age. This achievement involves both the concept of grammatical gender and the specific distribution of gender assignments in each language, something not governed by clear syntactic principles. More impressively, Meisel (1993) showed that French-German bilingual children demonstrate correct verb placement in each language by two years old. Again, this is strong evidence for the operation of grammatical constraints but also shows sensitivity to communicative contexts and cognitive dimensions. Hence, it suggests that both the semantic and formal rules are acquired simultaneously, a position that would not be supported by either a formal or functional position alone. To the extent that cognitive mechanisms influence acquisition, the view is a hybrid between formal and functional explanations. They state: "This is to say that although UG [universal grammar] does indeed, according to our hypothesis, function as a 'language acquisition device' (LAD), as it used to be called, one cannot hope to explain the patterns of language development unless various mechanisms of language processing and discovery procedures are also taken into account" (Meisel, 1990, p. 12).

Muller (1998) carried out a detailed analysis of the syntactic progress made by bilingual children learning German and one of French, English, or Italian, and proposed an interesting argument that bears on both monolingual and bilingual acquisition of syntax. She uses the word order rule for subordinate clauses in German as the target structure because it is a complex system with several variations. She reports that these children made systematic errors in this structure by adopting the simpler rules from their other language when speaking German. Nonetheless, she insists that children knew that the rules belonged to two different language systems and argues that children were transferring the construction from the other language because the German context was ambiguous. In this way, the transfer served as a "relief strategy" to help children deal with difficult and ambiguous structures.

There are two important features of this transfer. First, the direction of transfer is always from the language with the simpler or clearer structure to the language with the more complex or ambiguous structure. In the examples she used, children always transferred the word order rules from French, English, or Italian into German and never the other way around, irrespective of which language was more dominant for the child. Second, an examination of monolingual children learning German showed that they make the same word order errors, but they make fewer of them and these errors persist in speech for only a short time. Her conclusion is that there is cross-linguistic influence between the syntactic systems of the two languages for bilingual children. In this way, the syntactic development of bilingual children is never exactly like that of monolinguals learning each of the languages.

A different aspect of syntactic proficiency is reflected in how children can use syntactic cues to understand language, even semantic aspects of language. Gathercole has investigated syntactic mastery of Spanish-English bilinguals by examining three morphosyntactic features: the mass-count distinction (Gathercole, 1997, in press, a); the structure for grammatical gender (Gathercole, in press, b); and the rule for *that*-trace (Gathercole & Montes, 1997; Gathercole, in press, c). The first two are interesting because each is a syntactic feature of only one of the languages. The mass-count distinction is marked syntactically (i.e., morphologically) in English but not in Spanish, but the gender distinction is marked syntactically in Spanish but not in English. Native speakers of each language learn early on to use syntactic cues to make the appropriate classifications for these categories. The question was whether children learning both languages would learn the language-appropriate rule in each case, transfer the rule from one language to the other, or use a simpler semantic strategy. The third form, *that*-trace, is interesting because unlike the first two, this is normally considered a property of universal grammar. Therefore, if children were learning language according to some predetermined program, then the progress of the bilingual children in this case should be more like that of the monolinguals than it was for either of the first two more superficial features.

The study tested Spanish-English bilinguals and English monolinguals who were seven and nine years old, attending different kinds of educational programs, and belonging to different social classes. Comparison groups included both English and Spanish monolingual children of comparable ages. For all these structures, the bilingual children lagged behind their monolingual peers in learning the correct syntactic forms. The older children were performing better – that is, more like monolinguals – than the younger ones, and the amount of the relevant language to which the child was exposed was positively related to progress. Put another way, the older and stronger bilinguals resembled monolinguals in their syntactic sensitivity, but the weaker bilinguals took longer before they began paying attention to syntax. In all cases, however, the progression was the same and the structures were learned in the same manner and in the same order. The difference was that children learning two languages took longer to learn the subtleties of syntax than did children concentrating on only one language, and that the more exposure the child had to that language, the more quickly the structures were incorporated. This was even true for *that*-trace, undermining the explanation of acquisition as being primarily under the control of an unfolding universal grammar.

Finally, the precise manner in which languages interact as bilingual children endeavor to learn the syntax of two systems may depend on local features of both languages. Romaine (1999) cites a study by Mikeš in which he reports that children acquiring both Hungarian and Serbo-Croatian learn the locative case relations for Hungarian before they learn the corresponding forms for Serbo-Croatian. The form is simpler in Hungarian, and he argues that factors such as perceptual saliency and regularity can override general principles of syntactic acquisition when children are learning two languages.

How similar is the syntactic acquisition of a given language for children learning one or two languages? Some take a strong view on the similarity. Meisel (1993, p. 371) states: "The sequences of grammatical development in each of the bilingual's languages are the same as in monolingual children's acquisition of the respective language and is guided by the same underlying logic." Nonetheless, it is not exactly the same, and even Meisel (1990) is among those who mark the distinction by referring to "bilingual language acquisition" (cf. De Houwer, 1990, 1995; Grosjean, 1982). It is this particular uniqueness that puts the language acquisition of bilingual children in a position in which it may ultimately be able to adjudicate between competing conceptions of language and language acquisition.

Phonology

Evidence for the child's developing phonological system is apparent from the earliest vocalizations, the first playful sounds, and the initial repetitious sequences of simple consonant–vowel combinations. Although the prevailing theory used to follow the claims of Jakobson (1968) in arguing for a distinct break that separated explorations with sounds and acquisition of language, current views are more likely to endorse a description of continuity. There is a seamless progression from practicing sounds to learning words.

How do these early phonological skills and strategies adapt to a new language? The evidence shows that the basic perceptual processes for interpreting linguistic sounds become restricted in early childhood. Werker and her colleagues have investigated the perceptual acuity of infants in the first year of life to phonemic distinctions (and other phonological information) in languages that are either heard or not heard in their environment. Infants have a frustratingly small repertoire of behaviors that can be used reliably to signal a judgment about a category change, so this research has required creative efforts to obtain valid data. Their main method has used a reinforced head-turn response to indicate that the stimulus has changed. Typically, subjects are presented with pairs of sounds that are phonemic contrasts in some language not heard in their environment, and their ability to detect the difference is compared with the performance of adult speakers of that language and to adult native speakers of English. The results show a decline in the ability to perceive these distinctions between about six and twelve months of age (Werker & Tees, 1984; Werker et al., 1981). For example, Werker et al. (1981) found that six- to eight-month-old infants being raised in an English-speaking environment could make phonemic distinctions used in Hindi as well as adult Hindi native speakers but English-speaking adults could not detect these differences. By one year old, and continuing through childhood, children's performance is the same as that of adult native speakers of English (Werker & Tees, 1983). Beyond infancy, the perceptual processes that classify these sounds are applied only to phonemic categories in the language that is in the child's environment. These results have been replicated by researchers studying different populations of infants, listening to different linguistic contrasts, and measuring different response indicators (Best, 1994; Kuhl et al., 1992; Trehub, 1976). The capacity to distinguish phonemes in a nonambient language is apparently lost sometime during the first year of life.

An interesting extension of the sensitivity to the specific phonemic sounds of other languages is the way in which children respond to prosodic features of language use. It is well documented that speech addressed to children is acoustically adjusted in terms of such features as prosody and stress (e.g., Snow, 1977). Do children notice these adjusted features? In a study by Werker, Pegg, and McLeod (1994), Chinese and English infants who were four and one-half or nine months old listened to a Chinese-speaking adult address either an adult or another infant. All of the infants favored the speech directed to an infant. Even though the sounds of Chinese must have been very unusual for the English-learning infants, they could distinguish between the two forms of speech and clearly preferred that addressed to an infant. The perceptual abilities for speech by very young infants are remarkably sophisticated and appear to be independent of any particular language. Children are simply prepared to learn language, and the early attention to speech and the ability to classify its constituents is a crucial ingredient in that process.

When It Can Be Learned

It is almost axiomatic in popular science that children have a privileged ability to learn a second language. We accept this capacity of children as part of their natural endowment and simultaneously belittle our adult aptitudes in the realm of language learning. The ordinary way of describing this difference between adults and children uses such terms as a "special access" and "natural talent" possessed by children. The scientific jargon points to the presence of a "critical period" that enables children within its confines to enjoy a painless and successful journey to mastering a second language. Is there a critical period for learning a second language? Is there a boundary time beyond which the process of acquiring another language changes in both quality and quantity of presumed success? Although popular wisdom declares clear answers to these questions, scientific data are less definitive.

Science was not always so circumspect on this issue. Two reputable sources are usually credited with introducing the idea that language could fall under the jurisdiction of a critical period, constraining the acquisition of both first and subsequent languages by some maturational timetable. One of these sources was Lenneberg (1967), who noted that language recovery was virtually impossible if brain injury occurred after puberty. If injury occurred at an earlier age, there was a good chance that language would be restored. Although his argument has been widely extended to include limitations on second-language acquisition, Lenneberg was more cautious. He noted that some adults learn a foreign language perfectly well, and in fact offered an escape from fettering second languages into the constraints of a critical period: "since natural languages tend to resemble one another in many fundamental aspects, the matrix for language skills is present" (p. 176). With this observation, he acknowledged the possibility that it was the abstract structure of language that needed to be established in early childhood, and once accomplished, subsequent language learning might be possible at any age. Nonetheless, he is widely interpreted as arguing that all language learning is restricted after puberty because of maturational changes in the brain.

The other source is Penfield and Roberts (1959). Their book is a neurological study of the brain and its function in speech and language processes. As with Lenneberg, the majority of their evidence comes from the study of patients with various kinds of lesions, strokes, and impairments. The final chapter of the book is an epilogue, in which they pronounce on the implications of their theories for foreign-language instruction. They argue that there is a physiological difference between direct and indirect language learning. The former is how children learn their first language at home; the latter is what normally happens in classrooms. Further, in the absence of any evidence, they argue that these are neurologically distinct, that only direct language learning is effective, and that there is an age limit (although they do not specify what age) for this preferred method. Like Lenneberg, they acknowledge the possibility of successful adult language learning, but are essentially dismissive of the idea. They have no hesitation, however, in determining the correct model for language instruction in schools: "The time to begin what might be called a general schooling in secondary languages, in accordance with the demands of brain physiology, is between the ages of 4 and 10" (p. 255). Their arguments are based primarily on their conceptions of how language learning takes place, especially for young children learning their first language, although no evidence is cited. In the modern context, however, their conceptions of language learning are, to say the least, odd. They are rooted in behaviorist principles and molded by outdated social stereotypes. Dechert (1995) has examined several studies by Penfield and Roberts and demonstrated the extent to which their claims about second-language acquisition are based on incorrect and obsolete assumptions. The pervasiveness of these misconceptions in the argument challenges the authority of Penfield and Robert's conclusions.

The recent literature dealing with the question of a critical period for second-language acquisition is based on evidence that is more varied and more sophisticated than any available to Lenneberg or Penfield and Roberts. However, since this literature has been compiled and examined in several sources, it is not reviewed here (see, e.g., Bialystok & Hakuta, 1994; Birdsong, 1999; Harley & Wang, 1997; Singleton & Lengyel, 1995). Instead, a few issues will be selected for examination. These are (1) the logic of the argument, (2) the nature of the data, and (3) some alternative interpretations for those data.

Rationale for a Critical Period

The logical argument for a critical period for second-language acquisition depends on the interpretation of necessity and causality. There is no dispute that children are generally more successful than adults or older learners in learning a second language, and that over time, a younger start will normally yield higher levels of language proficiency. Including necessity in the argument means that this difference is inevitable, that it is caused by circumstances beyond the control of the learner. Furthermore, the differences in achievement that follow from embarking on language learning at different ages are universal. Adding causality to the story takes the position one step further. Not only is age of learning inevitably *associated* with this difference in outcome, it is the *cause* of the diminished success experienced by older learners. Specifically, the difference is caused by a biologically determined divide between older and younger learners that changes the potential for language learning on either side of it. This is the logic implied by a critical period.

Not everyone accepts this restrictive approach to a critical period. Long (1990), for example, has argued persuasively that there is a critical period for language acquisition, and that the source of the critical period can be traced to one (or more) of four domains: social, input, cognitive, and neurological factors. He carefully reviews the evidence for each and correctly documents its contribution to age-related differences in learning. There is no dispute about the details that he amasses; indeed, his discussion about the relation between age-related factors and success in acquiring a second language remains one of the most comprehensive to date. The debate is rather about the interpretation of those factors. "Critical period" is a technical concept and, as such, carries specific criteria. A correlation between age of learning and ultimate success is not, *prima facie*, evidence for a critical period. As the term is normally used in studies of behavioral development in various species (e.g., Marler, 1984, 1991), the relation between age and performance must be bound by necessity and causality. Only Long's neurological factor satisfies this criterion; the effects of the other three can be modified by experience and circumstance.

The set of cognitive factors is perhaps more dubious than the others for its simple classification on this dimension of necessity. Newport (1991) appeals to cognitive change as the most important element in an individual's declining ability to acquire language. She contrasts explanations that are based on a simple decline in ability and those that attribute decline to an increase in a competing ability. Both explanations, according to Newport, support claims for a critical period but differ in the locus of the maturational change. In the case of language, children's increasing cognitive maturity causes them to focus on larger portions of language input and apply more analytic procedures to those utterances. This, she claims, is counterproductive, because a simpler, more passive approach, like the one used by younger children, would be more successful. She calls this the "less is more" hypothesis. In this way, the cognitive domain, rather than neurological factors, sets limits on performance and creates a critical period. Her conclusion about a critical period in this case is consistent with the criteria set out for the construct, as it entails the required defining features.

Defining the Concept

What are the defining features of a critical period? Consensus, as always, is elusive. However, the concept of a critical period is well established in other fields, so using the term carries an obligation to employ it in a manner that is consistent with its previous applications. New definitions cannot be invented for each instance of age-related changes in learning. *Critical period* is a technical term and communication across disciplines requires respect for its established meaning.

Bornstein (1989) surveyed a broad spectrum of literature related to the functioning of a critical period, including diverse behaviors and species such as cocoon preference in ants, sexual imprinting in finches, egg recognition in birds, imprinting in chicks, acquisition of birdsong, aggression in mice, vision in cats, sociability in dogs, maternal responsiveness in goats, and social behavior in monkeys. From these cases, he identified fourteen dimensions that must be specified if a critical period is presumed to control learning. These dimensions were divided into four categories: *temporal contours,* relating to issues such as onset and offset times for the period; *consequences,* referring to observable features of the learning; *time scales,* describing the chronological path to learning, and *mechanism,* describing how the learning takes place. Although language acquisition can be shown to satisfy many of them, the criteria for mechanism are problematic. The main component of mechanism is specification of the system, defined as "the structure or function altered in the sensitive period" (1989, p. 184). For language acquisition, system must refer to linguistic representations, or the way linguistic competence is represented in the mind. What are these representations and how are they altered by maturational factors in the learner? The variety of theories of linguistic structure (Chapter 2) and possibilities for their representation (Chapter 4) make it exceedingly difficult to identify the object of study in discussions of a critical period.

Colombo (1982) reinforces the importance of specifying the system. In a survey of theoretical and methodological issues in sensitive period research, he states: "A problem frequently encountered in the critical period literature is the lax specification of what biobehavioral pattern, or portion thereof, is affected by the critical stimulation" (1982, p. 264). He singles out research in language acquisition to illustrate the point and notes that studies that have chosen different interpretations of the system, or of the nature of linguistic competence, have found different results regarding the operation of a sensitive period.

The absence of a definitive conception of the nature and structure of linguistic representations should not, of course, prevent language acquisition from being considered as a possible candidate for maturationally controlled learning. At the same time, the multidimensionality of language is a challenge to the need to specify exactly what is being affected by the putative critical period. Linguistic knowledge is diverse, and demonstrations of language proficiency, the observable dependent variable in all studies of a critical period, draw on its manifold aspects. So what, exactly, is the system targeted by the theory? Does a critical period apply only to that portion of linguistic representations that are considered fundamental or innate? Is phonology affected but not semantics? Do features of grammar reputedly governed by linguistic universals develop along a biological timetable but language-specific features do not? These are not trivial questions. To assert that there is a critical period for language acquisition necessitates clarity on precisely what the critical period controls. In the case of language, that specification is notoriously difficult to achieve. Yet, if language acquisition in humans is to be added to the list of phenomena governed by a critical period, then it must be shown to possess the characteristics of this learning paradigm.

Nature of the Evidence

What kinds of evidence would support the claim that language learning, at least in some measure, were subject to a maturational timetable? It is not enough to show that older learners achieve less than younger learners because there are many reasons this could be the case. Older learners have less time to learn, less sympathetic input, fewer opportunities for formal instruction, more difficult discourse demands, and a shorter period between the start of learning and the arrival of psycholinguists demanding a demonstration of what they know. All these conditions inevitably handicap older learners, but none of them has any connection to a critical period.

The data need to reveal the qualitative patterns of language acquisition that are unique to learning under the boundaries of a critical period. Primary among these is a clear discontinuity between the success of younger and older learners. If the relation between language proficiency and age of acquisition revealed a constant decline in ability as age of learning increases, then the decline could be attributed to any number of factors, including those mentioned above. If there were a clear demarcation, however, between learning success before and after the close of the putative critical period, then the evidence would strongly point to a significant change in learning potential at that point in time.

Several studies have addressed the linearity of this declining function, either directly or indirectly. In the landmark study by Johnson and Newport (1989), they claimed that the critical period was evident at age fifteen because the correlation between age of acquisition and proficiency in adulthood was strongly negative before that time but not significant after that age. However, two independent reanalyses of their data showed that this was not so. Elman et al. (1996) fit the entire data set into a single curvilinear function that showed an even progression across the whole age range examined in the study with no qualitative disruption at age fifteen. Bialystok and Hakuta (1994) moved the boundary to age twenty instead of fifteen and showed that both sides of the divide produced a significant (and comparable) negative correlation between age of acquisition and proficiency. Presumably, a few anomalous data points between the ages of fifteen and twenty had caused the different outcomes initially reported by Johnson and Newport (1989). In a different study, Birdsong (1992) also reported a negative correlation between proficiency and age of arrival for both early and late learners. Moreover, he was able to identify learners who had achieved native-like proficiency from both the early and late arrival groups. The Johnson and Newport study, then, does not provide the necessary evidence for discontinuity in learning potential at around puberty and is contradicted by other researchers.

Other studies have attempted to determine the shape of the relation between age of learning and proficiency. Hakuta, Bialystok, and Wiley (in preparation) plotted the self-reported proficiency of approximately a quarter of a million immigrants who arrived in the United States at different ages. There was a strong decline in proficiency as age of arrival increased from close to zero (birth) to about sixty years old, but no discontinuity in the function. Flege, Yeni-Komshian, and Liu (1999) gave a grammaticality judgment task to Korean learners of English and also found a decline in score with age of arrival. The nature of the decline, however, depended on the type of item. For lexically based judgments, there was a sudden dip at about twelve years old, but for rule-based judgments, the deterioration was gradual. They take this as counterevidence to a critical period. If the ability to learn a second language does not show a qualitative change at some specified point (e.g., puberty) but instead continues to decline across the lifespan as these data suggest, then the explanation may be more accurately sought in the effects of normal aging on language and cognition. These possibilities are discussed below.

A second kind of evidence is the documentation of what amounts to "special cases." These take a variety of forms, but the common feature is that unusual circumstances of language learning can produce patterns of language acquisition that are not normally included in the general repertoire of data. In this sense, special cases can include recovery from aphasia, acquisition of sign language by hearing-impaired individuals, and, most dramatically, people for whom normal language learning was delayed because of exceptional or abusive circumstances. The finding is normally that language learning in these cases is impaired if it begins later in life, probably past puberty. Snow (1987) makes a convincing case, however, that we should be suspicious of all these data, including those from the hearing-impaired learners who have normal cognitive and social backgrounds. Language acquisition that is removed from its normal context of a child growing up speaking at home, with the usual social, cognitive, and emotional support, is a different experience. It is not surprising that language acquisition under these altered conditions takes a different course, but there is no reason to attribute the difference to the nature of the learner's brain.

The most salient effect of an advancing age on the ability to learn a language is surely in the realm of phonology: the presence of a foreign accent. It is not surprising, then, that this aspect of language competence has been the subject of intense research on the topic of a critical period. Hence, the third kind of evidence is on the acquisition of native-like pronunciation, and the data, as always, are full of contradictions. For example, Patkowski (1994) and Bongaerts, Planken, and Schils (1995) elicited ratings of accent in nonnative speakers who began language learning at different ages. Patkowski reported a relation between native-like speech and age of acquisition and Bongaerts et al. did not. Both studies suffer from methodological difficulties, but each is offered to support an opposite side of the debate.

Studies that have used a more analytic approach to phonological acquisition have been clearer in their results. A classic finding in the first-language acquisition literature is that infants are able to distinguish between phonemically relevant contrasts in the ambient language by about one month of age (Eimas et al., 1971). This ability is obviously fundamental to the developing sound system that will shape the child's later speech. What is this discrimination like for languages that are introduced later? Research by Kuhl et al. (1992) and Werker and her colleagues (summarized in Werker, 1995) discussed earlier in this chapter sheds important light on this question. They have identified a significant change in the perceptual ability to make these phonemic distinctions somewhere between six and twelve months of age, depending on the study and the group tested. After the first year of life, constructing the sound system of a language is not assured by the natural, possibly innate mechanisms that guide newborns into the language they are about to learn. This change seems to carry the stamp of a critical period, although it applies only to phonology and it closes at twelve months old at the latest.

Flege and his colleagues (summarized in Flege, 1992) have pursued the acquisition of phonology in second-language learners who have begun learning the language at different ages. They have documented a U-shaped function for the authenticity of second-language sounds. The most native-like sounds produced in the second language are those that are either very different or very similar to the first-language phonology. Intermediate sounds are typically the source of the foreign accent and present the greatest problem for learners past about five to seven years of age. Before that time, the young language learner can create a new phonological category for the foreign sound irrespective of its relation to the known sounds in the first language. They attribute this change to perceptual and sensorimotor processes that are involved in the acquisition of language. The mechanisms for language acquisition, they insist, remain active throughout life. In their view, the differences in phonetic accuracy that are observed with age follow from the stabilization of the phonetic system: it is simply more difficult to establish new categories or reorganize old ones.

The argument against a critical period for phonology is difficult to wage because of a deeply grounded popular belief that makes it the last bastion of the critical period. There are simply too many examples, un-scientific though they may be, of an inverse correlation between the age of language learning and the strength and persistence of a foreign accent. However, we must be objective about the data.

There are two possible candidates for a critical period for phonology. The first comes from the infant research described above. In the first year of life, infants are capable of acquiring a complete sound system that represents any language in the environment. After one year, this universal sensitivity appears to end, and the incipient traces of foreign accent infil-trate the child's phonological structure. The first possibility, then, is that there is a critical period for phonology that ends in the first year of life.

The second potential point for a qualitative change in phonological ability emerges from studies reported by Flege and his colleagues. Gener-ally, the age at which foreign accents become perceptible is somewhere between five and eight years old (Flege & Fletcher, 1992; Flege, Munro, & MacKay, 1995). However, there are many exceptions to this generaliza-tion on both sides, namely, younger learners who retain a foreign accent and older learners who escape the apparent inevitability of phonologically distinct speech. Both of these possible points of departure, roughly one year old and eight years old, are substantially younger than the barrier that is usually set – puberty. Moreover, Flege and Frieda (1997) demonstrated that there was a significant influence on accent that came simply from the amount of the second language that was used on a daily basis for learners who all arrived at a very young age. None of these results fits the logical predictions that would be made if there were a critical period for language acquisition.

An alternative possibility is that there are multiple critical periods for different linguistic features that close at different times. More strictly, it may be that a critical period applies to phonology but not to other aspects of language such as syntax. This position has been advanced by some scholars (Scovel, 1988). The problem is that any theory we propose that involves the mind and all its complexity must be, as far as possible, consistent with what we know about how the mind functions. We would need to have a logical story about how and why the domains of language were not only represented separately but also subjected to different constraints. One story of this type has been advanced by Neville and her colleagues (e.g., Neville & Weber-Fox, 1994; Weber-Fox & Neville, 1996), who dissociate grammatical and semantic processing in terms of their vulnerability to age of language exposure. Their research is discussed below. Nonetheless, the simpler explanation for foreign accent that is consistent with the research evidence is that the age-related differences are the result of changing cognitive strategies to deal with sounds that are somewhat different from those in the first language.

A fourth type of evidence is a detailed study of grammatical competence based on some meaningful analysis of syntax. If there is a critical period for the acquisition of syntax, it is possible that it applies only to those aspects of language structure that, under formal linguistic theories, are considered to be more inherent, more universal, or more innate. These would normally be principles and parameters of language designated by universal grammar (UG). If the linguistic analysis is correct, and if there is indeed a critical period that restricts the acquisition of syntax, then it is possible that mastery of UG principles differs inside and outside the critical period. On different linguistic analyses, it could be argued that some types of features should be more constrained by a critical period than others, but no linguistic theory other than that of principles and parameters has made such a claim. Therefore, evidence for age-related sensitivity in the acquisition of these features would constitute support for a critical period. One such feature would be the subjacency principle that restricts the way units of sentences can be moved while preserving grammaticality. Here, too, the data are equivocal: Johnson and Newport (1991) reported a critical period effect for the acquisition of subjacency, while Juffs and Harrington (1995), studying a similar population of learners, found no age-related effects in acquiring this principle. Moreover, in a study by Bialystok and Miller (1999), an important factor in determining the acquisition of specific linguistic structures was whether the structures were the same in the two languages. Structures that were essentially the same were easy to learn and those that were different were hard to learn for all learners, irrespective of the age at which second-language acquisition began.

Finally, evidence for a discontinuity between the way that languages learned early or late are processed might be found by peering directly at the brain. The technology for functional imaging (discussed in Chapter 4) that produces diagrams of the blood flow pattern in the brain during online activity can be applied to this question. Although the data would not be logically decisive, it would be an important contribution to the argument if it were found that these patterns were different when using a language that had been acquired early or late. Kim et al. (1997) conducted such a study using functional magnetic resonance imaging (fMRI) and reported differences between early and late learners for activation in Broca's region but no differences in Wernicke's area. Nonetheless, they interpreted this as evidence for critical period effects. In a major research program, Neville and her colleagues (Neville et al., 1998) have produced images from fMRI studies showing that delayed acquisition of a language leads to an anomalous pattern of brain organization for that language in bilinguals.

Zatorre (1989) is skeptical that evidence showing different patterns of lateralization can be interpreted at all. He states: "One question which has not yet been asked, and which could clarify the entire matter of critical periods for language, involves whether or not linguistic abilities are really a separate set of skills, or if they form part of a broader perceptuomotor learning repertoire" (p. 141). Other researchers who have attempted to argue that language is continuous with other domains have usually placed it in a general cognitive context (see discussion of functional theories in Chapter 2). Zatorre's proposal is different because he suggests that language may be part of our ability to learn complex motor behaviors, and some of these may be acquired more easily in childhood. His advice is to find out whether there is a critical period for learning to ride a bicycle and, if so, to seek the common mechanisms that could explain how this ability to learn a new skill could also limit the acquisition of language. Although he presents this as a serious possibility, it provides little encouragement to those who seek the neurological basis of a critical period. Klein et al. (1995, p. 32) summarize the literature this way: "we find no evidence to support the hypothesis that a language learned later in life is represented differently from the native language; nor do we find differences in the neural substrates that subserve within- and across-language searches."

It is possible that data about cortical representations indicate an effect of causality opposite to that which we assume. Elbert et al. (1995) report that there was a greater representation of the fingers used for playing string instruments in the sensory cortex for musicians than nonmusicians, and that the differences were correlated with the age at which musicians began playing. The correlation with age was positive: older learners displayed more increased sensitivity than did younger learners. The experience of playing the instrument altered the way the tactile sensitivity of the fingers was coded in the brain. Representations depend on use and can change to conform to current needs and experiences. Gazzaniga (1992) makes a similar point in reviewing evidence from monkeys. These results reverse the usual direction of effect, suggesting that function (experience) can lead to changes in form (mental representations in the brain). Learning a second language may alter some mental configurations in the brain, but mental configurations did not necessarily lead to the particular pattern of language acquisition that was observed.

What Does It Mean?

Why are children invariably more successful than adults in acquiring a second language? If we discount the possibility that they are the beneficiaries of a biologically based critical period, what else could explain their success?

The conception of a critical period is compatible with formal theories of language acquisition. The premises regarding an autonomous processing model and innate dedicated knowledge are easily adapted to a constraint that sets maturational limits on the expression of these functions. Although nothing about a critical period *necessitates* those formal characteristics, they are logically consistent with a view of language acquisition that places it on a unique path with a particular timetable compared with other cognitive developments. In other words, for language acquisition to close off at some maturational point while other avenues of cognition remain open to development, language must be controlled, at least to some extent, by independent processing constituents. The only linguistic models that allow such independence are formal theories. Hence, the critical period hypothesis carries at least an implicit reliance on formal conceptions of language and language acquisition. However, as discussed in Chapter 2, formal theories provide at best an incomplete account of language acquisition. Minimally, linguistic competence, linguistic representation, and language acquisition are intimately connected to cognitive representations, social contexts, and general learning procedures. None of these latter contingencies should be subject to the effects of a critical period.

It is obvious, nonetheless, that success in acquiring a second language declines with age. If we abandon formal models, then it becomes possible to seek the explanation outside the strict domain of language. Some aspect of more general cognitive processing may be responsible for the decline in second-language learning ability.

Conceptualization

One approach to understanding age-related changes in language learning is to consider some principles of general cognitive processing and representational development (Bialystok, 1997a). New knowledge can be represented in one of two ways. The first is to extend the boundaries of known concepts to include the new information, considering this knowledge to be an exemplar of an existing concept. The second is to create a unique concept, signifying a structure that is sufficiently different from current knowledge that it is not adequately reflected in existing representations.

These options correspond, in a very rough manner, to the Piagetian processes of assimilation and accommodation, respectively, the essential mechanisms through which knowledge develops. Flege (1992) has shown a shift in strategy for learning phonological categories at about age five. Before that age, children readily establish new categories when new sounds are encountered, but after that age they rely more on extending existing, albeit inaccurate, categories to include new structures. The result of this is increased inaccuracy in the middle range of linguistic contrast. Features in the two languages that require very different categories for their representations cannot be ignored in this way and creating a new category is simply more imperative. At the same time, linguistic structures that are similar across languages are not as distorted by incorporating them into a phonetic category established by the first language. Hence, only the middle level of contrast is at issue in the decision about whether to assimilate the feature into an existing category or accommodate it by creating a new one.

The same may be true for syntax. As shown in the study by Bialystok and Miller (1999), structures that were different between the two languages were more difficult to learn than structures that were similar. It may be that learners attempted to assimilate these different structures into existing categorical schemata rather than create new representations.

The idea that experience and learning proceed by constructing categories through the processes of assimilation and accommodation may have surprisingly wide application. Eco (2000), in a discussion of the semiotic and conceptual bases of reference, reports that when Marco Polo traveled east he encountered an animal he had never seen before. Among its characteristics were that it had one horn emanating from the center of its forehead. Having no experience with this animal, he assumed it was (at last) a token of the category unicorn, a concept for which he had a mental structure despite the lack of instances in his experience. He recorded in his journal that he saw unicorns but that contrary to the common assumption, they were brown, hairy, and bulky rather than white, sleek, and slender. For him, this was certainly a unicorn, even if the descriptive features for the concept needed to be revised. He assimilated a rhinoceros into an existing category and simply made it fit.

Eco speculates what might have happened if the intrepid traveler had encountered a platypus. It certainly happened in the period of colonization that Europeans perceived this odd creature for the first time. The difference here is that the platypus has no obvious characteristic that would easily incorporate it into any existing category. It appears simultaneously as a mammal and a waterfowl, and so violates basic features of all existing schemata. In this case, the observer would need to establish a new category. Accommodation would be required to construct a mental representation for this anomaly that exists outside the boundaries of the existing category structures. Analogously, the rhinoceros functions like a phoneme that is moderately different from the categories established by the first language, but the platypus functions like a phoneme that is greatly different and necessarily requires its own representational category.

For Piaget, the back-and-forth play between assimilation and accommodation was part of the organism's attempt to strive for equilibrium, the elusive but harmonious stable state. Piaget noted that the balance between assimilation and accommodation changed with development. Accommodation predominated in the earlier stages, a time of rapid cognitive change. The balance later shifted to assimilation and what Piaget called a cognitive equilibrium. It is plausible that the stability of this cognitive equilibrium, surely the mental condition of older learners, leads naturally to a reliance on assimilation to attempt to make new knowledge interpretable within the existing structures. Older learners will try to use their present knowledge system as an organizing structure for the new material. New categories, or accommodation, will be created only when the misfit cannot be ignored.

Parenthetically, there is some evidence of a relation between children's progress in constructing categories and their ability to discriminate phonemes, supporting the above analogy. Lalonde and Werker (1995) compared the ability of ten-month-old infants to perform phoneme discrimination, visual categorization, and A-B search tasks. They found that when infants passed the threshold at which they were no longer able to discriminate among phonemes that did not occur in their own language, they were then able to solve the other two tasks. The common process here is categorization: when phonemic categories are established, so are visual and spatial ones. The difference is that categorization ability leads to the failure to discriminate irrelevant phonemes but to success on the other two tasks. The classification processes responsible for these developments appear to be general across domains and not specific to a body of knowledge such as language or space. The issue of domain general processes is discussed further in Chapter 7.

Returning to the main argument, assimilation and accommodation would create a situation in which age of learning influenced the development of mental representation because they altered the richness of the category structure that was being built up. This category structure, or knowledge, is what is reflected in proficiency with the language. Is there any reason to believe that there is a developmental shift away from forming new categories and relying more rigidly on existing structures? In a review of the literature, Davidson (1996) concludes that aging is associated with a greater reliance on existing schemas to interpret and recall events. Unlike younger adults and children, older adults did not notice small changes but assimilated patterns into existing schemas. He states: "in contrast to the results obtained with young adult subjects, . . . elderly subjects may rely more on their script knowledge in recalling a text. This suggestion is consistent with Hess' (1990) proposal that adults may increase their reliance on readily available knowledge structures as basic cognitive skills become less efficient with age" (1996, p. 47). This increased reliance on existing knowledge is functionally equivalent to a preference for assimilation over accommodation. This processing shift would make it more difficult for older learners to learn a new language accurately because they would be less likely to establish new categories for marginally different sounds, words, and structures. Hence, the overall proficiency in a second language that would be attained by an older learner is less than that for a younger one, although no critical period is involved.

Aging Cognition

Although most cognitive domains do not posit critical periods in development, there are nonetheless age-related changes in cognitive processing. One relevant change may be the categorization shift noted by Davidson (1996) described above. Other cognitive processes that have shown such changes are a decreased ability to learn paired associates (Craik & Jennings, 1992; Craik & McDowd, 1987), more difficulty encoding new information (Rabinowitz & Craik, 1986), and less accuracy in recalling details as opposed to gists (Hultsch & Dixon, 1990). Any of these could impair the ability to learn a new language as the learner ages. Kemper (1992) points out that older adults' second-language proficiency, like their first-language proficiency, could be affected by factors such as working-memory limitations, cognitive slowing, or attentional deficits. All these processes decline with age, and the decline is documented across the lifespan. Such a reduction in cognitive resources would surely affect the ability to learn a new language.

A different kind of approach can also lead to the position that language learning suffers the same age-related declines as other kinds of learning without implicating a dedicated module or a critical period. Churchland (1996) notes that in connectionist systems, where learning is defined as the establishment of new connections, all learning becomes harder with aging. Throughout life, it becomes more difficult to discover new patterns and to break out of old ways of associating. Therefore, it would become more difficult to learn language, just as it is more difficult to learn everything.

Restricting the Range

A possible compromise on the critical period hypothesis might be to limit the range of phenomena to which a critical period applies, restricting claims from second-language acquisition in its totality to only specific aspects of language competence. It is possible that the acquisition of phonology is controlled by different mechanisms and represented in different mental stores than is the acquisition of syntax. Thus, it may be that there is a critical period for accent but not grammar (Scovel, 1988) or grammar but not semantics (Weber-Fox & Neville, 1996). Although no one has ever proposed a critical period on the acquisition of vocabulary (but see Singleton, 1998), Neville and her colleagues have argued for a distinction between open and closed class words that captures the divide between semantic and syntactic processing. In a series of studies, they have used event-related potentials and fMRI to demonstrate different neural responses to these two word categories by different kinds of language learners. These effects have been obtained for hearing-impaired learners of sign (Neville, 1993; Neville, Mills, & Lawson, 1992) and Chinese learners of English as a second language (Neville & Weber-Fox, 1994; Weber-Fox & Neville, 1996). In the latter study, they specifically found differences from age of acquisition for syntactic judgments (closed class words) but not semantic ones (open class words). Their conclusion is that biological constraints influence the neural systems responsible for language and that these influences, or sensitive periods, vary for functionally distinct subsystems of language, notably, grammar and meaning.

This conclusion has implications beyond the issue of a critical period. Reliable evidence for a neurological and processing distinction between subsystems of language (especially grammar and meaning) addresses the debate about formal and functional approaches to definitions of language proficiency (see Chapter 2). It not only restricts the potential range of application of each approach by ruling out a substantial portion of language processing but also validates a hybrid model in which grammatical and semantic aspects of language are under the control of different systems. Formal theories would be vindicated in their jurisdiction over syntax (and possibly phonology) and functional theories would be supported as the proper explanation for semantics (and possibly pragmatics).

The interpretation in which a critical period applies only to certain linguistic structures raises a problem of integration. Returning to the central problem of system that was stated by Bornstein (1989) and Colombo (1982), the components of language that were divided by their impact from a critical period would still need to function as a coherent system. We use language seamlessly; the fragmentation that would result from positing individual domains the acquisition of which was under the control of dedicated factors seems, at best, a poor way to design a complex system.

Age-related differences in the ability to master a second language are real, but the cause of those changes cannot unequivocally be attributed to the effect of a critical period. It may be that first-language acquisition is biologically restricted by a critical period, but evidence for such a restriction on second-language acquisition is not convincing. The age-related decline in achievement is more protracted than would be predicted by a critical period and seems in fact to extend across the lifespan. This continuous and gradual change in ability is more amenable to cognitive explanations than to biological ones. Moreover, the learning pattern is consistent with predictions that are based on the assumption of decline in specific cognitive functions. No doubt, neurological changes are a crucial part of this decline and shift in cognitive strategy, but they are not wholly responsible for the consequences. The flexibility of cognition may be capable of overriding structural changes in cortical wiring.

It could be that the question about the existence of a critical period reflects a basic misconception about the nature of language learning. Aitchison (1996) argues that language actually takes twenty years to develop: five years to acquire basic structure, five years to master complex grammar and subtleties, and ten more years to establish a rich vocabulary. It is only our illusion of childhood competence and our impatience with adult struggling that compels us to seek explanations that free us from the slow and laborious process that is the hallmark of all worthwhile learning.

Learning Two Languages

Children who learn two languages in childhood, whether or not they learn them both at precisely the same time, have language learning experiences that undoubtedly differ in important ways from children who learn only one. How could it be otherwise? Monolingual and bilingual children move in different cognitive worlds, experience different linguistic environments, and are challenged to communicate using different resources, remaining sensitive to different abstract dimensions. The similarities are also striking in that all these children follow more or less the same processes on more or less the same schedule. A formal view of language learning pays too much attention to the similarities by focusing on the endpoint of language acquisition, proficiency, and is too dismissive of the variations in the experience. At the same time, functional theories leave too much to chance, requiring that input from each language conform to the interactive and cognitive needs that are the basis for the extraction of linguistic principles. Yet, the conclusion that general cognitive processes are at the very center of language acquisition is inescapable. It is not only adults past some putative critical period who must resort to using brute learning strategies to acquire language, but so must children at every age and at every stage of acquisition. All of this casts a large measure of variability, even uncertainty, into the language learning enterprise. It means that some people will flourish more in their language acquisition experience, some situations will nurture language learning better than others, and some combinations of languages will be more felicitous in promoting high levels of bilingual proficiency. So what is really at the heart of determining the outcomes of language learning? Segalowitz (1997, p. 107) accepts the complexity of the situation and deflects the position that there could be a single explanation for second-language acquisition: "This perspective shifts our focus away from the idea that there is one single, most important factor – some learner characteristic, some optimal strategy, learning environment, or innate endowment – that determines individual differences in L2 [second-language] attainment. It also suggests that what we perceive as language learning ability is not a fixed characteristic of a person but rather a complex reflection of the whole learning situation." It is observing the complexity of progress in children who learn two languages that compels us to adopt an interactive stance on the question of how second, and indeed first, languages are learned.

4

Language in the Mind

At the center of studies of the mind is the problem of representation. It has always seemed that if we could unravel the mystery of how knowledge is stored it would lead irrevocably to understanding how it is learned, how it is used, and, perhaps most intractably of all, how it is made conscious. The form that language takes when it is laid down as traces of long-term memory is a key to understanding its role in human development, intelligence, and socialization.

How is language represented? Are semantic features of words stored as entries in a lexicon or as part of our knowledge of concepts? How do words and meanings combine so that we can use language meaningfully and express thoughts verbally? Why do contexts change the way we interpret language? These are some of the questions that have fueled the inquiry into psycholinguistic processes and each one has a noble tradition in research and theory. Because the questions are difficult and the solutions impossible to observe directly, the research is intricate and the conclusions are inferential. However, the vast majority of that literature is based on a simplifying assumption: people have only one language. Again the story becomes more complex when these questions are asked about speakers who have two or more languages.

There is another complicating factor. Psycholinguistic research has typically approached research questions by examining and attempting to understand the stable state, namely, the adult mind. Developmental processes are always more difficult to observe and to understand. For monolinguals, questions about how children build up representations for language and representations for concepts are notoriously difficult to untangle. Children's early words and early meanings have a tentative existence on their own, as well as precarious connections to each other. These fragile systems must somehow evolve into the fabric that is our knowledge of language and the world. The mechanisms by which this happens and the stages through which it progresses are the subject of much research in developmental psycholinguistics. Again, the escalation in complexity is palpable if children are learning two languages.

These are the problems faced in the attempt to understand how bilingual children construct mental representations for language and concepts. Investigating this issue includes two sets of related questions that can nonetheless be examined separately. The first set of questions concerns the relation between the two languages. How is the mental organization of two languages different from that of one? What is the relation between the languages in the child's representational structure? Are the various levels of language, such as phonology, syntax, semantics, and pragmatics, isolated with the child's knowledge of an individual language or part of a shared resource? The second set of questions concerns the role of meaning and concepts in linguistic organization. How does each language connect with a system of meanings? Are the two languages alternative labeling systems for the same concepts? Does each language identify a different set of concepts and experiences for children? These are the questions that underlie the study of the development of mental representation for bilingual children.

In Search of Representations

Not long ago, questions of mental representation were among the most abstract and impenetrable of any in cognitive psychology. Although the nature of representation was fundamental to virtually every theoretical position, evidence for the mental organization posited by any particular theory was at best inferential and at worst entirely absent. The usual data consisted of measures such as reaction time differences to various problems, interference in performance between simple tasks, and behavioral consequences of cortical injury. More recently, there has been excitement over the possibility that brains could be observed, that cognition could be made visible, and that representations could be revealed.

Thinking Observed

Advances in neuroimaging techniques have led to the proliferation of research to uncover the intricacies of brain function. Three techniques have been especially powerful in advancing this research. The oldest of these is event-related potential (ERP), a measure of electrical activity in the brain during cognitive processing. The other two, positron emission tomography (PET) and functional magnetic resonance imaging (fMRI) are methods for identifying the cortical regions involved in an on-line assessment of cognitive performance. Data from PET and fMRI are able to localize cognitive functions with reasonable accuracy, but the "snapshot" time for the images is so long (up to one minute in some cases) that several component processes could be conflated into a single image. In contrast, ERP provides a more faithful record of the intensity and timing of cortical involvement in a specific task but little spatial information. Recent research has begun to combine these approaches to produce a more complete account of what the brain is doing when we are thinking. Critical reviews of these techniques, including a discussion of their strengths and weaknesses, are presented by Démonet (1998) and Rugg (1999). A summary of their contribution to understanding basic cognitive processes is offered by Cabeza and Nyberg (1997).

Research using functional imaging techniques has contributed importantly to theories of language representation and language processing (for overview, see chapters in Brown & Hagoort, 1999). These techniques, however, complicate the story by revealing details that appear to exceed the specificity of current theories. Wernicke's area, for example, has traditionally been considered the center of processing for language comprehension and fluency, but its role in comprehension turns out to be more varied. Robertson and Gernsbacher (1998) used PET scanning data to show that sentence strings stating unrelated facts (*A cat sat on a mat. A dog chased a cat.*) are processed primarily in the familiar left cortical regions, primarily in Wernicke's area, but the same texts that are made coherent by the insertion of anaphora (*The cat sat on the mat. A dog chased the cat.*) engage a significant degree of right hemisphere processing for their comprehension. Similarly, the role of Broca's area for production is not as simple as was once supposed. The structure turns out to be variable across individuals and difficult to delineate (Uylings et al., 1999) and the function is more diverse than usually credited by linguistic theories (Kimura, 1993). Consequently, there must be an interplay between the linguistic theories that guide studies in functional imaging and the interpretation of findings regarding how processing proceeds in different cortical locations. It is early days in these investigations, and flexibility and caution are both well advised.

On a smaller scale, these imaging techniques have been applied to investigations in bilingualism. The questions for this research have been some of the basic problems in language learning and use: how is the second language different from the first and how does its development interact with the cognitive landscape of the mind? Typically, the studies seek to identify the localization of the cortical areas used when solving tasks in each of the languages. Many of the studies suffer from a lack of control over essential factors such as language proficiency, method of language learning (especially for a second language), and task demands (see Zatorre, 1989, for discussion), but most include the age at which the second language was acquired as an independent variable. Even here, however, the degree of experimental control is questionable. The research motive is usually to determine qualitative changes that might ensue from the end of the (putative) critical period, but the age at which this window is assumed to close reaches nothing like consensus (see discussion in Chapter 3). Hence, designs in which language learners are considered to be early or late can scarcely be compared.

The research results are also without consensus. The study by Kim et al. (1997) mentioned in Chapter 3 used fMRI to identify the active processing regions for a first or second language in early or late bilinguals. They tested twelve individuals, six of whom had learned the second language in childhood and six at a later age (although scant information is given about the participants) and found representational differences only for late bilinguals and only in Broca's area. This constitutes only a small portion of the data collected, most of which did not discriminate between the two languages or the age of learning. Nonetheless, they concluded that a critical period determined the nature of linguistic representation for two languages. Different results were reported in a study by Perani et al. (1996). They presented a listening task to nine subjects who were native speakers of Italian and exposed to English as a second language after seven years of age. Subjects listened to texts in Italian, English, and Japanese, an unknown language. PET scans revealed that different cortical areas were involved for Italian than for the other two languages, even though one of them was completely unknown to the participants. An important difference between this and the study by Kim et al. (1997) is the experimental task, namely, covert speaking in the former (subjects were told to "imagine speaking" in each language) and listening in the latter. A study by Klein et al. (1995), however, used a variety of tasks, including comprehension and speaking, and obtained PET scans from bilingual subjects who had learned the second language after they were five years old. They found no variation in representation on any measure and concluded with a strong statement disavowing any differences in the representation of language as a function of either age of learning or the two languages themselves. Together, these studies manage only to point to the factors that may be relevant, but since the studies differed in most of the relevant factors (age, task, language status), it is impossible to determine their precise role in performance.

Conflicting results are also reported using ERP as the measure of neural functioning. Ardal et al. (1990) presented monolingual and bilingual subjects with a semantic processing task in which they had to detect incongruity. The patterns of ERP responding for this task are well known, so the question was to determine how bilinguals would compare with monolinguals and whether the two languages of the bilingual would elicit different patterns. They reasoned that if bilinguals were scanning a combined representation for two languages, as would be the case if two languages were stored in a shared system, then the time to solve the problem in both languages for the bilingual would be longer than that needed by comparable monolinguals. A delay only in the weaker second language would mean that the languages were represented separately and that processing was more efficient in the stronger language. Instead, the results revealed a third pattern: the bilinguals were slower than the monolinguals (suggesting a combined representation) but there was a significant difference between the stronger and weaker languages, with faster processing being observed in the stronger language (suggesting separate representation). These results indicate a pattern in which language representations are autonomous but processing differences distinguish the bilingual from the monolingual, even in the stronger language. Furthermore, the age at which the second language was learned did not affect performance. This pattern requires further clarification. Neville and Weber-Fox (1994) conducted a study requiring older and younger second-language learners to make acceptability judgments on sentences. They found that the neural response patterns while making judgments of semantic acceptability were the same for older and younger second-language learners, replicating the results of Ardal et al. (1990). In contrast, judgments of syntactic acceptability showed changes in ERP as a function of age of acquisition. Here the experimental methodology is essentially the same, but the linguistic process required by each task is different.

This is a small sample of the studies that have relied on methods of neuroimaging, but they illustrate the inherent confusion in this kind of research. Sample sizes tend to be extremely small, experimental tasks are virtually never the same across studies, and proficiency levels of subjects are rarely controlled. In a meta-analysis of five studies that had used PET imaging to isolate regions of phonological processing, Poeppel (1996) showed that there was little or no convergence on the cortical areas identified in each to be responsible for this function. One might ask whether the enterprise of exploring imaging as a method for understanding the functional relation of two languages in the mind is worthwhile.

There are two questions we must ask about this research. First, can images of the brain, even highly sophisticated ones, provide the necessary detail for determining how the brain is involved in something as multifaceted as language? Second, even if such information were available, what would it tell us about how humans learn and use language? There is no doubt that the insights achieved through these techniques are incomparable to evidence attained by behavioral methods. Nonetheless, we must risk the temptation of being seduced by the possibility of glimpsing the inner secrets of the brain. There is a dangerous reductionism at play here: the allure of observing the brain might lead one to conclude that one had also observed thought. This position, in fact, is explicitly held by those philosophers who consider the brain to offer the ultimate account for all cognition (e.g., Churchland, 1996). However, for those who remain more circumspect in their interpretation of these data, the images are just one visible consequence of thinking. From this more functional perspective, a formal account of neural activity offers an incomplete picture of thought. It is wholly unlikely that there is anything like a perfect mapping between the brain's function and the mind's creation, so seeing the function can only give us hints about the products of those machinations. Even if we were to detect correspondence between brain form and thought, Gazzaniga (1992) notes that neural configurations are just as likely to be altered by cognitive processes as cognitive processes are to be determined by neurological structures. We could not be sure which was the cause and which was the consequence. Therefore, we must treat this new technology with both respect and caution, reaping insights where we can but remaining sanguine about the limits of its revelations.

Behavioral Evidence

Establishing how languages are mentally represented is important because it is in the functional relation between the two languages, and between the languages and a conceptual system, that the competence of speakers lies. Functional imaging is adding a new dimension to these inquiries, but the majority of this research has been pursued through the less glamorous techniques of behavioral experimentation. On the surface, these methods appear to be more inferential than neuroimaging; one can never inquire directly about how languages are represented but only assume certain consequences to follow from particular hypothesized configurations. However, neuroimaging is less decisive than it might have seemed at first glance, at least using current techniques and theories. At present, then, behavioral research is the more fruitful path to unraveling the representation of two languages. It is more directly linked to proficiency, it can be obtained under more controlled experimental task conditions, and it is more interpretable in its implications for language functioning.

Behavioral research has been used to examine the problem of hemispheric localization for two languages using reaction time data, a traditional psycholinguistic measure. The assumption is that processing that contains more mental steps or travels over greater mental space will take longer to execute in measurable time where the unit of analysis is milliseconds. Using this logic, verbal input to the hemisphere in which language is represented should be processed faster than it would in the opposite hemisphere. In the latter case, the information must be transferred to the cortical region responsible for language processing in an additional step. Using standard assumptions about lateralization and linguistic representation, the left hemisphere should solve verbal tasks more quickly than the right. However, if a second language were represented differently, specifically in the right hemisphere, then presumably that relation would change.

This methodology, too, is not without its difficulties, and some cautionary notes are in order. One problem is in reliably establishing the reaction time differences in processing. There are two modality options for these studies: in aural presentation, a different stimulus is played to each ear and the subject reports which one was heard; in visual presentation, a written word is briefly flashed to a single visual field and the subject reports what the word is. In the aural tasks, called dichotic listening, the word processed first will be the one "heard." In the visual tasks, the time needed to respond to the words in each visual field indicates which presentation has more direct access to the cortical center for language. (There seem not to be any studies that have presented a different word to each visual field and timed the race to the brain the way aural studies do. It may not be possible: each eye delivers information from both visual fields, so unless the head were absolutely fixed in place, both eyes may pick up residual information from the other visual field and the signal to the brain would just be confusion. Auditory presentation is possible to confine to a single ear.)

Research has produced both outcomes: some studies show different response patterns for the two languages (Albert & Obler, 1978; Hynd & Scott, 1980; Schneiderman & Wesche, 1983; Vocate, 1984) and others show the same pattern for both languages (Albanese, 1985; Gordon &

Zatorre, 1981; Soares, 1982). In a study by Wuillemin, Richardson, and Lynch (1994), subjects named printed words that appeared on either side of a central fixation point. For the most proficient subjects, the words presented to the right visual field, hence processed in the left cortical hemisphere, were named faster than words presented to the left. Subjects who had slower reaction times overall were those who had learned English later and scored significantly lower on proficiency tests. However, the pattern of results could be an artifact of reading direction and proficiency. With the fixations in the center, it is easier to read to the right than to the left. (Parenthetically, the authors of this study submit that the data support a critical period because there was a right visual field effect only for younger learners. However, the relevant statistical analysis, namely, an interaction between age of learning and visual field was not significant, so the conclusion is unsupported in the data and unwarranted.) Similarly, dichotic listening has been challenged as a reliable method of accessing processing (see Zatorre, 1989). Although it is always necessary to interpret research results in light of potential interference from methodological impurity, it is particularly important when the object of study is accessed so indirectly.

Albert and Obler (1978) identified a number of factors that affected the cerebral dominance patterns of bilingual speakers, possibly accounting for some of the contradictory findings. These included the age and manner of acquisition for the second language, the usage patterns for each language, and language-specific factors. Hence, older learners may represent language differently from younger ones, spoken languages may be represented differently from those used only for reading, and some languages may gravitate to the right hemisphere for all speakers. In their view, then, there was not a single configuration for representing two languages across the two cerebral hemispheres, although their assumption was that the second language always occupied some portion of the right hemisphere.

A last source of evidence is more indirect. There are many documented cases of bilingual individuals who become aphasic (see collection by Paradis, 1995). The order in which their languages are recovered can be taken as some measure of the way those languages were initially represented. The classic position on this question, called Pitres' law, states that languages will be recovered in the order of familiarity, and recovery will begin by restoring comprehension and then production. Fabbro (1999), however, claims that the evidence does not support that view and insists that the extent of variability in these cases undermines the possibility that there are any rules. According to his analysis, 40 percent of bilingual aphasics have parallel recovery of all languages, 32 percent have better recovery of a mother tongue, and 28 percent have better recovery of a second language. For multiple languages, recovery can take place for unrelated languages (Italian-English) but leave a related language (Venetian) impaired. These examples caution us against expecting a clear and universal configuration of mental representations for language to emerge. They also warn us against attributing defective systems to those for whom language representations may be different from some extrapolation of a universal norm.

Beyond Methodology

What would it mean if it could be shown unequivocally that languages are represented differently as a function of being learned first or second and that age of acquisition determines how the second language will be represented? It is not surprising that representations change over time and with time. As competence builds in any area, presumably there is a reorganization of knowledge to accommodate the increasing expertise. New knowledge added onto this elaborated system will undoubtedly be represented differently from the more simple knowledge adduced in the earlier stages of learning. The later knowledge will have a different interpretation, a different structure, and a different relation to prior knowledge depending on the state of the existing knowledge. This is likely to be equally true for skill in playing chess, knowledge of dinosaur species, and the structure of a second language. For this reason, it would be surprising if second languages learned later in life were *not* represented differently from earlier-learned languages in some fundamental way, including their spatial location. What we need to understand about the representation of the second language is not where it is, but what it can be used for.

There may be another problem in this enterprise of establishing the nature and location of the formal representation for a second language. Most of the speculation is based on the assumption that the first language is localized in the left hemisphere. Although that is generally true, it is not absolutely or universally so. Lateralization is now considered to be a relative attribute rather than a categorical one, so that an individual is described on a dimension of lateralization (Binder et al., 1996; Milner, 1975; Penfield & Roberts, 1959). Some language processing under the most natural conditions for right-handed individuals still takes place in the right hemisphere. The situation is more variable for left-handers. Satz (1979) proposed that there are three types of cerebral organization of language for left-handers: for 15 percent, language is unilaterally represented in the right hemisphere (reversing the usual configuration); for 15 percent, it is represented in the left (exactly as it is for right-handers); and for 70 percent it is represented bilaterally. In fact, Delis, Knight, and Simpson (1983) describe a case of a left-hander with reversed lateralization, one of the 15 percent in Satz's typology, but claim it is the first clinical case of this type reported, underscoring the rarity of this organization. Nonetheless, irrespective of hemispheric lateralization, all these people learn and use language in ways that are functionally indistinguishable from that of right-handers, suggesting that the precise cortical configuration may be less important than we might have imagined.

The research that aims to determine the nature of linguistic representation, in particular, to decide whether representations for two languages are formally encoded as separate or integrated systems, may be misinformed. The questions about linguistic representation follow from three assumptions: first, that language is a coherent entity; second, that its representation can be located in (mental) space; and third, that the representation has a discernible structure. Any of these may be false, but even if only one of them is, the options for representation are completely changed. Regarding the coherence, or homogeneity, of language, every linguistic theory sets out a different set of criteria for the essential core of language. For Chomsky (1981), for example, language is principles and parameters, while for Goldberg (1995) it is relations between forms and functions (see Chapter 2). Clearly, there is no simple means of identifying what language is, hence no obvious target for describing the nature of its representation. Regarding the assumption that representations can be located in mental space, connectionist views of language processing presume that representations are distributed, hence occupy no identifiable place (Allen & Seidenberg, 1999; Bates & MacWhinney, 1989). Finally, the assumption that there is an organizing and identifiable structure to language and its relation to cognition may also be false. Indeed, as Weinreich (1968) pointed out, what organization there is might well change over time and even include several alternative structures for a single learner at a single point in time. For these reasons, the options discussed below do not reflect all possibilities but are the logical solutions that respect the three assumptions. One must begin somewhere, and making theoretical assumptions places needed constraints on theorizing. But it is equally important to be clear about what those assumptions are so that the alternatives can be properly evaluated and generalizations duly restricted.

We are committed, then, to a framework that sets out limited alternatives. Within these constraints, how can two languages be represented in the mind? This question takes on a different sense when it is asked of either children or adults. Not surprisingly, the research addressing the question is conceived differently as well for these two groups. Regarding the relation between the two languages, the debate for children's representations is whether or not the two languages are rcpresented separately or in the same system and, relatedly, whether or not children *realize* that they are using two different languages. For adults, the question is similar but the solutions tend more toward determining the architecture through which the two languages are related and the extent to which activation spreads across both languages when using one of them. It would be ridiculous to suggest that adults were unaware that the languages were different, but the nature of the relation between them in the mind of the adult bilingual is much less obvious.

Regarding the relation between language and concepts, studies with children have focused primarily on lexicon (reviewed in Chapter 3) to determine the extent of overlap in children's labeling in the two languages. The issue for adults is, again, more complex. The research on this problem has tended to examine the organization through which the lexicon indicates meaning, either directly or indirectly, in its associations with conceptual structures. We begin by examining some of the proposals offered for the way in which these three entities, two languages and a conceptual system, might be organized for adults. Presumably, the adult organization represents the end state toward which children's developing representational systems must progress. This means that the proposals for describing children's representation of language and meanings must be congruent, at least potentially, with those established for adults.

Adults and the Problem of Concepts

Types of Bilinguals

One of the earliest discussions of how language is represented in the minds of bilingual speakers is the three-fold analysis proposed by Weinreich (1968). He based his well-known distinction between coordinate, compound, and subordinate bilingualism on three different arrangements of words and their concepts. Although these categories have become virtually synonymous with his name, it is interesting to note that Weinreich did not invent them; he attributes these terms, especially subordinate and coordinate bilingualism, to Roberts (1939), a linguist who was scarcely heard of again. In fact, Weinreich's own labels for these options are the unhelpful nomenclatures type A, type B, and type C. The more familiar and informative names are borrowed from Roberts.

Weinreich's contribution in proposing these categories is that he explored how words and concepts could be related to each other in bilinguals and how the various arrangements reflected important differences in the bilingual experience. The two primary varieties of bilingual representations are type A, later called coordinate, and type B, renamed compound. In coordinate bilingualism, the two words signify separate concepts, whereas in compound bilingualism, the two words converge on a single combined concept. Thus there are two configurations for expressing a set of meanings. Weinreich implies that compound representations can grow out of coordinate ones: "Once an interlingual identification has occurred . . . it becomes possible for the bilingual to interpret two signs . . . with a single signified [concept] and two signifiers [words], one in each language" (1968, p. 9). Compound bilingualism is the preferred option, but he acknowledges that the arrangements can coexist. A bilingual speaker may have combined concepts for some words but not for others.

The third variety of bilingual representation is subordinate. In this case, the meanings for new words refer to words in another language, not to concepts. This situation arises when a new language is learned through a known language, probably the way Latin has been learned by generations of students. Nonetheless, Weinreich seems to assume that even in this case the representation can evolve into one of the other forms and he identifies the nature and success of this transition as an area that should be the subject of further research.

Although the category of subordinate bilingualism was eventually dropped, largely because of refinements to the concepts proposed by Ervin and Osgood (1954), there was some early interest in investigations of the distinction between compound and coordinate bilingualism (Kolers, 1963; Lambert, Havelka, & Crosby, 1958). These studies often adopted different names for the configuration of words and concepts in the two languages (see De Groot, 1993, for summary), but the conceptualizations were clearly modeled on Weinreich's original classifications. The line of research was eventually abandoned because the categories were too vague to operationalize and the data were too inconsistent to interpret. Experimental results changed as a function of the subject's fluency (e.g., Opoku, 1992), the experimental task (e.g., Durgunoğlu & Roediger, 1987), word type (concrete vs. abstract) (e.g., Kolers, 1963), and the relation between the languages (presence or absence of cognates) (e.g., De Groot, 1992). The diversity of results led De Groot (1993) to conclude that all the arrangements were plausible and likely co-occur in the mind of individual speakers. This is not much different from Weinreich's original observation that the three types of organization could combine in a single individual speaker.

Storing Languages and Meanings

More recently, the experimental study of the mental organization of words and concepts has become very sophisticated (examples and overviews in Bijeljac-Babic, Biardeau, & Grainger, 1995; Grainger, 1993; Grainger & Dijkstra, 1992; Smith, 1997). Studies that have focused on the relation between the languages have addressed two central problems. First is the familiar question of whether the lexicon for two languages is represented separately or together. The second is the relation between languages and a meaning system.

Regarding the first question, the evidence appears to favor independent representation for the two languages. This evidence includes the absence of priming effects across languages in lexical decision tasks (Durgunoğlu & Roediger, 1987; Kirsner et al., 1984), word association patterns within and between languages (Van Hell & De Groot, 1998), interference on Stroop tasks (Brauer, 1998), and patterns of independent language recovery from aphasia in bilinguals (Paradis, 1997). Nonetheless, a plausible case for an integrated lexicon has been submitted by Dijkstra and his colleagues (Dijkstra & Van Heuven, 1998; Dijkstra, Van Heuven & Grainger, 1998; Dijkstra, van Jaarsveld, & Ten Brinke, 1998). They have developed a connectionist model, called the Bilingual Interactive Activation Model, which has been successful in predicting performance of subjects in tasks such as lexical decision and in simulating these performances on the connectionist network.

Whether the two lexicons are independent or integrated, all these current models agree that both language sources are active when one of them is being used (Grainger, 1993; Grainger & Dijkstra, 1992; Guttentag et al., 1984; Hermans et al., 1998; Smith, 1997; Van Heuven, Dijkstra, & Grainger, 1998). This raises a further question: if both languages are activated, then how can language performance proceed fluently in only one of them? Some solutions to this puzzle are discussed below.

The second representational problem is the relation between the languages and a meaning system. An important model of this type is the one developed by Kroll and her colleagues (Kroll, 1993; Kroll & De Groot, 1997; Kroll & Stewart, 1994). This model also helps to resolve some of the conflicts regarding the separate or combined representations for lexicon in two languages. According to Kroll and De Groot (1997), the lexical representations for the two languages are independent but the conceptual representations are shared. Experimental results aimed at determining the nature of the representation, then, depend on whether the task requires access to the conceptual representations or can be solved by more shallow access to lexicon. Moreover, the nature of the relation between words and their meanings changes as a function of fluency in each language. As language proficiency increases, the connection between a word and its meaning becomes more direct, relying less on a mediating connection through the first-language lexicon. In a similar proposal, Altarriba and Mathis (1997) follow most of the same principles as those outlined in the model by Kroll and her colleagues but place semantic access at a much earlier stage of proficiency in the second language.

These are only a sampling of proposals in the productive area of research investigating the representation of language and meanings in bilingual adults. It is beyond the scope of this discussion to examine this issue in detail. Its importance is mostly in terms of what it contributes to our understanding of the representation of language and meanings in bilingual children. Several points can be made in this regard. First, the models that are most successful in accounting for the varieties of data offered are multidimensional (e.g., Grainger & Dijkstra, 1992; Kroll & de Groot, 1997). Simple dichotomies, such as whether languages are represented individually or in combination, and whether concepts are linked directly to the second language or are mediated by the first, fail to receive empirical support. Adequate descriptions of the organization of mental representations include the effect of such factors as level of proficiency and the circumstances of second-language learning. Moreover, it appears likely that multiple arrangements can even coexist in the mind of an individual speaker (e.g., De Groot, 1993). Accordingly, there is no reason to expect the situation to be any simpler for children. Efforts to choose one of two possible arrangements, for example, one system or two, as the defining configuration for children of a specific age (or even specific proficiency level) are doomed to failure (cf. point made by Grosjean, 1998). Instead, it seems more likely that young children learning two languages experience the same complexity in mental representation as adults do, linking languages and concepts in dynamic ways, and restructuring the system as needs change and fluency evolves.

Implications of Complex Representation

One consequence of adopting a detailed model for linguistic representation is that one becomes committed to positing a production model at a comparable level of specificity. If linguistic and conceptual representations

are described on a gradation that takes account of relative language proficiency, task demands, and the like, then explanations of how languages
are used must be equally specified. How is it that learners can use one
language and not another, or invoke the other language when needed, or
resist interference from perhaps a stronger language? Green (1998) addresses some of these issues with a model based on inhibitory control, an
executive system for activating or inhibiting individual linguistic representations (lemmas). Some implications of this proposal are discussed in
Chapter 7, where processing differences between monolingual and bilingual children are considered.

Whatever the state of mental organization turns out to be for children,
it must eventually develop in conformity with the adult model. It is
difficult to investigate these issues of mental representation for children,
especially very young children in the earliest stages of language learning,
and this is undoubtedly one of the reasons for the paucity of data on the
topic. In contrast, there is a great deal of data generated from research
with adults, so it is reasonably clear what the adult model must look like,
at least in broad outline.

An example of this point is that the two languages for adult bilinguals
are functionally independent, even if there is also joint activation and
shared conceptual representations. Adults are not confused by the fact
that two linguistic systems share processing space for knowledge and
communication. Therefore, if a different configuration is posited for children, then it must be accompanied by a mechanism that would allow it to
reshape itself into that of the adult. This is a problem for models that posit
a single combined representation of languages for bilingual children. If
bilingual children's earliest representations of their two languages are
shared, then how do they separate into the two systems that define the
adult mind? If the words are initially unmarked for the language to which
they belong, then how do they migrate to the appropriate representation
for the individual language? Where does the language tag come from?
Why does it appear later in language development than the initial learning
of the word?

Since we know that the adult bilingual has a differentiated mental
representation regarding the distinctness of the two languages, it is simpler to suppose that children's mental representations follow a similar,
albeit more primitive model. The problem of explaining how the representations can undergo a fundamental shift seems to be more intractable than
accepting that the young bilingual already has the basis for the adult
representational model in place. However, with an infinitely smaller reper-

toire of language to be represented and a vastly impoverished conceptual system, the child's representations just look different from the adult's.

Weinreich (1968) actually raises the question for children: "It has been asked, for example, at what age children become aware that they are learning two languages. One writer claims that not until the age of three does a child take note of its bilingualism. Another observer recorded the first consciousness of bilingualism at 1;6 and full awareness of it at the age of 3;0. A third child was reported to know the names of the two languages at the age of 2;1. Whether the early or late cognizance of his or her bilingualism correlates with the individual's subsequent behavior in regard to interference remains to be investigated" (p. 77). Although Weinreich never investigated that problem, subsequent researchers did, and it is to those inquiries that we now turn.

Children, Language, and Thought

Consider the following utterances that have been reported in the speech of young bilingual children:

> 1. Siri: *mer* milk, *mer* mama (More milk, more mama)
> 2. Siri: *klappe* hand. M: Hm? Siri: clap hand.
> 3. S: *takk* (thank you). M: You're welcome. S: finish. M: You finished? S: *ja*.
> (from Lanza, 1988, English and Norwegian).

> 1. You *mette* honey? (You're putting honey?)
> 2. He *manger.* (He eating.)
> 3. *Il a* finish. (He is finished).
> (from Paradis & Genesee, 1996, English and French).

> 1. *Ei ole enam* some more (There isn't any more some more).
> (from Vihman, 1985, Estonian and English).

What should we conclude about the knowledge these children have of the two languages they are learning? Do they believe that all languages are interchangeable? Is their linguistic representation a single repository of expressive devices to be selected as meanings require? Do they recognize the differences between the languages but fail to respect their appropriate contexts of use? Or are these children simply being strategically clever and recruiting whatever resource is necessary to achieve the principal goal of expressing their thoughts? The answers to these questions hold important keys to fundamental problems in mental representation. Understanding how language is represented is preliminary to understanding how language develops and how it is used. The same two issues discussed for adult representations underlie the study of children's development. The first is the relation between the two languages themselves; the second is the relation between the languages and the conceptual system of meanings.

When bilingual adults infuse their speech in one language with words or structures from the other, we typically attribute the intrusions to a limited competence that has forced the speaker to look elsewhere for the resources to carry on the conversation (cf. Bialystok, 1990). Such explanations, however, reveal nothing about the underlying representation that allows this exploitation of knowledge to take place. Whether we assume that the mental representations of language engaged by these adult bilinguals are organized around discrete or combined representations, we do not entertain the idea that the adult bilingual was oblivious to the difference between languages or incapable of distinguishing between them. Yet, on the same evidence of language mixing, the usual deduction is that children are simply unaware that they are using two language systems. Clearly, the conclusion of linguistic confusion requires more convincing evidence.

One Language, One Mind

It is uncontroversial that young children who are learning two languages go through at least an early stage in which their utterances show an apparent disregard for the integrity of the two individual languages. At the one- and two-word stage of acquisition, bilingual children regularly produce verbalizations like those quoted above, or, in the case of single-word utterances, simply select the wrong language for the situation or the addressee. The simplest interpretation is that these children are unaware of the linguistic violation; the differences between the languages are either not noticed or not considered relevant. Eventually, of course, the two systems will separate, or the children will realize that language choice matters very much indeed, and their speech will be purified, at least in terms of some linguistic homogeneity.

This explanation was formalized in early research on the problem by Volterra and Taeschner (1978). They proposed a three-stage model to account for the evolution of two distinct languages in children's minds. In the first stage, the child has only one lexical system comprising words from both languages. This is reflected in the wanton disregard for language choice illustrated in the cited examples. The second stage marks the beginning of the development of two distinct systems for lexicon, but syntax remains undifferentiated. Finally, the systems disentangle their syntactic rules as well as vocabulary, and the child has discrete linguistic options.

The three-stage model captures the descriptive properties of the developing speech of bilingual children. Moreover, it has been endorsed and supported by researchers using both empirical data and analytic argument (Arnberg, 1987; Grosjean, 1982; Leopold, 1970; Redlinger & Park, 1980; Saunders, 1982; Swain & Wesche, 1975; Taeschner, 1983; Vihman, 1985). The assumption is that language competence is more general than the knowledge of any particular language. The differentiation of this competence into specific linguistic systems is a developmental achievement that signals the growth of linguistic knowledge. As Leopold (1954, p. 24) stated, "infants exposed to two languages from the beginning do not learn bilingually at first, but weld the double presentation into one unified speech system." Grosjean (1982) pointed to Leopold's diary of Hildegard to illustrate the nature of this evolution from a single conjoined system into discrete linguistic competencies.

The majority of the research examining the early representation of two languages considers the evidence from syntax and lexicon, but there are exceptions. Schnitzer and Krasinski (1994) conducted a longitudinal case study of a bilingual child between the ages of one year, one month and three years, nine months to describe the phonological systems of the two languages, Spanish and English. The results were more heterogeneous than they might have wished – for example, they found an initial single stage for consonants but not for vowels with a great deal of variation in vowel production. Their explanation for bilingual phonological development required incorporating a wider range of factors, and they suggested that such features as articulatory maturation be included to account for inherent differences in the difficulty of producing specific sounds. They concluded that the child passed through four stages during this time. The first stage is a single system, although it is incomplete and inconsistent; the second includes a distinction between the languages; the third is characterized by stabilization of the vowels; and the fourth introduces interference between the systems. Although these stages are built out of developments of phonological accuracy, they are reminiscent of the stages proposed by Volterra and Taeschner (1978) which were primarily proposed to account for the development of syntax.

In this research, children's failure to function consistently in a single language is taken as evidence that they do not consider the two languages to be separate entities. Since it is premature to attribute linguistic awareness to these children, who in many cases are less than two years old, their "consideration" of what these languages are is simply a reflection of their mental representation. But is the methodology for investigating the question again intruding into the results? Is there confusion between distinction in the mental representation and the metalinguistic ability to describe the two language systems? In a study by Levy (1985), a bilingual two-year-old was asked such questions as, "How does mommy say X," and predictably responded with non sequiturs. Similarly, Fantini (1985) was willing to credit his bilingual son with understanding the distinctiveness of the two languages only when he was able to *comment* on the differences. For example, when he was almost three years old, the child said that people spoke English on the airplane. Using a criterion as explicit as a metalinguistic statement certainly leaves no ambiguity that the child has noticed something important about the languages, but the absence of such declarations does not unequivocally indicate that the child lacks this awareness. What does a child of two years old understand such a question to mean?

Separated at Birth

It is one thing to notice that children appear to use languages interchangeably in the early stages, but it is another to argue that this behavior indicates a lack of differentiation in children's minds. For this reason, several researchers have challenged the interpretation of children's language mixing and questioned the plausibility that it indicates an undifferentiated repository of all linguistic knowledge.

One of the arguments for reconsidering the conclusion that languages are combined in children's early linguistic representations is parallel to one that was used earlier to explain the development of word meanings in young (monolingual) children. Children's overextensions of words to refer to similar objects, such as using "doggie" to label squirrels, is more likely evidence of strategic resourcefulness than of conceptual confusion (see discussion in Chapter 2). Similarly, children with two incomplete language systems may well attempt to exploit their combined resources when specific words or structures are lacking in the language required for the present needs.

In the differentiated view, children's linguistic representations are organized according to the two languages, but terms and structures from the other language are selected if they are required to fill a gap in the language the child is attempting to use. Just as young monolinguals will use a close but incorrect label for an object they want to talk about, so too will bilingual children use an item from their other language when it is necessary to express their current meaning (De Houwer, 1990; Deuchar & Quay, 2000; Goodz, 1989; Lanza, 1992, 1997; Lindholm & Padilla, 1978; Meisel, 1989; Pye, 1986). Using detailed analyses of children's utterances and relating the incidence of mixing to specific linguistic, contextual, and pragmatic factors, these studies support the view that young bilinguals are able to distinguish between their two languages and use them appropriately. Although much of this research is based on case studies, sometimes with only one subject, there is typically a detailed analysis of the child's lexicon in each language included. For example, Deuchar and Quay (2000) list the separate Spanish and English vocabularies for their bilingual subject and can make unambiguous attributions when the child combines lexicon from both in a single utterance. Their conclusion is that the child, who was approximately two years old at the time of the study, is operating from two systems but exploiting the resources of each where necessary. This argument has been extended to the ability of trilingual children to establish three independent linguistic systems from the first stages of languages acquisition (Mikeš, 1990).

Genesee (1989) contends that the deciding evidence for whether children's language mixing reflects a common source or a strategic tool comes from the distribution of language mixing in the use of the weaker language. For most bilingual children, one language is the preferred or stronger language, and the other is weaker. On any explanation of language mixing, one would expect the stronger language to intrude into the weaker language. Therefore, the stronger language will predominate in all contexts and with all interlocuters. The weaker language, by definition, takes more effort for children to produce. If the two languages are represented in a single system, children should be expected to produced structures and items from the weaker language equally in contexts requiring either of the two languages. Conversely, if children distinguish between the two languages and attempt to select appropriately, then there should be significantly greater use of the weaker language in contexts requiring that language than in contexts requiring the stronger language.

Some evidence supports this hypothesis. In a study by Petersen (1988), a bilingual English-Danish child used English morphology with both English and Danish lexicon, but never mixed Danish morphology with English lexicon. In this case, the child's dominant language was English and it was used to adapt the lexical structures in both languages to the syntactic context. This difference presupposes an ability to distinguish between the languages, since lexicon is freely mixed in both directions.

Research by Genesee and his colleagues has investigated this issue more directly. In one study, Genesee, Nicoladis, and Paradis (1995) examined five French-English bilingual children who were between the one- and two-word stage in their language acquisition. All these children were being raised in the one parent, one language model. They found mixing to occur primarily from the dominant language into the weaker language and concluded that these children could reliably and consistently differentiate their languages. In another study examining four children between one year, seven months old and three years old, Nicoladis and Genesee (1996) studied children's use of the correct language with each parent as well as their selection of translation equivalents, words for which the child possessed the lexical item in both languages. If children can name a concept in both languages, then selecting the appropriate language indicates that children recognize this difference. The researchers uncovered an early stage in the second year in which the children showed little or no language differentiation when speaking to their parents. At this time, fewer than half of the translation equivalents were used correctly; after languages could be appropriately selected for each parent, more than 80 percent of the translation equivalents were used correctly. Thus, they conceded that there is an initial period when bilingual children do not differentiate their languages pragmatically, at least as evidenced by language choice. This, of course, does not necessarily resolve the more fundamental question of how those languages are represented in the mind. The earlier stages of language learning also provide children with fewer resources in each language, increasing the temptation to borrow from a neighboring system.

Other researchers take a more dogmatic position on the earliest stages of language use. Lanza (1992) reports a case study of language acquisition of English and Norwegian in a two-year-old. There was considerable language mixing at this age, especially on functors, where grammatical terms from the dominant language were incorporated into utterances in the weaker language. In this sense, the dominant language sets out a syntactic frame, similar to the matrix described by Myers-Scotton (1997) that determines the grammar for both languages. Lanza argues, however, that lexicon is a more neutral aspect of language and that lexical mixing would therefore provide a better indicator of language differentiation. She finds no reason to posit an early stage in which children operate from a single system. Rather, the languages are distinct from early on and the patterns of mixing are the same as those found in older bilinguals.

Lanza (1997) introduces another dimension to the explanation of language switching. She identifies five discourse strategies that characterize parental responses to children's mixed utterances. These strategies – minimal grasp, expressed guess, adult repetition, move-on, and code-switching – vary on a continuum describing a monolingual context on one end (minimal grasp) to a bilingual context on the other (code-switching). Lanza argues that children and adults negotiate the point of the dimension in which they are functioning by means of these parental responses. Children then respond with greater or lesser degrees of code-switching to comply with that sociolinguistic context. Although she reports data to support the notion that degree of code-switching was predicted by the parental discourse strategy, a study by Nicoladis and Genesee (1998) failed to replicate the relation.

The observation that language mixing decreases with increased competence is also consistent with a strategic explanation and need not evoke explanations of undifferentiated linguistic representation. De Houwer (1990) points out that children who mix languages may be making sociolinguistic errors of language choice but they are not necessarily making psycholinguistic errors. Meisel (1989), too, states that code-mixing is part of pragmatic competence and commonly occurs when one of the languages is dominant. Mixed utterances are stable over (developmental) time, suggesting they are normal features of bilingual language use. Further, they are used more with a bilingual parent than monolingual interlocutor, suggesting that children are aware at some level of the social context that permits these combined utterances.

As a final note, it is not incompatible with the distinct language view to find some very early origin for children's language competence in which there is not yet separation between the languages. This may be regarded as a compromise between the two positions, one in which the undifferentiated system is both very early and temporary. Nicoladis (1998) develops this position and presents data from a case study of a young child, tracing his development from the time he was one year old with a vocabulary of seven words and following him for a period of six months until it contained 122. Her interest was in whether the child first learned to distinguish between the languages for individual words he used or the contexts in which he needed to use each of his languages. The context was simply defined by the parent with whom he was interacting, as the family followed a one person, one language rule. She found that the child distinguished between the contexts about one month before showing control over word distinctions, although other studies have reported the opposite (Quay, 1995). The order is really not important; the critical finding is that there is reasonable evidence that children's very earliest stages of using two languages do not show this differentiation, but by one and a half years old (much younger than the age for achieving differentiation in the unitary language models), they are clearly operating from two systems.

Developing the Systems

Consider now how language competence would develop if bilingual children began language learning with distinct representational systems for each language. The two language representation systems may or may not interact with each other, and this creates two possibilities for development. If the languages interact, they would likely influence each other and the bilingual child's acquisition of each language would be qualitatively different from a monolingual child's acquisition of each respective language. Paradis and Genesee (1996) call this the interdependence view. Alternatively, if the linguistic resources remain relatively isolated from each other, then bilingual children should respect the typical path of development for each of the two languages individually, and each would be comparable to that of a monolingual child. This option is called the autonomous view (Paradis & Genesee, 1996).

Paradis and Genesee (1996) evaluated these options by studying three French-English bilingual children at three intervals in their third year of life. Their analysis investigated the way in which three syntactic structures were acquired in each of the languages. The three structures, finiteness, negation, and pronominal subject, are instantiated differently in the two languages, so influence from one of the languages onto that structure in the other language would be readily apparent. In all cases, children's acquisition of these structures followed the patterns established by monolingual children learning each of these languages independently. Hence, the researchers concluded that not only were the two languages separated in the mind of the bilingual child from very early in acquisition, but also were they distinct and autonomous and did not influence the acquisition of the other.

A different kind of evidence for the early representation of two languages comes from the assumptions children make about the meanings of new words. In the development of word meanings, several constraints are assumed to apply to children's strategies for learning the meanings of new words. These constraints prevent children from applying a new label to a concept that already has a name. Consequently, a novel word will be connected with an unnamed concept (Clark, 1987, 1993; Markman, 1989; Merriman & Bowman, 1989). If the two languages of the young bilingual are represented as a common source, then children should be reluctant to accept two names for the same concept, or doublets, even if the names each belonged to a different language. In a common representation, this difference between languages would be irrelevant.

Pearson, Fernández, and Oller (1995) investigated this possibility with young English-Spanish bilinguals. They found that these children, who ranged in age from eight months to two and a half years, had on average about 30 percent of doublets in their vocabulary. That is, almost one-third of their lexicon represented linguistic options for naming the same concepts. More important, there was no observable change in this ratio as children passed between the stage boundaries that Volterra and Taeschner (1978) claimed marked the shift from a single to an independent representation of the two languages.

An extension of this research approach is to study whether bilingual children will behave like monolinguals on experimental tasks aimed at establishing their adherence to these constraints. Au and Glusman (1990) and Merriman and Kutlesic (1993) found that bilingual children and adults were willing to abandon these constraints when the words came from two different languages. This is consistent with the report by Pearson et al. (1995) showing that bilinguals were better than monolinguals in tolerating overlap between words from different languages.

The more significant effect, however, would be to show that monolinguals and bilinguals differ in their adherence to the constraints when inferring meanings within a single language. This point was not examined in the study by Pearson et al. (1995), because they considered only cross-language labels and only bilingual children. Merriman and Kutlesic (1993) found little difference between monolingual and bilingual children in observing the constraints when they were presented with novel words in English. Both groups were reluctant to accept a novel name for a concept they could already name in English. However, Davison et al. (1997) report different results. They tested monolingual and bilingual children who were three and six years old using three different criteria for mutual exclusivity. They found that the monolinguals were more constrained than the bilinguals on two of them and that the groups were equivalent on the third. Their conclusion was that bilinguals were less tied to the word-meaning constraints than were monolinguals. It is not clear why the two studies reported different results, but some factors may be the level of proficiency in the two languages for the bilingual groups and the criteria used to determine the presence of mutual exclusivity. Regardless of the contradictory results using a single language, several studies have replicated the finding that bilingual children are released from these constraints when thinking across languages. Hence, these children consider that linguistic distinctions are sufficient cause to accept a new label for a known concept. Logically, languages would need to be understood as distinct systems for these patterns to occur.

Grosjean's (1989) proposal that bilinguals can move along a continuum from monolingual mode to bilingual mode (discussed in Chapter 3) may obviate the entire need to compare the representational independence of bilinguals with that of monolinguals. In the bilingual mode, language mixing and switching is normal and comprehensible, so there is no assumption of confusion or absence of differentiation in the underlying representation. Nonetheless, the underlying competence that permits this movement along the dimension from bilingual to monolingual modes is undoubtedly different in important ways from the underlying competence of monolingual speakers. Cook (1997) makes a similar claim about the uniqueness of *multilingual competence,* arguing that it is different both from that of a monolingual and from the combination of two monolingual systems that have simply been collated into one.

Consistent with this view that bilinguals function in two languages in a way that is not captured by any processing carried out with monolinguals, it is not surprising that bilingual children intersperse linguistic forms. Research investigating the cognitive processes used by bilingual adults in language and memory tasks has recently converged on the conclusion that the two languages for bilinguals, even highly proficient ones, are both always active to some degree (Dijkstra, van Jaarsveld, & Ten Brinke, 1998; see also discussion in Chapter 7). It is not surprising that bilingual children, with their fragile linguistic and conceptual systems, will select words and structures from the other language when it is feasible and expedient, even though the languages enjoy distinct representations and the child accepts that they are different.

These analyses point to the importance of the social context in defining the speech of bilinguals. Therefore, another factor that needs to be seriously considered before condemning bilingual children to linguistic chaos in the earliest stages of language acquisition is an analysis of what they actually hear. Adult speech is less linguistically pure than we might wish to believe; foreign words are frequently interpolated for effect, emphasis, accuracy, or social affiliation. Even in situations that are essentially monolingual, children are likely to hear fragments of adult speech that contain language mixing. In a bilingual context, the situation is undoubtedly exacerbated. A home that functions in two languages will inevitably create a situation in which family members switch between the languages, and there is nothing to prevent that switching from occurring within single discourse contexts, single conversations, and even single utterances.

What is the influence of these mixed speech patterns on children's language acquisition? Several researchers have noted that the model of language mixing presented by parents might predict the extent to which children engage in language switching (De Houwer, 1990; Genesee, 1989). Theoretically, the argument depends on establishing contingencies between parental speech and children's language acquisition. Beginning with the collection of studies by Snow and Ferguson (1977), researchers have continued to examine this question in increasing detail (e.g., Prior, 1996; Sokolov, 1993). Studies of monolingual children show that there is a certain influence, although it is limited in scope and usually confined to specific kinds of features or structures. The effect is pervasive enough, however, to acknowledge that the language children hear has a role in shaping the language they will speak.

The premise in applying this principal of the influence of parental speech into analyses of children's language is that it is possible to describe the child's linguistic context in terms of the specific people or situations in which each language is heard and used. The most common model for raising bilingual children is the one parent, one language arrangement, the "Grammont system" described by Ronjat (1913). This, the story goes, is the ideal situation: input is relatively equivalent, languages are clearly separated, and communication is highly motivated. Building on this, Lanza (1988) proposes a more detailed prescription for how the linguistic environment should be arranged for prospectively bilingual children. She notes the importance of metalinguistic comments as well as clear separation between the languages to maximize the child's evolving competence in both languages.

How realistic is this model? Goodz (1989) conducted an investigation of young bilinguals who, according to parental testimony, were being raised in this way. Parents assured researchers that they were scrupulous about honoring the household rules of linguistic choice and that their speech to the child was pure and unadulterated. In recorded observations from the home, however, Goodz found otherwise. Despite their protestations to the contrary, parents did mix languages, and children's own integrated utterances may well have been a reflection of the language modeled for them at home.

Representing Two Languages

The discussion so far has centered on a somewhat esoteric difference between two interpretations of an essentially uncontroversial fact, namely, that children learning two languages in childhood begin by using them together before being able to keep them apart. The cognitive issue in deciding between these alternatives is whether the mental representation in the earliest stages of language acquisition respects the distinction between the languages or not. The discrepancy is not trivial. The origins of linguistic knowledge have always been a forum for playing out competing theories of the nature of language and its relation to the rest of cognition. Some of these conflicts were raised in Chapter 2. Is language a biologically programmed module, unconnected to other domains of thought? Is language constructed from experience and modified through general cognitive processes? Normally, the arguments are waged theoretically, but in the case of bilingual children, it may be possible to observe aspects of early language development that are normally transparent in the monolingual.

The same question applies to the problem of representation for two languages in adult bilinguals, but the assumptions and evidence are different. In deciding on the proper architectural configuration for two languages in the adult mind, the options vary along a continuum of mutual interactivity between the languages. The continuum indicates the distinctiveness with which each language is represented but, more importantly, activated, during language processing. The most salient test cases assess the degree to which the language *not* in use is involved, however peripherally or implicitly, while functioning in the other language. The options, therefore, reflect the overlap between the two languages.

Even in the cases of most overlap, however, there is never any intimation that the adult speaker is ever in a state of linguistic confusion. Consequently, determining the proper representational format and pattern of activation need not have any implications for the behavioral experiences of using two languages: the bilingual adult could remain blissfully unaware that the unused language has been activated at all. Nonetheless, the research with children is quick to conclude that they are incapable of distinguishing between two languages if they are represented together or mixed together in speech. Establishing how young bilinguals build up representations for their knowledge of two languages must include more subtle evidence than combined language utterances and more sophisticated argument than inference from speech behavior to mental representation.

The nature of linguistic representation for two languages bears as well on issues in linguistic theory. There is no direct connection between formal or functional linguistic theories (see Chapter 2) and either of the two positions for early linguistic representations. There is, however, a logical association that biases each linguistic approach to one of the two representational alternatives. In the differentiated language systems hypothesis, the child's earliest and most basic notions about language are already demarcated for the specific language to which they pertain. Abstract information about individual language systems is somehow incorporated into children's initial linguistic knowledge. Because this information is so abstract, it is difficult to imagine how it could be extracted from experience (especially if bilingual adults are heard speaking both languages); consequently, it is more plausible that it is part of children's preconceptions of language and its structure. The differentiated systems hypothesis, therefore, follows more logically from a formal linguistic theory in which abstract linguistic knowledge, codified as some measure of universal grammar, however weak in scope, constrains children's language acquisition.

Conversely, in the unitary language system hypothesis, children's early linguistic representations are not specified for a particular language. Instead, a single system of meanings and structures eventually evolves into the two separate languages. Functional linguistic theories are more compatible with this kind of development. Children's experiences allow them to represent knowledge in a reasonably general way, and these representations are refined and specialized through further learning and experience. This view places a greater responsibility on general cognitive processes that must establish linguistic knowledge from somewhat undifferentiated representations.

Just as the dichotomy between formal and functional interpretations led to no clear choice in the matter of deciding on the criteria for language proficiency (see Chapter 1), so too the absolute division between single and combined representational systems leads to a false divide. Elements from each are required for a complete description.

Interpreting the Evidence

The evidence has proven to be more intricate than any model predicted. Not surprisingly, the simple theoretical dichotomy has no parallel in children's actual experiences or in results from research studies. The weight of evidence favors the differentiated language view, but the overwhelming degree to which language mixing occurs cannot be so easily dismissed, even with the entirely reasonable explanation that it reflects children's need to communicate. A more elaborate alternative that combines aspects of both approaches is needed to reconcile the differences between them and ultimately provide a better fit with the observations of the way in which children begin to learn two languages.

The resolution must consider several lines of argument. The first and most obvious is the one that Weinreich (1968) alerted us to in his early contemplation of this problem. There is no reason that several organizations cannot coexist, and that even these organizations change over time and with development. We know that knowledge is dynamic; we must allow the representations of knowledge to be dynamic as well. There is no reason that two language representations cannot share certain elements and not others, and that the shared elements cannot change over time.

The second argument follows from the research with neuroimaging techniques (described above) that have attempted to establish the configurations of cortical involvement in representing and processing language. The irresistible conclusion is that the patterns are less universal than we might have hoped. If this is the case, then we need not assume that representational structure is universal, either. There may well be a range of normal variation that defines how knowledge of language is represented, and across different individuals, that organization may be quite different. It would not be surprising, for example, if such individual variations reflected differences in experience and language learning history.

Third, the different results that have been obtained by studies using different methodologies often reflect differences in the demands placed on the subjects by the tasks. In all cases, the broad domain of interest is language, but language is vast and multidimensional. Tasks that assess syntax frequently yield different patterns of results than do tasks that assess semantics, and control over semantics is often unrelated to mastery of phonology. Even within one level of linguistic analysis, for example, syntax, there are arguments to support the idea that distinctions between divisions such as universal and language-specific structures correspond to different kinds of representations.

These variations might reveal more about the testing methodology than the representation of linguistic knowledge. There is a difference between the structural details of knowledge representation in the brain and the functional use of those representations in processing. The two might not be related: representations that are spatially distinct might be highly interfering during processing and others that are combined may not interact. Some methodologies provide more access to spatial information about representational distinctness (e.g., PET, fMRI), while others provide access to information about functional activation (judgment tasks, inter-ference tasks).

It is generally assumed that the representational form, whatever it is, applies to all aspects of the language, but there is no forceful argument that should make this so. We know that language representation is divided to some extent, even across cerebral hemispheres. The right hemisphere involvement in language may not monitor fundamentals such as syntax, but it is no less crucial to normal language functioning than are the more linguistically central processes that reside in the familiar left hemisphere. Even here, some of the earliest insights into how language is represented in the mind concern basic divisions of responsibility. The earliest progress in this area was to isolate the comprehension functions in Wernicke's area and the distinct production functions in Broca's area. Although these descriptions are now considered to be oversimplifications, it remains the case that the different aspects of language processing are housed in these cerebrally distinct locations.

Finally, the resolution may be achieved by examining changes in pro-cessing rather than changes in representation as children develop. In the inhibitory control model proposed by Green (1998) described above, the representation of two languages in the bilingual mind is distinct, but both languages remain active during any language use. It is the responsibility of an inhibitory process to suppress the nonrelevant language and allow the required one to carry out the task. Part of children's development in the early years may be in refining this inhibitory control so that it effectively eliminates intrusions from the unwanted language. If both languages are always active (whether they are represented in a single or independent lexicon), then two factors would lead to their combination in children's early speech. The first is that the need to communicate would compel the child to recruit whatever resources are available. An alternative lexicon that is already active would be an irresistible resource when gaps are encountered in the language being used. The second is that the inhibitory processes required to suppress to nonrelevant language might be too frag-ile to prevent all intrusions for very young children. As these inhibitory processes become more viable, children's speech can remain more reliably fixed on the language being used. This possibility is discussed further in Chapter 7.

Toward Distinct Representations

The correct description for the representation of language must include all the elements that are supported by substantial empirical evidence, even if they appear on the surface to be mutually contradictory. The broad outline of the solution must be that representations of language are always dispersed over both language-specific representations and general cognitive domains of thought. The language-specific aspects of representation undoubtedly include constraints that make language acquisition possible, but the general cognitive involvement is essential for the development of language as an instrument of socialization and thought.

Developmental forces are exerted onto all these representations as children elaborate their formal knowledge of language and its structure, expand their resources for using language to direct and communicate thought, and mature in their social interactions so that language becomes central to their place in the world. All of this is multiplied for bilingual children. They draw on their compound representations that pertain to knowing and using language as they continue to develop more complete linguistic representations for each language they are learning. It is not surprising that they sometimes, especially initially, incorporate elements that may seem inappropriate into their speech. What is more important is that by about two and a half years old, they function effectively in the two languages. Most of the evidence for language mixing after that age comes from lexical insertions, and that is arguably the most trivial aspect of language use and easily explained by strategic devices to continue communicating. Following these schematic considerations, the mental representation of two languages for a bilingual is clearly different from that of a monolingual but certainly not the simple compounding that would result from compiling two systems into a place normally occupied by one. The two languages are distinct and the representation for them is unique. This remains true even if the languages are forced to share space in a complex mind. It is their functional configuration that determines learning and cognition.

5

Thinking About Language

The vocabulary we use to express our ideas is more than just a reference system. Words have power, and when words come into favor, they can take on a life of their own. Words can then *determine* our ideas, because they focus our attention on certain concepts at the expense of others and invoke assumptions that may never be made explicit. If the words are successful, they can spread across contiguous interest groups, entering the consciousness of what is eventually a widely dispersed research community. Just as language changes as it spreads to different cultures and different places, so too technical language changes as it is embraced by researchers occupied with different kinds of questions. One inevitable consequence of this terminological imperialism is a lack of consensus about the meaning of the term. Terms can be used by researchers from different traditions in ways that have little commonality, although the meaning differences are not necessarily detected. This was the case for the term *critical period*: a stable meaning needed to be established before it could be evaluated for its role in language learning (see Chapter 3).

This has also been the fate of the term *metalinguistic*. The prefix "meta" came into prominence in the 1970s and was applied to a variety of cognitive functions, such as metacognition and metamemory. Since then, it has been used by psychologists, linguists, and educators with little regard for its meaning in other contexts. Indeed, the prefix has been liberally attached to any concept or activity that requires some extra knowledge or effort. But what does it mean when it is used to describe an aspect of language knowledge or use?

One of the first references to metalinguistic awareness as a unique construct was made by Cazden (1974, p. 29), who defined it as follows: "The ability to make language forms opaque and attend to them in and for themselves, is a special kind of language performance, one which makes special cognitive demands, and seems to be less easily and less universally acquired than the language performances of speaking and listening." Although Cazden signaled the ways in which metalinguistic uses of language were to be differentiated from speaking and listening, she did not identify what was "special" about their cognitive demands.

For the past two decades, abilities described as "meta" have occupied a prominent place in the developmental literature. The largest share of this research attention has been devoted to metalinguistic development. Researchers have continued to redefine the term "metalinguistic"; to develop tasks to assess and quantify its presence in children; to assign it responsibility for achievements from literacy to Piagetian formal operational thought; to distribute it among individuals on the basis of their intelligence, schooling, and social class; and to locate it in a variety of theoretical frameworks for teaching, learning, and thinking. Some of the research fields that have installed metalinguistic functioning into their explanations for performance include cognitive development (e.g., Hakes, 1980), language acquisition (e.g., Gombert, 1992), literacy acquisition (e.g., Yaden & Templeton, 1986), second-language acquisition (e.g., Birdsong, 1989), language instruction (e.g., James & Garrett, 1992), and theory of mind (e.g., Wellman, 1990). Most important for our purposes, it has been identified as one of the ways that bilingual children distinguish themselves from their monolingual peers (e.g., Hakuta, 1986). If metalinguistic ability could do even a fraction of what has been attributed to it, it would indeed be one of the most significant achievements of childhood. But what is metalinguistic awareness?

In spite of the impressive array of consequences that have been attributed to metalinguistic abilities, little agreement can be found on specifying what it is, how it develops, and what function it plays. Therefore, some discussion of the construct itself must be logically prior to speculation about how it figures in the mental lives of bilingual children.

Defining "Metalinguistic"

It may be that bilingual children develop metalinguistic awareness in a different manner or at a different rate from monolingual children, as some studies have reported. The claim, however, is difficult to interpret because it is not clear what metalinguistic awareness is or why its development is important. We begin, therefore, with an attempt to clarify the construct and its role in children's development. This context will provide a background against which we can evaluate claims about how children develop metalinguistic awareness.

The term metalinguistic is used as a qualifier for at least three different entities: knowledge, ability, and awareness. It is also used to qualify an experimental procedure, as in a metalinguistic task. Presumably, however, the distinctive features of a metalinguistic task will follow from a clarification of what is being tested, that is, the meaning of the knowledge, ability, or awareness that is indicative of this achievement.

The differences among the uses for metalinguistic as it applies to knowledge, ability, or awareness are never made explicit. Often the phrases are used interchangeably, but intuitively they point to different constructs and set different constraints on the meaning of metalinguistic. Together they may reveal a significant set of conditions that apply to the underlying common concept. The additional claim here is that they convey an implicit ordering in the way in which metalinguistic is conceptualized along a dimension of processing demands. Since the goal here is to ultimately define metalinguistic constructs in terms of their processing demands, finding a means of defining these contexts by virtue of their processing demands is an important starting point.

Metalinguistic Knowledge

How is metalinguistic knowledge, or knowledge *about* language, different from what might be called more simply knowledge of grammar? If it turns out that metalinguistic knowledge is simply what less formal theories would call grammar, then the concept does not serve a useful purpose. Knowledge of grammar is linguistic knowledge that has been made explicit. Is metalinguistic knowledge more than this?

One difference between linguistic and metalinguistic knowledge may be in the level of generality at which rules are represented. If the rules are a record of the structure of a particular language, such as how to form past tense, what word order is needed for different sentence types, how relative clauses are constructed, then they essentially *are* the grammar. Although such knowledge of grammar may be part of metalinguistic knowledge, it is insufficient to justify a concept at the level of theoretical importance occupied by metalinguistic. Metalinguistic must be more. Hence, metalinguistic knowledge minimally needs to include the abstract structure of language that organizes sets of linguistic rules without being directly instantiated in any of them. This would include insights such as canonical word order and productive morphological patterns. Knowledge of these abstract principles is distinct from knowledge of a particular language and supports a separate concept to describe it.

The implication of this condition is that the content of metalinguistic knowledge must be broader than any that applies to knowledge of a particular language. When one has metalinguistic knowledge, one has knowledge of language in its most general sense, irrespective of the details of specific linguistic structures. Children would understand, for example, that the order in which words are linked can change the meaning of a sentence or that modification to the verb in the sentence can change the time at which a stated event occurred. If there are cognitive benefits from acquiring metalinguistic knowledge, they accrue because it is abstract knowledge and not particular knowledge. On this view, metalinguistic knowledge is the explicit representation of abstract aspects of linguistic structure that become accessible through knowledge of a particular language.

Metalinguistic Ability

For metalinguistic ability to have significance, it must be recognizable as a distinct achievement while integrating seamlessly into other aspects of linguistic and cognitive skill. This simultaneous need for uniqueness and commonality is perhaps the most elusive of the criteria for a proper definition of "metalinguistic." The attempt to define a cognitive skill thus becomes intertwined with architectural questions in cognitive science such as the modularity of mind.

Logically, metalinguistic ability describes the capacity to use knowledge about language as opposed to the capacity to use language. Hence, the definition of this ability is contingent on the definition of the previous construct, metalinguistic knowledge. By giving it a separate label, a distinct knowledge base, and a unique course of development, the tendency is to assume as well that metalinguistic ability is independent of the ability responsible for using language for purposes such as conversation. This assumption leads to a false dichotomy: knowledge of language is forced to separate from the ability to use language. Is it reasonable to assume that metalinguistic ability is distinct from the linguistic ability that drives ordinary listening and speaking?

Consider a case in which metalinguistic ability is posited to be an independent skill for using knowledge about language. This conception is appealing because most descriptions of language use, and certainly language acquisition in the early stages, exist just fine without any additional construct requiring children to know *about* language. In this sense, metalinguistic ability is something that is added on, an optional embellishment, but not part of the basic machinery that drives language acquisition and use. If such an additional skill is required, it may or may not be equivalent to the linguistic ability that allows people to learn to speak and understand language. It could develop on its own course, through its own experience, and manifest itself in its own contexts. In fact, it may have little to do with linguistic ability.

A view of this type that sets metalinguistic ability apart as an autonomous skill has the theoretical advantage of being unconstrained by accounts of linguistic development. In other words, if metalinguistic ability is a mechanism separate from linguistic ability, then explanations of how it functions and how it develops can be unique to this skill. It makes it easy to explain why all children learn to speak but some children struggle to acquire metalinguistic concepts. It also allows metalinguistic ability to be the reserve of some privileged few: the more intelligent, the more educated, the more multilingual, and so on. At the same time, it requires us to regard the ability to use knowledge about language as distinct from the ability to use language.

In contrast to this view is one in which metalinguistic ability is located firmly within the confines of linguistic ability. It may be derivative of linguistic ability, but it is not a different kind of thing. Whatever parameters are needed to explain the development and use of linguistic ability are also needed to account for metalinguistic ability. Although the parsimony of this view is more satisfying than the fractiousness of the previous one, it leaves the entire concept of metalinguistic vulnerable to the charge of vacuity. If it is not a different kind of thing from linguistic ability, then presumably it does not need a different kind of label and certainly does not need a different theory to account for its development.

A proper definition of metalinguistic ability must be a compromise between these two positions. The ability must be sufficiently unique from the linguistic skill that is responsible for ordinary language use that it can be detected independently and traced over an autonomous developmental course. At the same time, it cannot be so isolated from linguistic ability that they have no common origin. Intrinsic to definitions of metalinguistic ability, then, must be the means of relating it to linguistic ability, and explanations of the nature and development of metalinguistic ability must be reconcilable with the facts and theories of linguistic ability. We are not free, in other words, to posit parameters for metalinguistic ability that are not consistent with parameters for linguistic ability.

Metalinguistic Awareness

The third context, metalinguistic awareness, probably raises the most awkward of all the issues attendant to definitions of "meta" abilities – the problem of consciousness. Conscious knowledge implies an involvement in on-line processing. My knowledge of the route I take from my home to the university is explicit but it is only conscious when I am in the process of moving from one place to the other. To this end, consciousness, or awareness, needs an additional mechanism – attention. The combination of attention and explicit mental representations can produce the phenomenal experience of awareness.

The nature of consciousness has resurfaced in discussions of philosophy of mind as one of the central problems to be solved. However, it is not clear that a compelling explanation that ultimately solves the problem of human consciousness is any closer now than it was for Descartes. But more to the point, it is not clear that solving this problem will have much consequence for the way in which we conceptualize learning and understanding and the way that we use the term "consciousness" to do so.

Consciousness can be used to refer to both knowledge (as in conscious knowledge of events) and awareness (to be conscious of one's knowledge of events). Searle (1992) takes an even broader view and claims it to be characteristic of mental abilities: human functioning is conscious by its very definition. Just as liquidity is a property of H_2O molecules (albeit within a certain temperature range), so too, argues Searle, consciousness is a property of human brains. The problem with defining consciousness in this way and applying it to the present contexts is that it does not set out contrasting positions that are clarified by the distinction. If knowledge can be conscious, what is unconscious knowledge? If awareness is conscious, can there be unconscious awareness? Regarding mental abilities, Searle refuses to even entertain the possibility that there could be unconscious mental processes. Therefore, both metalinguistic and linguistic ability must be equally conscious. If a term does not distinguish between two kinds of events, in this case conscious from unconscious processing or metalinguistic ability from linguistic ability, then it does not contribute to theorizing. For this reason, the concept of consciousness is unproductive as a condition in defining metalinguistic because it fails to make relevant distinctions.

What is left for metalinguistic awareness is attention. Metalinguistic awareness implies that attention is actively focused on the domain of knowledge that describes the explicit properties of language. Defined this way, metalinguistic awareness is a momentary phenomenon, something achieved at a point in real time because attention has been focused on certain mental representations. This definition displaces the explanatory burden to the problem of attention. However, because attention is a general function implicated in all cognitive processes, metalinguistic awareness becomes part of ordinary cognition.

The Relevance of "Meta" for Second-Language Acquisition

Each of the three contexts in which "metalinguistic" is used provides a criterion for defining the term. Metalinguistic knowledge must be both explicit and abstract in that it is stated at a higher level of generality than are the specific details of any particular language. Metalinguistic ability must be continuous with linguistic ability; it cannot be isolated from it and operate according to independent principles of development and use. Nonetheless, it must be demonstrably distinct from the ability to use language in ordinary conversation. Finally, metalinguistic awareness must be incorporated within a theory of attention that explains how certain features of a mental representation come into active processing and how attention is distributed to some but not all aspects of the mental representation.

With these three considerations, metalinguistic is a potentially important concept in explaining the acquisition and use of language. Moreover, it has clear relevance for understanding second-language acquisition. Consider some of the implications. First, metalinguistic knowledge provides an important constraint on theories of language acquisition. According to this view, the knowledge that is made explicit during language acquisition is not knowledge of specific grammars but knowledge of linguistic principles. Linguistic knowledge can be relevant for subsequent language acquisition only if it is represented in an abstract and general sense, so if metalinguistic knowledge is to influence second-language acquisition it must meet this condition. Hence, metalinguistic knowledge is constructed from language acquisition and applied to second-language acquisition precisely because it is explicit and universal. Second-language learners need not relearn the fundamental principles of language structure because these are already known from the metalinguistic knowledge that grew out of first-language acquisition. To the extent that a learner has metalinguistic knowledge, second-language acquisition is facilitated because a language template is available.

Regarding metalinguistic ability, a theory of second-language acquisition must find some measure of continuity between first-language acquisition, second-language acquisition, and formal linguistic ability. Just as it makes no sense to separate the ability to use metalinguistic knowledge from the ability to use linguistic knowledge, so too the ability to learn a second language must be continuous with first-language acquisition. Without this condition, there would be no means of connecting linguistic and metalinguistic ability. There would be little point, in other words, in making metalinguistic ability convergent with linguistic ability if the ability responsible for learning a second language were allowed to dissociate from both of these. Therefore, metalinguistic ability provides continuity to theories of language acquisition because they are all based on the same underlying processes responsible for using language. To this end, the linguistic computations and manipulations that are endemic to using language in precise or specialized ways are aided by the learner's metalinguistic ability.

Finally, the definition of metalinguistic awareness focuses the problem of language processing on the concept of attention. Attention is decisive in distinguishing between linguistic and metalinguistic processing and provides a means of identifying an important cognitive basis of language use. The idea that processing involves the selective attention to different information, and that performance may vary as attention is redirected in different ways, helps to account for the observable differences between linguistic activities such as speaking and listening on the one hand and solving grammar problems on the other. In this sense, the inclusion of metalinguistic awareness into a description of linguistic performance helps to explain some of the ways in which second-language use might be different from first-language use. Presumably, allocation of attention is different for the two activities, and this attention is directly dependent on the types of mental representations or knowledge that the speaker has of each language. This interpretation also allows us to dispense with the problem of consciousness because attention can be explained without need for this illusive and defiant construct.

This analysis of the three concepts illustrates the role that metalinguistic processing might have in understanding second-language acquisition. The exploration was predicated on the assumption that the learners were adults and that the languages were being learned sequentially. What about children?

Bilingual children often learn their two languages simultaneously. In this case, there is no clear designation of a first or second language but rather a single acquisition process in which two linguistic systems are constructed instead of one (but see discussion in Chapter 4). Does metalinguistic development change when children are learning two languages? If metalinguistic concepts are central to child language acquisition (as theorists have argued) and involved in second-language acquisition (as claimed above) then surely they are germane to children learning two languages in childhood.

Metalinguistic: The Process

Most descriptions of metalinguistic abilities (regardless of which of the three contexts is being examined) have emanated from a structuralist assumption. Structuralist models lend themselves to illustration by means of boxes and arrows indicating the components and their connections, or Venn diagrams allowing some overlap among components. From this perspective, metalinguistic is a distinct domain that can be defined by identifying the boundaries that distinguish it from similar concepts. Hence, metalinguistic skills separate from linguistic skills by virtue of some characteristic property or demand, for example, attention to form rather than meaning; metalinguistic knowledge is identifiable from linguistic knowledge because of its representational form, for example, it is more explicit; and metalinguistic tasks are those that assess metalinguistic rather than linguistic performance, for example, talking about language rather than simply using it. The options always seem to be clear and the choices are generally binary. The logic is that crossing the threshold on any of these factors into the adjacent domain makes that performance metalinguistic. The description is structuralist because there always is some threshold or border, so the underlying metaphor is essentially spatial.

The approach is unsatisfying because it demands that categorical judgments be made about divisions between cognitive events that are not clearly distinct. Not all metalinguistic tasks or abilities are created equal, so the definition for metalinguistic should provide a means of evaluating gradations in the construct. By making the choices binary, the options are limited to deciding that the knowledge to solve a task is explicit or implicit, that an ability is linguistic or metalinguistic, that a process is carried out with or without awareness. Mental activity is surely more subtle than that. Binary choices are brute mechanisms that leave little room for understanding how processing works (Bialystok, 1998).

A different way of conceptualizing metalinguistic behavior is to incorporate the criteria uncovered in three contexts into a notion of processing that is scaled on continua in which the values for these dimensions, or criteria, adjust gradually. There is no absolute threshold beyond which processing can be claimed to be "metalinguistic" since all language use involves some measure of these features. Instead, the criteria for individual language processes are relative measures of processing that are more or less metalinguistic. Children's development moves them along these dimensions into language uses that are more demanding (or more metalinguistic), but there is no specific point at which a threshold is crossed and the child is declared to have achieved metalinguistic awareness. Put another way, metalinguistic ceases to be a description of a domain (referring to awareness, tasks, or abilities) and becomes a designation for a process that can move one into these domains. The spatial metaphor of structuralism is replaced by the intensity metaphor of processing.

The shift to a processing description to demarcate the territory for metalinguistic is consistent with the earliest attempt to define this construct. Recall that the definition from Cazden (1974, p. 29) cited above includes the phrase, "one which makes special cognitive demands." From the beginning, it seems, Cazden assumed that at least part of the critical features for distinguishing metalinguistic skills would be based on processing demands.

Using this processing approach, questions that aim to compare the two groups most important for our purposes, monolinguals and bilinguals, for their metalinguistic achievement need to be reformulated. Without categorical designations for children's metalinguistic achievements, the comparison between groups becomes a relative matter. Moreover, if the processing bases for metalinguistic performance are independent of each other, then differences between monolinguals and bilinguals may occur for some but not all of these. Although such results would be important for children's development, they would not necessarily translate into higher levels of metalinguistic behavior for certain groups.

The analysis and control framework introduced in Chapter 1 and described elsewhere (Bialystok, 1991a, 1993) is an example of a conceptualization of metalinguistic behavior that is derived from underlying processes. Two cognitive processes are identified and implicated in all aspects of language processing. The relative involvement of each process is theoretically independent (although practically they are correlated) and varies from minimal to stringent demands. As the levels required for each of these processes increase, language behavior appears to be increasingly metalinguistic. However, no specific boundary in the evolution of either process signals a category shift into metalinguistic performance.

Identifying Processing Components

The framework identifies changes in mental representation and attention to those mental representations that underlie increasingly metalinguistic (and literate) uses of language by children. These changes are attributed to the development of the two processing components. The first, analysis, is the ability to represent increasingly explicit and abstract structures; the second, control, is the ability to selectively attend to specific aspects of a representation, particularly in misleading situations. Together, these two processes enable children to move from simple conversation to the intentional language use involved in reading and metalinguistic problem-solving.

Analysis of representational structures is responsible for the child's ability to create mental representations of linguistic information at increasingly detailed levels of structure. Knowledge that had been implicit can be redescribed so that it is represented in an explicit structure that allows access to the detail and components of that knowledge. Karmiloff-Smith (1992) articulates a theory of cognitive development in which representational redescription plays a central role. Although not identical to the process of analysis that comprises one part of the present framework, there is much common ground in the two descriptions. An important similarity in both positions is that the evaluation of explicitness is relative: knowledge constantly undergoes a process of explication and elaboration that moves it gradually along a continuum of analytic representation. This processing component captures the need for metalinguistic behavior to be based on knowledge that is more explicit or more formal than that needed for more ordinary linguistic performance. Accordingly, it satisfies the criteria set out by definitions of metalinguistic knowledge and metalinguistic ability.

Control of attention is the process that allows the child to direct attention to specific aspects of either a stimulus field or a mental representation as problems are solved in real time. The need for control is most apparent when a problem contains conflict or ambiguity. In these cases, two or more mental representations may be constructed, each of which bears some relation to the problem. The correct solution typically requires attending to only one of these possible representations, thereby inhibiting or resisting attention to the other. The tendency to attend to the (incorrect) competing representation may either simply slow down the problem-solving or mislead the child to the incorrect solution.

As with the process of analysis, the demands for control are continuous across problems (or situations of language use) and the ability to exercise it increases gradually in development. Most language use situations present some degree of ambiguity. Even the simple act of carrying on a conversation provides the speaker with at least two alternative signals to which attention can be paid: the use and structure of the formal symbol system and the set of meanings that the symbol system has been invoked to represent. These alternatives are scarcely noticed in conversational uses of language since the meaning is so clearly the relevant level of representation and attention for language comprehension and production. Other uses of language, however, in particular those normally invoked as meta-linguistic tasks, demand high levels of control in that misleading information is deliberately included into the problem. A number of researchers have included a need for attention to forms and control of processing into their criteria for designating performance to be metalinguistic (Bowey, 1988; Lundberg & Tornéus, 1978; Tunmer & Herriman, 1984). Higher levels of control, furthermore, are associated with processing that is more intentional (cf. Jacoby, 1991). The ability to control attention over linguistic representations satisfies the criterion for awareness set out by the definitions of metalinguistic ability and metalinguistic awareness.

Demands of Metalinguistic Tasks

When the three metalinguistic constructs are defined in these processing terms, then any situation of language use that places these cognitive demands on performance is a metalinguistic task. A variety of tasks carrying different values on these processing demands, therefore, may qualify as being metalinguistic. A selection of such tasks in terms of their processing demands is illustrated in Figure 1.4. Roughly, the tasks are positioned into the quadrants by virtue of the relative demands they make on each of the processes. There is a relation between these processes, however, that has implications for both how we understand the processes and how they define the tasks.

The task demands are not completely independent. Tasks demanding high levels of one tend to demand high levels of the other, frustrating the attempt to examine each process in isolation from the other. Mental representations can be reliably studied by researchers only if they can be accessed by the language user. Theoretically, it is possible for language learners to have highly analyzed representations of language, but with no access to those representations, perhaps because of limitations in attentional control, we would not know that. This paradox is similar to one encountered in memory research. Although models of memory make a distinction between encoding and retrieval processes and attribute different factors to their execution, encoding is difficult (but not impossible) to examine in the absence of retrieval. Essentially, the researcher needs to find indirect means of determining what has been encoded without relying on the individual to retrieve the memory directly. The same is true for determining the levels of analysis of mental representations. Researchers must find a means to assess the degree of analysis without requiring the person to articulate the knowledge or to indicate its structure explicitly. This methodological dilemma means we may underestimate the level of analysis that learners possess because we are incapable of measuring it directly.

Another implication of the correlation between the processes is that there is a logical contingency between them. Attention presumes attention *to* something, so greater levels of attentional control are invoked only when there are greater levels of representational complexity. Simpler representations can be processed through simpler attention mechanisms. The need for more controlled attention is signaled by the evolution of more abstract or more complex representations. Consequently, the normal expectation would be that increases in levels of analysis precede increases in levels of control. Put another way, increases in control occur in response to increases in analysis.

Finally, this relation between the processes imposes an ordering on the three contexts for metalinguistic. Because of the potential contingency between analysis and control, the context resting primarily on analysis must be considered earlier in the progression than those resting more strongly on control. Hence, the development would be from metalinguistic knowledge to metalinguistic ability, culminating finally in metalinguistic awareness. There is a presumption here that control is more criterial in that it provides more clear or conclusive evidence that the processing involved in solving a specific task is metalinguistic. If this is the case, then it may be reasonable to exclude tasks that assess only metalinguistic knowledge from the battery of instruments that detect metalinguistic abilities. Metalinguistic knowledge in itself is only weak evidence for the kinds of skills and processes that are included in these other constructs.

Returning to the problem of defining how "meta" is an issue for language abilities, the approach is to define the processes implicated in using language in various ways and in solving various language tasks. As the demands for analysis increase, language use begins to involve more metalinguistic knowledge; as the demands for control increase, language use begins to involve more metalinguistic ability and metalinguistic awareness. Operationally, then, one difference between the three uses of "meta" is in the type of process they implicate.

Even with this processing definition, it is not possible to categorically state where "meta" begins. Because all linguistic problems require different levels of involvement of each of these two processes, it makes little sense to declare certain problems as metalinguistic while others are not. Instead, problems can be compared for their demands on these two processes by considering relative weightings on each. A developmental consequence of this conceptualization is that each of these two cognitive processes can develop in response to different experiences. Bilingualism may be one such experience.

Is It Better with Two Languages?

One of the first research areas that claimed consistent advantages for bilingual children over their monolingual peers was the domain of metalinguistic awareness. It is plausible that having two different language systems for examination may make structural patterns more noticeable and hasten the child's attention to the systematic features of language. In an important early examination of the role of metalinguistic concepts in children's language acquisition, Clark (1978, p. 36) speculated that "learning two languages at once, for instance, might heighten one's awareness of specific linguistic devices in both." Tunmer and Myhill (1984) went further and postulated metalinguistic awareness as the *mechanism* by which bilingualism exerts its influence on any aspect of cognition. They argued that fully fluent bilingualism increased metalinguistic abilities and those in turn led to higher levels of reading acquisition and academic achievement.

As we have already seen with the problem of defining the term, it is not clear what is entailed by metalinguistic functioning or what is measured by tasks that are described as metalinguistic. Indeed, the descriptor "metalinguistic" has been used to denote tasks varying widely in their purview, from on-line repair of speech to judgments about structure to manipulation of forms according to some arbitrary rules. Gombert (1992) conveys a sense of this breadth in his detailed discussion of the wide range of metalinguistic tasks that have been used in research. Hence, conclusions about broad abilities that are more developed in bilingual children need to be postponed until the performance of these children can be examined more analytically. What do we mean by metalinguistic in this context and what are the research findings with bilingual children solving tasks described as metalinguistic?

Any linguistic skill is a candidate for a metalinguistic counterpart in development. Therefore, metalinguistic abilities (or tasks) are sometimes classified according to the aspect of linguistic skill from which they derive, creating subcategories of metalinguistic proficiency in syntax, word awareness, and phonology. Some would also make a case for metapragmatic ability (Bates, 1976; Blum-Kulka & Sheffer, 1993; Pratt & Nesdale, 1984) but those cases are not discussed here. The development of phonological awareness has special status because it has been tied to the acquisition of alphabetic literacy. Therefore, this aspect of metalinguistic development is discussed only briefly and revisited in Chapter 6.

Most metalinguistic tasks used to compare monolingual and bilingual children assess either word awareness or syntactic awareness. Word awareness is normally investigated by assessing children's ability to recognize linguistic units that correspond to individual words, and syntactic awareness by some form of grammaticality judgment task. In both cases, the tasks require children to focus on a formal property of language and demonstrate an ability to make judgments about its structure.

The research body as a whole has yielded conflicting results about the relative state of development in these areas for monolingual and bilingual children. Some studies declare the advantage to be in one or the other of the groups, while other studies proclaim that there is no difference at all between groups. Ultimately, the tasks used in this research need to be examined in terms of criteria that are more analytic than a simple categorization, such as "word awareness." The proposal here is that the pattern of results begins to make sense when task demands are considered in terms of their connection to specific cognitive processes.

Word Awareness

Two related insights are required for children to fully appreciate the abstract level of linguistic structure designated by words. The first is awareness of a segmentational process that isolates words as a significant unit. Tasks assessing this aspect of word awareness typically ask children to count the number of words in a sentence or define what a word is to demonstrate knowledge of the appropriate boundaries. The second is awareness of how words function to carry their meaning. This aspect, sometimes called lexical or referential arbitrariness, indicates the extent to which children understand the conventional relation by which words convey designated meanings. The importance of this distinction is discussed below.

Ben-Zeev (1977) developed a creative task to assess children's awareness of the formal properties of words early in this research agenda. The task, symbol substitution, assessed children's level of awareness of referential arbitrariness. She said to children, "In this game, the way to say *we* is with *spaghetti*. How would you say, *We are good children?*" Defying all sense, children had to say, "Spaghetti are good children." She found that bilingual children were significantly more reliable in making this substitution than were monolinguals. For some reason, it was easier for them to ignore the meaning and deal with the formal instructions.

What this task points out is that monolingual children are more wedded to the familiar meanings of words than are their bilingual peers. It is as though the meaning is inherent in the word, an immutable property of it. In contrast, bilingual children are more willing to accept that the meaning of a word is more convention than necessity, more agreement than truth. We are free to break the agreement if we so choose.

The logic of this analysis follows from the explanation proposed by Piaget (1929) in the investigation of his famous sun-moon problem. He asked children if it would be possible to change the names for the sun and moon, and if so, what would be up in the sky at night. The final question was the most difficult: what would the sky look like at night? Although most children could accept the rules of the game sufficiently to say that the names could be changed and that the sun would be up in the sky at night, the majority insisted that the sky would be light. (It would be *dark*, of course. Only the names have changed.)

If Ben-Zeev's analysis of the symbol substitution task is correct and her results are reliable, then bilingual children should find the sun-moon problem easier than monolingual children do. In both cases, the solution depends on understanding the very nature of representation, a fundamental part of any metalinguistic consideration. The first systematic test of this hypothesis was carried out by Cummins (1978). He found the predicted bilingual superiority, a finding that has since been replicated by others (Bialystok, 1988; Ricciardelli, 1992).

This area of linguistic understanding, namely, the nature of the relation between words and their meanings, consistently emerges as superior in bilingual children. In his famous diary study of his daughter, Leopold

(1961) identified the ability to recognize and appreciate this arbitrary basis of meaning in language as a direct benefit of bilingualism. Bilingual children, he suggested, are able to make a distinction between words and their meanings before monolingual children grasp this idea.

This general idea of the nature of reference has been investigated in other ways as well. Feldman and Shen (1971) taught groups of monolingual and bilingual children new names for things, where the new names were either the real names for other objects (as in the sun-moon problem) or nonsense words. Both groups of children learned the new names equally well, but only the bilinguals were successful in using the new or nonsense names in sentences. In other words, only the bilinguals accepted that the new names *could* be used arbitrarily in a real linguistic context. Similarly, Ianco-Worrall (1972) asked monolinguals and bilinguals about the viability of changing the names for known objects, and only the bilinguals agreed that names for things could be changed.

Cummins (1978) administered four metalinguistic tasks of word awareness to bilinguals and monolinguals. There were performance differences between the groups on only some of the tasks, or on some parts of the tasks. For example, one task tested whether a child considered a word to be stable even when the object the word referred to had ceased to exist, such as the continued existence of the word "giraffe" if there were no giraffes left in the world. This task showed a bilingual advantage, especially by the older children. In another task, children were asked whether particular words had the physical properties of the objects they represented, for example, "Is the word *book* made of paper?" Here there were no differences in performance between bilinguals and monolinguals. Cummins concluded that bilinguals had a greater linguistic flexibility but not a greater reasoning ability for problems that extended beyond the domain of language.

Ricciardelli (1992) compared the performance of first-grade children who were either English monolinguals or Italian-English bilinguals on a battery of cognitive and metalinguistic tasks. There were five metalinguistic tasks – three assessed aspects of word awareness, one syntactic awareness, and one a concept of print task. The design also divided subjects according to their level of proficiency in each language, creating a large number of language groups with relatively few subjects per group. For this reason, the statistical analyses may not accurately reflect the structure of the group differences. In addition, the statistical analyses were conducted in a somewhat unconventional manner. Nonetheless, the results showed a significant bilingual advantage on the syntactic awareness task and one of the word awareness tasks. The other two word awareness tasks produced higher bilingual performance but it was not statistically significant.

Results of studies like these do not always favor bilinguals. Rosenblum and Pinker (1983) found no differences between bilinguals and monolinguals in their ability to substitute a nonsense word for an actual word, but there were differences in their explanations. Monolingual children focused on the attributes of objects and explained that the name of an object, such as a table, could be changed to *shig* because it still had four legs. Bilingual children justified their answers in more abstract and general terms, explaining that the name of an object was arbitrary and could be changed under certain conditions.

A study by Edwards and Christophersen (1988) added an important dimension to these investigations. These researchers considered the effects of both bilingualism and literacy, treating each as a continuous variable rather than a discrete binary category. They assessed performance on several metalinguistic measures and found different effects for each of the independent variables. In a task requiring children to identify the number of discrete words in a sentence, higher levels of literacy were associated with higher task performance. Conversely, performance on two tasks assessing referential arbitrariness was significantly related to level of bilingualism. These tasks involved the familiar attempt to have children change the names for the sun and moon (and cats and dogs as well in this case) and to answer questions about the tangible properties of words, such as, "Does the word *bird* fly in the sky?" At the same time, neither literacy nor bilingualism was related to children's ability to make simple grammatical judgments about sentences and phrases.

Contrary results notwithstanding, there is still an impressive body of research that points to a bilingual superiority in tasks that are generally addressed to concepts of word (Bialystok, 1987, 1988; Edwards & Christophersen, 1988; Yelland, Pollard, & Mercuri, 1993). None of the research has ever found a blanket advantage for bilinguals on all tasks – it is normally confined to certain tasks, and sometimes to certain parts of some tasks. It is not uncommon for studies employing a battery of tasks to report quite different results for each. However, this is a good thing. If it were the case that one group consistently outperformed the other irrespective of the task demands, it might signal an inherent difference between the groups, for example, differences in intelligence or language proficiency. Instead, the array of results requires us to examine the pattern closely to determine the conditions under which bilinguals express a processing superiority.

Syntactic Awareness

The need to make a judgment about the grammatical acceptability of a sentence is probably the prototypical metalinguistic task. Nonetheless, there is some controversy about whether the standard version of this task (that is, judge the grammaticality of a simple sentence presented in one's native language) is metalinguistic at all. For Chomsky, at least, it is simply part of native speaker competence. Perhaps for this reason, the paradigm is used frequently both as a measure of syntactic awareness and as an index of language proficiency. As a test for syntactic awareness, the assumption is that errors can be detected only if attention is directed to the form of the sentence, and since usual processing of language takes greater account of meaning, the redirection to form constitutes an aspect of metalinguistic functioning. As a test of language proficiency, the assumption is that only native speakers can make reliable judgments about sentence acceptability, so a comparison between nonnatives and natives in their judgment decisions provides an index of how proficient or "native-like" the learner is.

These tasks have been used successfully with children. Galambos and Hakuta (1988) compared monolinguals and bilinguals for their ability to solve two kinds of metalinguistic tasks. The first was a standard task in which children were asked to judge and then to correct the syntactic structure of sentences. The second asked children to determine the ambiguity in sentences and then to paraphrase the various interpretations. The research was conducted longitudinally and showed that bilingual children had a consistent advantage over monolinguals in the syntax task but only the older children were better than the monolinguals in the ambiguity task. They also report specific effects of the children's level of language proficiency and details of the task items. These are important constraints on the results – bilingual effects are not simple and not pervasive.

A more extensive study based on the same principles was conducted by Galambos and Goldin-Meadow (1990). They presented monolinguals and bilinguals with a range of problems assessing syntactic awareness. In a series of sentences, children were asked to note any errors, correct the errors, and explain why they were errors. The ability to solve each of these constituent questions, respectively, was considered to be ordered for difficulty from lowest to highest levels of awareness. They found that noting and correcting errors developed systematically in all children in the ages studied (four and a half to eight years) but that explaining the errors appeared to be a qualitatively different skill from these. There was little relation between the errors that could be corrected and those that could be explained. This bifurcation between the explanation condition and the other two tasks was recapitulated through the effects of the bilingual experience on performance. For noting and correcting errors, the bilinguals progressed faster than monolinguals and showed significant advantages at all ages tested. For explaining the errors, however, there were no compelling advantages for the bilingual children. Galambos and Goldin-Meadow (1990) interpreted the developmental progression as moving from a content-based to a structure-based understanding of language, and bilingual children were more advanced than monolinguals in all of these. They note as well the clear division between the explanation and the other two tasks both for their developmental patterns and their influence from bilingualism. Their conclusion emphasizes that bilingualism alters the rate of development but not its course.

Grammaticality judgment tasks have been manipulated to create more precise tools for investigating children's linguistic and metalinguistic competence. The manipulations usually involve altering the detail of examination required (Galambos & Goldin-Meadow, 1990; Galambos & Hakuta, 1988) or the length or complexity of sentences in an effort to elicit judgments from younger children (de Villiers & de Villiers, 1974; Smith & Tager-Flusberg, 1982).

A different kind of manipulation can alter the difficulty of attending to the grammatical form by introducing misleading material. This manipulation was first used by de Villiers and de Villiers (1972) and developed into an experimental task to identify differences between judgments made by monolinguals and bilinguals by Bialystok and colleagues (Bialystok, 1986a, 1988; Bialystok & Majumder, 1998; Bialystok & Ryan, 1985). Standard judgment sentences require subjects to decide whether or not there are grammatical violations. The extent to which subjects can do this is an indication of their level of grammatical analysis. If the sentence also contains incorrect semantic information, then it becomes more difficult for subjects, especially for young children, to ignore these errors and attend only to the well-formedness criteria. These manipulations are discussed in greater detail below. For the present purpose, the finding that has been consistently replicated is that sentences that contain distracting semantic information are very difficult for monolingual children to judge for their grammatical acceptability, but bilingual children are more successful with these items. Again, there is a bilingual advantage on a narrowly defined metalinguistic task but not a global advantage over the paradigm.

Gathercole (1997) used a grammaticality judgment task to determine whether Spanish-English bilingual children could use syntactic cues to distinguish mass nouns (such as water) from count nouns (such as cups) (described in Chapter 3). She found that older and more fluent bilinguals performed like monolinguals but the younger and weaker bilinguals paid little attention to the syntactic cues. The young bilingual children were not using the formal information as effectively as the monolinguals were, and in this respect, at least, were less developed in a specific metalinguistic function.

In another study, Gathercole and Montes (1997) used a more traditional grammaticality judgment task to determiné whether Spanish-English bilingual children could make appropriate decisions about sentences containing violations of *that*-trace. They found that monolinguals were better than bilinguals for both judging and correcting the sentences, but that the performance of the bilinguals was significantly influenced by the amount of English input they received at home. This research identifies some areas in which bilinguals do *as well* as monolinguals, but none in which they do better.

Phonological Awareness

Research on children's development of phonological awareness has largely been conducted from the perspective of the impact of this ability on the acquisition of literacy (see discussion in Chapter 6). A small number of studies has examined the development of phonological awareness in bilingual children, but the studies are difficult to evaluate because children were either minimally bilingual or sample sizes were very small. Rubin and Turner (1989) compared the phonological awareness of English-speaking first-grade children who were either in French immersion (giving them a modest command of French) or English programs and found an advantage for the French-immersion children. Using a similar population, Bruck and Genesee (1995) compared monolinguals and beginning bilinguals longitudinally from kindergarten to first-grade children on a variety of tasks. They found an advantage for the bilingual children on onset-rime segmentation in kindergarten but it disappeared in grade one. In first grade, there was an advantage for the monolingual children on a phoneme counting task.

Using children whose bilingualism was even more limited, Yelland,

Pollard, and Mercuri (1993) asked children to judge whether pictured objects had long names or short names. They found an advantage for bilinguals in kindergarten but it disappeared by the end of grade one. Nonetheless, they also examined some aspects of early reading and found that the grade-one bilinguals maintained an advantage over monolinguals in word recognition.

A study by Campbell and Sais (1995) offered more rigorous evidence because the children, preschool Italian-English bilinguals, were reasonably competent in both languages. There were four tasks included in the battery. In two of the tasks, children were required to choose a word that did not fit in a set because of either a semantic or phonological (first sound) mismatch. The semantic detection task is not a measure of phonological awareness, but the two together, which required children to change the criterion for membership in the group, namely, from meaning to sound, indicate their access to these structural properties of words. In addition, there was a phoneme deletion task. The bilingual children performed at a higher level than the monolinguals on the phonological tasks but did no better than monolinguals on a letter identification task. These are promising results for bilinguals, although the results must be interpreted cautiously since the sample size was small and language and cognitive differences between the groups were not well controlled. Moreover, the children were tested only in preschool and previous studies showed that these early advantages disappeared in first grade.

We conducted a series of studies to explore the development of phonological awareness in monolingual and bilingual children across a larger range of age and task complexity (Bialystok, Majumder, & Martin, in preparation). In the first two studies, children were five, six, and seven years old (corresponding to kindergarten, first grade, and second grade) and were fully bilingual in English and French. The task, called phoneme substitution, was a difficult problem in which children needed to replace the first sound in a target word with the first sound from another word to produce a new word. For example, the word "cat" could be converted to "mat" by substituting the first sound of "mop" into the target word. Children were told, "Take away the first sound from 'cat' and put in the first sound from 'mop.' What is the new word?" (There were also conditions in which the sounds k and m were given to the child, but the results were the same.) The results showed no difference at all between the monolinguals and the bilinguals in their ability to solve this problem.

In the third study, two groups of bilingual children and three different phonological tasks were included to increase the range of assessment.

Children were again five to seven years old and were monolingual or bilingual with either Spanish or Chinese as their other language. The three tasks were different in the demands they made on explicit phonological awareness and the involvement of other cognitive components in their solution. First was the sound-meaning task: children were required to select which of two words matched a target for either the sound (rhyme) or meaning (synonym). For example, the experimenter could ask the child, "Which word sounds something like dog, frog or puppy?" This task requires only minimal levels of sound awareness. The second was a segmentation task in which children had to determine the number of phonemes in common words. This task is the purest assessment of phonological awareness because the solution requires explicit attention to the sound structure of words, but the task itself does not invoke many extraneous cognitive processes. Finally, a version of the phoneme substitution task was used to assess children's ability to make computations with the segmented sounds. There was a bilingual advantage on only one task and for one group – the Spanish-English bilinguals solving the segmentation task. Hence it appears that there is some advantage to bilingual children in learning about the sound structure of spoken language, but it is evident only on relatively simple tasks and apparent only for children whose two languages bear some resemblance to each other. The majority of results from these studies indicated no advantage for bilingual children. Again, although reliable advantages for bilingual children occur under some circumstances, they are constrained by other factors. Bilingualism itself is insufficient to fundamentally change the path of metalinguistic development.

Interpreting the Research

Two kinds of explanatory factors are needed to systematize the findings from the research described above. The first is a set of descriptors reflecting the individual differences among the children who comprised the participants in the research groups. These include differences in language proficiency, intelligence, and level of bilingualism. The second is a set of descriptors reflecting task differences in the measures used to assess the particular metalinguistic performance. These can be examined in terms of the processes of analysis and control.

Individual characteristics of research participants are a crucial part of experimental design. Obviously, we construct experiments expecting that all sources of extraneous variance have been properly identified and controlled, either through sampling procedures or statistical methods. Nonetheless, it was subject characteristics that turned out to be the watershed between early research that showed cognitive deficits for bilinguals and modern research that at least allows for cognitive advantages (see discussion in Hakuta, 1986). Still, monolingual and bilingual groups are never the same. At the very least, the bilingual children usually have a stronger and weaker language, and testing in one or the other has inevitable implications for the kind of performance that is observed.

One factor that has been productive in pointing to differences between cases in which bilinguals differ or not from monolinguals is the level of balance in the child's proficiency in the two languages. Although most studies that include this difference as an experimental factor for the bilingual group consider only two levels, balanced and unbalanced bilinguals, Tunmer and Myhill (1984) identified at least four configurations that depended on the proficiency level in *each* language. They argued that all four were importantly different from each other and could be expected to influence the development of linguistic and metalinguistic skills. This approach is one way to uncover the more graduated development of metalinguistic abilities and come closer to understanding their essence.

Studies that have included at least some version of the child's level of proficiency have usually found it to be a significant determiner of performance. The effects of proficiency range from finding bilingual advantages only for fully balanced bilinguals (Bialystok, 1988; Ricciardelli, 1992), or a greater advantage for fully balanced bilinguals (Cromdal, 1999), to disadvantages for partial bilinguals (Gathercole, 1997). This is essentially the pattern predicted by Cummins' (1979) threshold hypothesis, in which he sets out a minimal level of bilingual competence to avoid deficits and a higher level to enjoy advantages. Further, for children who are partially bilingual, there are differences between groups at different levels of second-language proficiency. Hakuta and Diaz (1985) report greater changes in metalinguistic competence in the earlier stages of achieving bilingual proficiency, a result not replicated by Jarvis, Danks, and Merriman (1995), who instead claim, along with the previous studies, that the greater advantages emerge with greater competence. Nonetheless, Hakuta (1987) reported that for Hispanic children in American schools higher levels of bilingualism predict performance on a series of nonverbal tasks but not metalinguistic tasks. In some cases, the level of proficiency in the language of testing provides an independent prediction of success, irrespective of the level of bilingualism (Galambos & Hakuta, 1988). Both absolute levels of language proficiency and the relative balance between languages are crucial factors in determining outcomes for bilingual children. Understanding these effects and resolving contradictory findings, however, will require a more detailed description for values on these factors than is usually available in binary classifications.

Task characteristics are more difficult to document. No two tasks are identical and the commonality between them is often a matter of conjecture. Some statistical techniques are useful for extracting the underlying similarity based on patterns of response to sets of tasks. For example, Wagner et al. (1993) used confirmatory factor analysis to isolate the components of phonemic awareness tasks, allowing them to make a distinction between analytic and synthetic tasks. Yopp (1988) also classified a large number of tasks, but she used a dichotomy between simple and compound tasks, each bearing a different relation to the acquisition of alphabetic literacy. Others, too, have attempted to find a means of grouping phonological tasks in some meaningful way (e.g., Adams, 1990). All the analyses arrive at different distributions and are based on different criteria, so it is difficult to make any comparative assessments among them.

The analysis and control framework provides another means of interpreting task differences in an attempt to find pattern in the bilingual effects. As discussed above, there is inevitably a correlation between the demands that specific tasks place on these processes because tasks that involve more information and more irrelevant information (control) also require more detailed consideration (analysis). This is simply the nature of real-use situations for language and is part of what makes ecological studies an important part of research. Nonetheless, it is possible to place a wedge between these two processes to validate their individuality and unique contribution to processing. Ricciardelli (1993) conducted a study in which participants were given a battery of tasks that were based more heavily on either analysis or control. A factor analysis showed that the tasks in each category accounted for unique portions of the variance and were therefore assessing different underlying processes. This degree of functional independence justifies applying this framework to the resolution of disparate findings regarding the metalinguistic performance of monolingual and bilingual children.

Applying the Framework

Typically, metalinguistic problems are difficult because they require explicit attention to form, an aspect of language that is usually transparent. We pay scant attention to grammar when we engage in conversation, barely notice structure when we read text, and often consider formal knowledge of the rules of grammar to be a needless frill. In metalinguistic problems, however, these abstract structures become the target of our consideration and the criteria by which performance is judged. To the extent that metalinguistic tasks probe explicit knowledge of this abstract but rule-governed feature of language, they rely on analysis of representational structures for their solution. The point about the process of analysis is that knowledge can be accessible to different levels of explicitness and detail depending on task or situation demands, but that the representation of that knowledge must include the possibility for that explicit access. Hence, the grammatical knowledge that may implicitly guide speech needs to be represented more analytically to be useful for solving metalinguistic problems. Put another way, performance on metalinguistic problems reveals something about the explicitness with which linguistic knowledge has been represented.

Most metalinguistic tasks that assess syntactic awareness require high levels of analysis for their solution simply because the object of study is the grammar of the language. The tasks are explicitly focused on the formal properties of language; however, the level of explicitness or analysis required for the response can vary. In grammaticality judgment, for example, the purpose of the task is to determine whether or not individuals can evaluate the use of specific grammatical structures by requiring them to detect violations of the rule. Logically, one would need to know the rule *at some level* in order to realize that the rule had been broken. What it means to "know" the rule, or what "level" of knowing is assumed, however, can vary along a range of explicitness or consciousness. In the study by Galambos and Goldin-Meadow (1990), for example, a gradation of tasks requiring subjects to note whether there were errors, correct the errors, and explain the errors showed these to lead to different degrees of performance. Although all three tasks are metalinguistic, the responses to each require increasingly high levels of representational analysis for their solution.

Metalinguistic problems that require the highest levels of control of processing are those in which the solution depends on paying attention to some aspect of the language input that is not salient, not usual, or not expected. To count the number of words in a sentence, for example, the child must overcome the natural strategy of paying attention to meaning and instead pay attention to the word boundaries (Fox and Routh, 1975). In the symbol substitution problem developed by Ben-Zeev (1977) in which children are required to substitute arbitrary words into sentences and create nonsense, the natural tendency to attend to meaning prevents young children from solving this problem. Piaget's (1929) sun-moon problem is a further example of this type of task demand. Children are reasonably successful at deciding what the sun and moon would be called if they switched names and which one would be up in the sky at night. The difficult question is in saying what the sky would look like, because children must resist paying attention to what the word usually means. To solve this problem, children must dissociate the word from its conventional meaning, ignoring a fundamental part of using language.

These problems are all difficult because their solution demands unusual attentional strategies that must be executed in the context of compelling alternatives. It is extremely difficult to ignore meanings. Stroop (1935) demonstrated long ago that if you show subjects printed cards with names of colors written in different colors of ink and ask them only to say what the color of the ink is, the color word itself provides hopeless interference when the two do not match. Similarly, metalinguistic problems that introduce misleading information are difficult because the usual attentional strategies must be inhibited or overcome in order to intentionally execute the processing strategies needed for the problem.

All metalinguistic tasks and, indeed, all uses of language, rely on processing that includes both representational analysis and attentional control. Knowledge of language is represented in some form, and task demands guide the way attention must be allocated to perform adequately. This interpretation is based on a view that considers language processing to be part of general cognitive functioning, but it is still compatible with descriptions that treat language more as a specialized modular function. Even in more modularized views, the processing demands that solicit linguistic knowledge reflect variations in task demands and representational details. Pinker (1994) clearly advocates explanations that are grounded in the uniqueness of a linguistic module, but still explains language acquisition and language processing in terms that require specifying the nature of the linguistic representation and the kind of mental processing used. His explanation for the acquisition of irregular past tense verbs, described in Chapter 2, illustrates how linguistic modules are not immune to the need for specification of the nature of representation and attention.

The empirical application of this framework is that these task characteristics can be manipulated to create metalinguistic problems for which the demands on each of these processes are relatively controlled and therefore measurable. The research approach has been to present children with versions of tasks that alter the balance in which the two processes are required for the solution to a problem. For example, a grammaticality judgment task consisting of simple well-formed sentences can be manipulated to increase the individual involvement of analysis and control (Bialystok, 1986a). A standard sentence, such as, "Why is the dog barking so loudly?" makes few demands on either the abstractness of representational structures or the control of attentional processes, and children easily recognize it as an acceptable sentence. The demands for analysis are increased by introducing grammatical errors to the sentence, such as, "Why the dog is barking so loudly?" Children need to detect the violation in structure and respond that the sentence is unacceptable. The demands for control are increased by introducing distracting information that is irrelevant to the solution, such as, "Why is the cat barking so loudly?" Children are trained to respond only to grammaticality, but the error in meaning is a compelling magnet for their attention and it is difficult to respond that these sentences are grammatically correct. Interestingly, the processes of judging the grammaticality of sentences that are meaningful but ungrammatical and sentences that are nonsensical but grammatical elicit different patterns of ERP activity (Neville & Bavelier, 1999).

Another example of a paradigm that manipulates the demands for analysis and control is a task used to assess children's concept of word (Bialystok, 1986b). In the standard version, children are required to count the number of words in a sentence. The intention is to determine children's concepts of what constitutes a word. Because the items are presented in meaningful sentences, the challenge to control of attention is to ignore the cohesive meaning that rises out of the sentence and focus instead on the individual words, some of which (like functors) have no meaning on their own. Scrambling the order in which the words occur so that attention is not directed away from the individual units in the sentence can reduce the control demands for this task. Similarly, the analysis demands depend on the complexity of words that are being used. If children have a simple hypothesis about word boundaries, for example, equating words with syllables, then monosyllabic words will be easy to identify but bisyllabic words will be mistakenly counted twice. The more explicit, or analyzed, the child's concept of word, the more accurate will be the response under conditions that use various types of words. In this study, four levels of word complexity were included: monosyllabic words (*cat*), bisyllabic words (*princess*), polysyllabic words (*pajamas*), and double morpheme words (*snowman*). Therefore, the task included eight conditions: items based on high control (sentences) or low control (scrambled) and four levels of lexical analysis.

A consistent finding in this research is that bilingual children perform better than their monolingual peers in tasks that demand high levels of control, but there is no consistent bilingual advantage in tasks for which the solution relies primarily on high levels of analysis of representational structures (Bialystok, 1986a, 1988, 1997b). On the grammaticality judgment task described above, correct solutions to the analysis problem (grammatically incorrect but meaningful) increased with the acquisition of literacy for both monolingual and bilingual children with no difference in improvement between them. In contrast, the control problem (grammatically correct but anomalous) is solved better by bilingual children. This dissociation was replicated in independent research with Swedish-English bilinguals (Cromdal, 1999). On the concept of word task, there was a clear bilingual advantage for items that were presented as sentences, the high control version of the problem. The analysis manipulation for different types of words revealed no group differences in performance for the simpler types but began to show a group difference for the more complex words. For double morpheme words, the bilingual children were significantly more successful than the monolinguals.

Considering these studies together, bilingualism was related to higher levels of control and literacy was related to higher levels of analysis. In some cases, bilingual subjects also performed better in tasks demanding higher levels of analysis. This occurred most often when the level of bilingualism was controlled so that the more balanced, or fully bilingual, children were those who showed an advantage on all the tasks (Bialystok, 1988). However, children who are more fully bilingual may also be more literate in the language of testing. A more detailed version of this hypothesis regarding a bilingual advantage in control is proposed in Chapter 7.

Another way of interpreting this pattern is in terms of the three contextual uses for "meta" that were identified earlier. The progression from metalinguistic knowledge to metalinguistic awareness reflected an increase in the amount of attentional control required to carry out the tasks indicative of each context. In this respect, monolingual and bilingual children essentially perform the same on tasks that assess metalinguistic knowledge but begin to diverge on tasks that are more directly aimed at assessing metalinguistic ability or awareness. Put another way, monolingual and bilingual children begin with equivalent levels of metalinguistic knowledge, but bilingual children can achieve higher levels of metalinguistic awareness.

The results of these studies on metalinguistic awareness are consistent with those found in other research that was not specifically designed to test the analysis and control framework. Interpretations from those studies are more speculative because the tasks were not constructed on the basis of their representation or attention demands, but they provide converging evidence for the relevance of these two processes in metalinguistic functioning. Cummins (1978) reported that bilinguals were more able than monolinguals to accept that the word "giraffe" would exist without giraffes in the world but that the groups were the same in discussing the analytic properties of words. Cummins' explanation was that the group difference was in flexibility, not in reasoning, a description compatible with the processes of control and analysis, respectively. Edwards and Christophersen (1988) found a literacy advantage for counting words in sentences but a bilingualism advantage for a task on referential arbitrariness. In the research by Galambos and Goldin-Meadow (1990), the bilingual advantages were in the first two levels of the task involving the least explicit knowledge, or analysis. The explanation task required the most detailed levels of analysis of knowledge and yielded no difference between monolinguals and bilinguals. Turning to adults, a study by Scribner and Cole (1981) examining the effect of literacy and bilingualism among the Vai people of Liberia produced complex but compatible results. In a large battery of tasks administered to adult male members of a community where literacy, bilingualism, and schooling produced mindboggling combinations of groups, it was generally the case that tasks that included misleading information (such as logical reasoning tasks containing distracting or irrelevant information) were solved better by bilinguals, but tasks that included explicit knowledge of grammar (such as correcting grammatical errors) were solved better by literates. Finally, the research by Gathercole (Gathercole, 1997; Gathercole & Montes, 1997) showed that tasks based more heavily on knowledge of particular structures did not necessarily yield bilingual advantages, but tasks based more on processing did. Therefore, even when tasks were not designed to isolate the processes associated with analysis of representational structures and control of selective attention, there is still a pattern in which bilinguals routinely surpass monolinguals if the problem relies mostly on selective attention but are not necessarily any better than monolinguals if the problem is based on detailed levels of analysis of linguistic knowledge.

Why the Difference?

Across all the studies examined, it is impossible to conclude that there is an overall difference between the way in which monolingual and bilingual children develop metalinguistic concepts. By considering the acquisition of word awareness, syntactic awareness, and phonological awareness, there is evidence in each case for bilingual advantages and disadvantages in certain tasks. An interpretation that fits a good part of the data from these studies is that reliable bilingual advantages occur only for those tasks that are based primarily on the ability to selectively attend to information when there is competing or misleading information present. Although bilingual children sometimes displayed more advanced linguistic representations by being able to solve problems based on high levels of analysis, they did not always do so. Other factors, such as the cognitive stage of the child, the relation between the two languages, and the child's relative proficiency in each of the languages, likely intervene to determine the outcomes of those problems.

Why would bilingual children excel in problems requiring control of attention? Galambos and Goldin-Meadow (1990) suggest that the metalinguistic advantages exhibited by bilingual children occur because bilinguals need to focus on form in order to differentiate their two language codes. This focus on form could provide an essential experience from an early age in which some abstract feature of the language, specifically, which language is being used, must be attended to. With that experience, bilingual children may simply find it easier to treat language as a formal system and examine its properties.

It is easy to point to unique experiences that bilingual children have from an early age, many of which involve assessing formal aspects of the language they are using, as explanations for the metalinguistic or even cognitive differences in their development. To some extent, however, these explanations are descriptions just as much as the phenomena they are intended to explain. The explanation ultimately must be able to account not only for the processes in which differences between the two groups occur but also for those in which no differences are found. This is a more difficult explanatory problem. The evidence from the development of metalinguistic concepts provides an important clue that any explanation will need to incorporate: metalinguistic concepts are essentially a reflection of linguistic ability, and the complexity of results in which bilinguals have an advantage in solving only some subset of these problems suggests that the explanation will ultimately be broader than an account of linguistic processing. Differences in metalinguistic and other linguistic skills are a reflection of more general cognitive processes. Evidence that bilingualism affects these cognitive processes to produce different developmental patterns for monolingual and bilingual children would be a truly profound outcome.

6

Link to Literacy

The pinnacle of young children's educational development is the acquisition of literacy. Literacy is the ticket of entry into our society, it is the currency by which social and economic positions are waged, and it is the central purpose of early schooling. In some sense, we send children to school at about the age of five so that they will learn to read. Future academic success depends on how well they master that skill, and academic success in our part of the world determines much about children's futures. So we would not want to do anything to jeopardize the success our children will experience in learning to read. In Western middle-class families, we deliberately attempt to bring our children into the world of literacy almost from the time they are born. If we found out that having two languages made learning to read problematic, we would endeavor to keep our children monolingual. Parents are like that.

The extensive research on the acquisition of literacy by monolingual children has provided an important framework from which the special circumstances of bilingual children can be examined. Despite the ubiquity of bilingual children in the school system, however, surprisingly little research has been expressly dedicated to this population. Much of what follows attempts to extend the existing literature on literacy development with monolinguals to the experience encountered by bilingual children.

As usual, "bilingualism" is in need of some deconstruction. As we saw in Chapter 1, there are myriad ways in which a child can be bilingual, and these seem to be particularly important in the way each one influences the child's acquisition of literacy. Literacy itself changes with languages and contexts. Two languages may be written in either the same script or in a different script, in the latter case doubling the amount the child needs to learn in order to decode basic text. Also, as we shall see, children's early experiences with stories is crucial in preparing them to read on their own.

Bilingual children may have access to stories in one or both of their languages, and this difference too is bound to be decisive. Hence, the bilingual experience varies in crucial ways that can have significant consequences for how bilingual children learn to read.

The progress in acquiring literacy by bilingual children will depend in part on social, political, and educational factors that define the child's environment at the time that literacy is introduced. Children may be exposed to two literacies in school, where both the majority language and a second language are used together, as happens in immersion programs. These children tend to be native speakers of the majority language and typically accept the second language without hesitation or cost to the first language. Although reading is officially taught in the second language, these children usually have strong background skills to develop literacy in the majority language.

Children whose first language is the minority language are in a different situation. They need to learn literacy skills in the majority language, which they may or may not speak well, and they may have opportunities, either formal or informal, to learn or maintain written proficiency in their first language. The social and cultural pressures that define these situations are considerably more intense than they are for immersion education. Detailed descriptions of some of the circumstances in which children from various first-language backgrounds attempt to acquire the literacy skills in either their first language, typically not the language of their current community, or their second language, the majority language, are presented in the collection by Durgunoğlu and Verhoeven (1998). The chapters in that volume provide rich accounts of the social and political contexts that shape children's experiences in these situations.

Despite the formidable burdens presented by the social context, children must nonetheless master the cognitive skills that lead to reading. Each language bears a slightly different relation to its printed form, each writing system represents the spoken language in a somewhat different manner, each social group places a different premium on literacy and provides different levels of access to it, and each educational system resolves the pedagogical issues independently. In spite of all these differences, children must ultimately learn how to read texts, and that is a cognitive problem. The focus in this chapter is on those cognitive aspects of learning to read.

The intellectual path to literacy appears to move relatively seamlessly from children's first encounters with written texts to the wondrous moment when they are independent and autonomous readers. Within this journey, however, it is possible to isolate three stages, which, although not clearly distinct in their boundaries, represent three levels of skill in the ability to deal with written text. At each stage, there are specific concepts that the child needs to acquire to move on toward the goal of independent reading. The first is the period of preliteracy in which children are building up concepts of symbolic representation and learning about the writing system. The second is early reading. At this stage children learn the rules for decoding the written system into the familiar sounds of the spoken language. Finally, in fluent reading, the meaning of the text takes priority and children can begin to use written texts for receiving and expressing ideas they did not have before. When we say that children are readers, or prereaders, it is helpful to be more precise by placing them at one of these levels. In all cases, children have some familiarity with texts, probably enjoy having stories read to them, may well have memorized some of the stories, but have different levels of skill in managing to deal with the texts on their own.

First Steps

It is an exciting moment when children discover that they can read. It is a discovery that is truly its own reward, and in most middle-class communities, roundly reinforced and praised. But children do many things that are "like" reading before that epiphanic moment – they can sometimes recognize company names on familiar signs, they can often print their name, they can usually name the letters of the alphabet. When does reading begin? Does it count as reading if it is aided by the presence of supportive pictures or familiar company logos?

There is a view of reading, called emergent literacy, in which children are considered to be on an irrevocable path to reading from their first experiences with language. All the steps and stages on the way, beginning with children's first utterances, are part of literacy. This view has been most vigorously defended by Sulzby (1986) and Teale (1986). Teale (1986) makes the strong claim that learning to read is the acquisition of culture, and is therefore a central part of children's socialization from the earliest encounters with text. Indeed, studies of the family context of language use have left no doubt that the family support and the early exposure to literacy have profound influence on the child's development of literacy skills (Dickinson & Tabors, 1991; Heath, 1982; Snow, 1983; Snow & Goldfield, 1983; Wells, 1985). Others, too, subscribe to the notion that there is an unbroken continuum in children's linguistic development that begins with the tentative ability to use and understand simple words and ends with the confident mastery of written text. Garton and Pratt (1989), for example, trace a path from children's increasing command of syntax, discourse, and vocabulary in spoken language through to their emergence as independent readers.

If the view of emergent literacy is correct, then the magic is removed from the process of learning to read. Instead of being a specialized skill acquired through diligent effort and special instruction, it is a natural consequence of gaining proficiency in language. Children will learn to read as surely as they will learn to speak, because reading grows out of the same abilities that are part of children's use of language. The view requires that there is a social context that supports literacy, but even with minimal guarantee of such, reading is natural and assured.

In this interpretation of literacy, there should be no special contingencies that intrude for children who happen to speak more than one language and are learning to read in both of them. Providing that social conditions are appropriate and the contextual situation is supportive, it would follow that bilingual children should equally enter into the literate world of both (or more) languages. There may be divergences between the child's two languages because of difference in the literacy environments. For example, the child may be read stories in one but not the other language or the opportunity to speak one of the languages is so limited that the child fails to advance into the sophisticated structural forms that characterize written text. But normally, the developmental progress children make with one or more languages should be sufficient for the emergence of literacy.

Most explanations of reading acquisition, however, ascribe specialized knowledge and specific training to the process of children learning to read. Reading is neither as natural nor as assured as learning to speak, and without specific tutelage, it may not occur at all. The controversy about the "naturalness" of reading is not trivial.

The question of the relation between reading and speaking has surfaced in at least one extremely consequential debate, namely, the battle over method. The premise behind the "whole language" approach is that the meanings in written text are predominant, just as they are in spoken language, and anything that distracts children from those meanings, such as attending to sound-symbol relations, is ultimately detrimental to fluent reading. The "phonics" approach, in contrast, is predicated on the notion that reading is decoding, and therefore endeavors to equip children with tools for interpreting the symbols on the assumption that the meanings will emerge on their own. To be fair, few reading programs ascribe dogmatically to one or the other position, recognizing merit in each agenda. However, there is a tradition of reading programs designed to implement the philosophical premises of one these methods.

The consequence of an overly zealous adherence to a phonics approach is a reading program which lacks interest and in which children are unmotivated to persevere. Phonics, as some of us remember from our own school days, has virtually nothing to recommend it in terms of its ability to instill intrinsic motivation in aspiring young readers. However, the consequence of an unqualified commitment to whole language is the failure to learn the basic tools of decoding. Letters make sounds, and failing to inform children of this simple truth could make reading new words and unfamiliar texts an unnecessarily painful experience. This neglect may well be an abrogation of responsibility by educators charged with teaching children how to read. A passionate spokesperson against whole-language methodology was Liberman and her colleagues (e.g., Liberman & Liberman, 1990; Liberman & Shankweiler, 1991). Leaving no room for ambiguity, Liberman and Shankweiler (1991) offer a chilling indictment of programs that fail to teach children the basic principles of sound-symbol correspondence:

> . . . the current vogue for the so-called . . . "whole language," "psycholinguistic guessing game," or "language experience" approaches are [sic] likely to be disastrous. Children taught this way are likely to join the ranks of the millions of functional illiterates in our country who stumble along, guessing at the printed message from their little store of memorized words, unable to decipher a new word they have never seen before. (p. 14)

Background Preparation

In views that do not take reading to be a natural extension of speaking, children must acquire skill in several areas of competence as preparation for learning to read. Adams (1990) presents an excellent review of these prerequisites for reading and their development. Part of these preparatory skills includes the need to build up concepts and experiences about the social, linguistic, and cognitive dimensions of reading (Bialystok, 1996; Bialystok & Herman, 1999).

Dale, Crain-Thoreson, and Robinson (1995) suggest that the prerequisite skills for reading are systematically related and then use these interrelations as the basis for a two-phase model of reading development. In the first phase, multiple skills are invoked in the initial preparation for literacy, including verbal, spatial, and analytic abilities. The second phase is specifically linguistic, and children with more advanced language competence begin to pull ahead of their peers and move more rapidly through the stages of literacy. This conception is satisfying because it is not a compromise that attempts reconciliation by finding a place for all the factors but is a sensible attempt to connect the various factors in a more large-scale causal explanation of reading. Linguistic competence is not neglected but is given a precise role at a certain stage in the process. Similarly, the social and experiential factors are not irrelevant frills but are instrumental in establishing certain skills at an earlier stage.

All these dimensions of experience are different for bilingual children than for monolinguals: the social context is always unique to a specific language; the linguistic insights one gleans are crucially dependent on factors such as the structure of language and one's proficiency with it; and the cognitive implications of using language are tied to the purposes for which the language is used. Therefore, not only would bilingual children develop the background concepts for learning to read differently from monolingual children, but they also would develop these concepts separately for their two languages, depending on their experience with each. If the research that connects these insights to literacy is correct, then there are serious implications for bilingual children who are learning to read. A different history in developing the prerequisite concepts will lead to a different experience, and possibly different success, in mastering the skill.

Social Context of Reading

It is uncontroversial that learning to speak is essentially a social activity: children learn language through interactions with the verbal members of their community, especially their parents. The influence of these interactions is easily traced to the first days of infancy, long before the idea of learning language has formed itself in the mind of even the most aggressively ambitious parents. We know, for example, that by four weeks old, infants can discriminate among the phonemic categories that structure all the natural languages. This was first reported by Eimas et al. (1971) but subsequently replicated many times. Further, as discussed in Chapter 3, infants by about ten months old can distinguish between the phonemic contrasts that appear in the language they are about to learn but not in a novel language (Kuhl et al., 1992; Werker & Tees, 1983), indicating the ability to distinguish between languages. Additionally, the kinds of verbal interactions in which children are engaged and the nature of language uses they encounter in their early experiences shape their own adoption of language as a means for different social and communicative functions (Heath, 1983). Exposure to a particular language and particular forms of language is uncontroversial in its formative role in children's acquisition of spoken language.

It is less obvious but equally true that learning to read is also a social activity. Long before there is any "story" to consider, children's early experiences with picture books set the stage for the activity of reading. During these interactions, children learn about the mechanics of reading (how to turn the pages and proceed through a book), the pleasures of reading (curling up with a parent in a quiet space), and the interest of reading (the story or talk that goes on around the book). Ninio and her colleagues (Ninio & Bruner, 1978; Snow & Ninio, 1986) have documented the ways in which these experiences shape the child's approach to reading as an activity and contribute directly to children's development of literacy skills in the next few years. The routines that are learned during storybook reading prepare children for independent reading.

The stories that are part of these early social experiences help to develop the more cognitive and linguistic skills that enable children to read. Reading aloud to preschool children provides a rich opportunity for exposure to the conventions and style of language used in creating stories (e.g., Snow & Tabors, 1993; Teale & Sulzby, 1986). Purcell-Gates (1988, 1989) examined prereaders' understanding of the reading register by asking kindergarten children to pretend to read aloud the story of a wordless picture book. She found that children who had been read to regularly at home had greater facility with the style of language used in books than did children who were not. The well-read-to children also gave richer "readings" of the wordless picture book by providing more explicit background information and clearer reference to characters and events depicted.

Herman (1996) extended this research by examining the development of story-telling ability in preschool children exposed to two languages. All of the children in the study were bilingual, and according to formal assessments of proficiency, such as vocabulary size, were equally competent in both languages. Their experiences in the two languages, however, were different. All of the children were being schooled in French but they had different levels of support for English at home. Following the methodology of Purcell-Gates (1988), Herman (1996) asked children to tell the story from a wordless picture book and evaluated their stories in terms of syntactic accuracy, semantic richness, and discourse coherence. There was a significant relation between children's ability to use the literate register in English and the amount of exposure to English storybooks they had at home. All children performed the same in French, but children's experience with French stories was the same because it was part of their daily routine at school. What was different for these children was their experience with English stories at home, and this affected their ability to tell the pretend story in English. In other words, exposure to stories in a given language determines children's ability to use the literate register of that language, even when conversational proficiency is controlled.

The results of the study by Herman (1996) point to an important qualification on how we conceptualize bilingualism and its effects on children's development. Even though all the children in the study were bilingual, and all the children belonged to middle-class families and attended high-quality preschools, only some of the children showed an advantage in a specific literacy task from the bilingual experience. The importance of reading stories to children turns out to have implications beyond the general effects of introducing literacy – it develops as well a language-specific competence in the language of those stories.

Cognitive Prerequisites

Written text is a symbolic system for recording spoken language. Learning to read, then, requires understanding the meaning of symbolic representation. For some symbolic systems, children do this easily: by two and a half years old they can use information in a picture to find where an object is hidden in a room (DeLoache, 1987). But writing is different. Vygotsky (1978) described the difference between representational systems that provide transparent recordings of meanings, such as drawing, or conventional representational systems, such as writing, as first-order and second-order symbolism, respectively. First-order symbols can be read directly, and changes in the representation indicate a change in meaning. A drawing of a dog, for example, can be changed to represent another dog, or a part of a dog, or a smaller dog, by changing the drawing. Altering the word "dog" by changing the font, removing a letter, or reducing the print has no effect on the referent concept dog. This difference between representational systems is not obvious to children, especially because their early experiences are entirely with first-order representations. Learning how to interpret symbol systems that are indirect, second-order, or opaque is an important cognitive achievement, and it must certainly precede learning to read.

The Invariance of Symbolic Notations

It is not immediately apparent that children find this aspect of reading difficult. Before children can read, they seem to understand perfectly well what the function of the writing system is and how it carries meanings. They can do things with the writing system that support this interpretation of competence – they can name letters, recognize signs, and print their names. But do they know why the printed word says what it does?

Interesting research by Ferreiro (1978, 1983, 1984) provided an early sign that we may be overestimating what children understand about writing systems. In informal experiments with children who were prereaders, she found that they had persistent misconceptions about how print referred to language. They believed, for instance, that the print needed to embody characteristics of the word it signified so that big words were written with big letters, and groups of many objects were represented by repeated letters or words. In general, they looked for aspects of meaning in the visual properties of the printed forms, just as one would do in first-order representation. However, these children were familiar with basic concepts of print: they could answer simple questions about print, such as those often used in reading readiness assessments, and could perform early literacy tasks such as printing their own names. Nonetheless, they seemed to be mistaken about how these forms led to meaningful written language. These findings have been replicated with children learning to read in different languages. Tolchinsky (1998), for example, studied the early attempts at writing of children who were about to learn to read in Catalan or Hebrew. Although their writing efforts contained many conventional features of the appropriate writing system, they still expressed incorrect beliefs about some of these basic principles of written text.

We pursued some of these ideas in more formal experiments (Bialystok, 1991b). If children understand the relation between print and meaning, then they know that the meaning is derived completely and exclusively from the print. This is a fundamental principle of reading – it is the letters that tell the story. The idea is easy to test. We selected children for the study by screening them for their knowledge of print. All the children were able to identify letters, say what sound they made, and print their name, but none was yet able to read independently. These children were then given the moving word task. We showed the children pictures of common objects and named them, for example, a king and a bird. Then a card was introduced on which was printed the name of one of the pictures. The experimenter told the child what was written on the card: "This card has the word *king* on it. I'm going to put the card right here." The card was then placed under the picture it named, although that correspondence was never explicitly drawn to the child's attention. The child was asked what was written on the card. Some confusion then erupted, and a stuffed animal on the table (or sometimes two stuffed animals, or sometimes a stuffed elephant with a bad cold who sneezed a lot) created a disturbance which resulted in the card being displaced so it was under the other picture. Then the child was asked for the second time what was written on the card. The experimenter then noticed that the materials had been changed, commented on it to the child while returning the card to its original position, and asked the child for the third time what was written on the card.

The issue in this task is whether or not children understand that the meaning of the printed word is determined entirely by its structure and not influenced by its position on the table. If children understand this, they will see that the contiguity between the card and a particular picture is irrelevant. The important response, therefore, is what children say is written on the card when it is under the wrong picture. Recall that all the children were included in the study because they displayed considerable knowledge of print – they knew the letters and their sounds. Nonetheless, preschool children who were four and five years old provided the correct answer to the second question when it was under the wrong picture only about 40 percent of the time.

On the surface, the task appears to be simple. The children in the study do not know how to read, but they know about letters and they are told what the word on the card says. Why do they think the word changes when it is moved under a different picture? What they fail to understand is *why* the word says what it does. They have not fully realized that those letters that they can recognize and name are themselves the route to what the written word is. Print is symbolic; the letters are the code.

Achieving this insight requires separating the formal structure of print from the meanings encoded in it. In other words, children must be able to attend simply to the forms and accept that they are representations of the language. This is analogous, in some measure, to the insight children achieve in understanding the separation between spoken language and the meanings represented by those forms. An important development in that domain, discussed in Chapter 5, is the knowledge that words do not embody the properties of their referents (e.g., the word *fire* is not hot) and that the conventional association between specific words and meanings could be changed through consensus (e.g., the sun-moon problem). As we saw in Chapter 5, bilingual children arrive at this understanding earlier than monolingual children do. If the structure of the insight is the same, then perhaps bilingual children go on to understand the separation of written forms from their meanings earlier than monolingual children do as well.

We tested this hypothesis in two studies, one comparing monolingual children with French-English and Chinese-English bilinguals (Bialystok, 1997b) and another comparing monolinguals with Hebrew-English bilinguals (Bialystok, Shenfield, & Codd, 2000). In both studies, the bilingual children correctly reported what was under the card when it was under the incorrect picture over 80 percent of the time. Their performance was more than a year in advance of that of the monolingual children.

Correspondence Rules for Understanding Print
Another aspect of understanding the symbolic function of print is to know how the representation works: *how* does print encode meanings? In alphabetic languages, the system functions because letters represent sounds. It follows, then, that words that have more sounds will need more letters to represent them. If children realize that the purpose of the letters is to stand for these sounds, then whether or not they can read they should be able to match long strings of letters with words that have long sequences of sounds. Similarly, short words with few sounds should correspond to written strings containing few letters. Again, this insight is a prerequisite to reading: it does not explain or predict reading but it is impossible to think that a child could read (at least in an alphabetic script) without understanding this relation.

We examined the emergence of this insight in children who were selected again for their knowledge of letters, sounds, and print, but who were still prereaders. The task, the word size task, required children to match printed words to spoken words under various conditions, sometimes accompanied by pictures or written materials. For half of the items, there was incongruity between the size of the word and the size of the object it named. For example, in the pair *train-caterpillar*, the longer word names the smaller object. Previous research showed that making judgments of word size under these conditions of conflicting semantic and phonological cues is very difficult for children at this age (Papandropoulou & Sinclair, 1974). Our study confirmed these results and showed that children with much background knowledge of print could not use the property of sound-symbol correspondence to choose the between long and short words (Bialystok, 1991b).

But what about bilingual children? The knowledge required to solve this problem is more specialized than that needed for the moving word task. In that problem, children need only to understand that something about writing a word down makes the notation a representation for that word, and no information beyond the text is necessary to interpret the word. In this task, children also need to understand what it is about the writing system that encodes the word: why does the word say what it does? We administered the word size task to bilingual children who had different kinds of literacy experiences in the two languages (Bialystok, 1997b). The children in one group, French-English bilinguals, were fluent speakers of two languages, but the stories they were read in each were written in the same script. Children in another group, Chinese-English bilinguals, were speakers of two languages but also had experience with the written text of two completely different writing systems, alphabetic and character. The question is whether one or both of these bilingual experiences would influence the way in which children came to understand the principle of alphabetic writing.

The writing system was instrumental in determining the results. The French-English bilingual children performed exactly the same as the monolingual controls; there was no advantage in this task for either speaking two languages or hearing two kinds of stories written in 'the same writing system. The Chinese-English bilinguals were different from both of these. The younger children in this group found the problem to be very difficult and scored the lowest of any of the children in the study, performing at about chance on all the measures. They seemed to be confused by the rules used in two completely different writing systems and were unable to effectively solve the problem in either language (all bilingual children were tested in both languages). The older Chinese-English bilinguals, however, had sorted out the correspondences used in the two writing systems and they scored significantly better than any of the other children in the English word size problem. The experience of working through representational rules in two different systems clarified the rules for both, making them more explicit and more accessible.

Why was the task so difficult for the younger Chinese-English bilinguals? The Chinese character system differs from the Roman alphabetic system in two ways: the individual forms are different, presenting a learning problem, and the correspondence rules are different (form to sound vs. form to morpheme), presenting a conceptual problem. Either or both of these may have been responsible for the different pattern of discovery experienced by the Chinese-English bilinguals. We examined these possibilities by presenting the same problems to bilingual children for whom the writing system of the other language differed from the English writing system in only one of the two ways. Hebrew is written in a Semitic script, and although the forms are completely different from Roman letters, the writing system is alphabetic. Therefore, children who are bilingual with English and Hebrew are like the French-English bilinguals in that both of their writing systems follow an alphabetic system, but like the Chinese-English bilinguals in that each of their writing systems uses forms that are completely different from each other and need to be learned separately. The experience these children have as they learn the alphabetic principle, therefore, should help to interpret the differences found for the Chinese-English bilinguals in the previous study.

We examined this question with Hebrew-English bilingual children of the same age and selected according to the same criteria as those in the previous study (Bialystok, Shenfield, & Codd, 2000). This time, there was no disadvantage for the younger bilingual children (in fact, there was evidence of a small advantage) and a clear and consistent superiority of the older bilingual children compared with the monolinguals solving these problems in each of the languages. The need to learn two different visual forms for representing sounds helps to draw the child's attention to those sound-symbol correspondences. The need to learn two different correspondence rules, however, as in learning both a character and an alphabetic language, increases the difficulty of the task and may result in a general confusion by the younger children.

Why do the bilingual children have a more complete understanding of the symbolic relation between print and meanings than monolinguals? Both groups of children are well versed in the storybook routine and have had extensive experience listening to adults read them stories. Presumably, many of these children follow in the book while the story is being read. Children's storybooks normally contain both text and pictures and it is quite normal for children to attend to the pictures while the adult reads the text. What the results of this study show is that at worst, children do not even realize that it is the print and not the pictures that tells the story, and at best, they do not know *how* it is that the print tells the story. Clearly, this is a critical insight for becoming an independent reader, and it is an insight that bilingual children achieve earlier, or more easily than monolinguals.

The difference in the effect that bilingualism had on children's performance in the two tasks is also telling. It is not surprising that the word size task is strongly influenced by the nature of the writing system; the task directly assesses children's understanding of a crucial aspect of that writing system. It is more surprising that bilingualism, irrespective of the writing system, leads to such large differences in performance on the moving word task. The interesting possibility is that the advantage the bilingual children demonstrate in this task is solely a reflection of their knowledge of oral language. The experience of managing two spoken systems and the concomitant insight about separation between form and meaning places these children in a privileged position with respect to a central cognitive notion that leads to reading.

Insights about the way in which print refers to text are obviously part of the preparation children must acquire en route to literacy. However, there is no straight line from these preliminary skills to the attainment of autonomous literacy; it is simply one prerequisite that must be in place. There is no research at present that provides data on how the attainment of these prerequisite skills predicts the point at which children will be able to read, and certainly no group data that examines overall patterns in this path for monolinguals and bilinguals. Furthermore, as we saw with the two tasks discussed above, the way in which bilingualism influences these developments changes with the specific concept being assessed and the nature of the bilingual and biliterate experience. Evidence that bilingual children acquire the cognitive insights essential for dealing with symbolic representations earlier than monolinguals do does not lead irrevocably to a conclusion that the path into literacy would be different in either rate or manner for the two groups. But the evidence is one piece of a puzzle and it is a piece that is difficult to dismiss.

Early Reading

The Role of Phonological Awareness

The one predictor that has consistently proven to be effective in accounting for children's early ability to read is the attainment of phonological awareness (review in Adams, 1990). Numerous studies have provided persuasive evidence that children's ability to segment and manipulate the sounds of speech predicts their initial progress in learning to read. Early research by Bradley and Bryant (1983) demonstrated that three-year-olds who were more skillful with rhyme were more successful several years later when they learned to read. Training studies have confirmed the importance of phonological awareness by teaching these skills to children and comparing their progress in reading with children who did not have the benefit of that instruction (Castle, Riach, & Nicholson, 1994).

Subsequent research has refined the relation between phonological awareness and reading by examining the component skills of each activity more precisely. Phonological awareness is a broad concept, and the connection to reading may depend on some subset of skills implicated by the larger construct. McBride-Chang (1995) administered a battery of tasks to children in third and fourth grades. Using a regression analysis, she showed that phonological awareness was composed of at least three components: general cognitive ability, verbal memory, and speech perception. Other researchers have shown how different aspects of phonological awareness have different impact on subsequent linguistic concepts. Yopp (1988), for example, grouped phonological awareness tasks into two major categories and identified different roles for each in the children's development of literacy.

Other research has shown that the specific components of phonological awareness are not equal in their impact on learning to read. Byrne and Fielding-Barnsley (1993, 1995) reported that teaching children to identify phonemes was more beneficial for reading than was teaching children to segment words, and Muter, Hulme, and Snowling (1997) found segmentation to be more relevant than rhyming. Stanovich, Cunningham, and Cramer (1984) assessed ten different phonological awareness tasks for their contribution to reading and found much variability among them. Wagner and his colleagues (Wagner et al., 1993, 1994, 1997) have used processing analyses to identify the aspects of phonological awareness that are relevant for reading by examining the underlying cognitive processes used in each. Not surprisingly, therefore, the various components of phonological awareness contribute differentially to the larger and more diffuse task of reading.

Other studies have considered the relation between phonological awareness and related cognitive abilities. No matter how important phonological awareness turns out to be, other cognitive and linguistic skills must still bear some significant responsibility in explaining early reading. Gottardo, Stanovich, and Siegel (1996), however, found that phonological awareness not only continued to predict reading ability after working memory and syntactic processing had been accounted for but also was the only factor in the model that remained significant irrespective of the order in which data were entered into a regression analysis. This is powerful evidence for the supremacy of phonological awareness among the many factors that contribute to reading.

Bowey and Patel (1988) have challenged the standard view on the relation between metalinguistic awareness and reading and ascribed a more modest role to phonological awareness. They investigated the possibility that metalinguistic awareness does not have a unique role in explaining variation in reading ability. They used two metalinguistic tasks, one phonological (the phonological oddity task developed by Bradley and Bryant, 1983) and the other syntactic (grammaticality judgment of simple sentences), as well as two measures of general language proficiency (vocabulary and sentence imitation). A regression analysis showed no explanatory role for the metalinguistic scores in reading achievement once language proficiency had been accounted for. However, the opposite was also true: there was no significant contribution for language proficiency once metalinguistic skill had been related to reading achievement. The implication of this result is that metalinguistic ability is not qualitatively different from general language proficiency, a conclusion compatible with the position discussed in Chapter 5. Nonetheless, following the general conceptualization of metalinguistic awareness described in Chapter 5, the tasks used in this study were only minimally metalinguistic, making limited demands on both analysis and control, and hovered within a narrow range of component types. Generalizations to broad claims about metalinguistic effects on development would seem to be premature on the basis of these tasks. Indeed, Bowey and Patel (1988) acknowledge that it is still possible that particular metalinguistic abilities contribute to specific aspects of reading skill. These results provide further evidence that progress in uncovering the complexity of these skills and their interrelations will proceed through detailed analyses of specific components and not through broadly based classifications.

It seems clear that phonological awareness is an important part of learning to read, at least for alphabetic languages. The relation between phonological awareness and reading in nonalphabetic scripts, however, suggests little effect in these cases (Mann, 1986; Read et al., 1986). Nonetheless, even for alphabetic languages, the effect of phonological awareness is not simple. Most researchers have come to agree that there is an interactive relationship between the development of phonological awareness and the acquisition of reading competence (Ellis, 1990; Liberman et al., 1977; Morais et al., 1986; Perfetti et al., 1987, 1988). Morais (1987), for example, distinguishes between phonemic awareness, relating to major speech boundaries, and phonetic awareness, relating to individual sounds, and assigns each a different role in the development of literacy. Specifically, phonemic awareness sets the stage for literacy, and literacy,

particularly alphabetic literacy, leads to the emergence of phonetic awareness. Stahl and Murray (1994) characterize such relations as "reciprocal
causation." In an interactive relationship, a single effect works in two
directions, but in reciprocal causation, the effects themselves are different.

Although some aspects of metalinguistic development proceed
differently for bilingual children, the development of phonological awareness appears to be minimally affected by bilingualism (see Chapter 5). It
may be, however, that the impact of bilingualism on this development is
more subtle than can be revealed through group designs. Just as the relation between phonological awareness and reading is interactive, so too the
relation between phonological awareness and bilingualism may be
bidirectional and interdependent. What is beyond dispute is the crucial
role that phonological awareness plays in learning to read an alphabetic
script. It is less clear what role, if any, this metalinguistic skill plays for
learning to read in scripts that are not recorded by rules that are strictly
phonological, or what the involvement is when children are learning two
languages or two scripts. It is important to establish, then, how children
develop phonological awareness and what the relation is between phonological awareness and the written code children are attempting to
master.

Bilinguals and the Awareness of Sounds

There are three questions to consider in determining the relation between phonological awareness and literacy for bilingual children. First,
does early bilingualism promote the development of phonological awareness? Such an effect may be most evident in children who are raised with
two languages simultaneously and have encountered two sound systems
from an early age. Second, do phonological awareness skills developed in
one language transfer to another? If children who learn their languages
sequentially, or for whom one language is stronger or more practiced than
the other, can profit from the analysis of sound structure in the first or
stronger language, then learning to read in the second or weaker language
may be made simpler. Third, does the specific language change the role
that phonological awareness plays in learning to read? The importance of
phonological awareness in learning to read is that alphabetic reading requires the segmentation of words into sounds and learning the correspondence between letters and those sounds. However, alphabetic languages
differ in the transparency of those correspondences. The transparency of
the sound-spelling system in a given language may determine the ease with
which children can apply phonological insights to reading. For bilingual

children whose two languages differ on this dimension, there may be an advantage when children learn the less transparent system because of their experience with the simpler (more transparent) system.

Advantages in Phonological Awareness

The possibility that bilingual children establish higher levels of sound awareness by virtue of speaking two languages was examined in Chapter 5. There is little evidence to support the conjecture in its simplest form. Although the research is scant, the results are sufficiently vague and fragile that there is no basis for such a conclusion. Still, there is evidence that something is different about the ways in which monolinguals and bilinguals approach problems that assess their level of phonological awareness. Problems that provide simple tests of children's awareness of the sound structure of language show bilingual advantages providing the task does not include high-level cognitive computations and the two languages of the bilingual children are in some manner related. Still, bilingual children think about language differently from the way monolingual children do. At the very least, they have a greater repertoire of phonemic distinctions, and the points of difference between their two languages may well make such distinctions more salient. At the same time, phonology is a relatively transparent feature of spoken language, that is, in terms of its structural significance, and the fact that two spoken languages are based on different phonological structures may be irrelevant in building children's awareness of language.

The Language Connection

The importance of phonological awareness may not be immediately evident in young children who already speak two languages, but it may exert its influence when children learn a second language. Although such children may have no higher levels of awareness of sound structure than monolinguals, they may enjoy a distinct advantage in acquiring access to the sound system of a new language because the insights have already been achieved in another language. Such an effect would constitute something like a high-level transfer function, in which an abstract understanding of structure, in this case, structure of sound, facilitated uncovering the sound structure of a new language.

Some support for this possibility is found in a study by Ciscero and Royer (1995). Their participants were children in kindergarten and grade one who had various mixtures of competence in Spanish and English. It is difficult to classify the children as monolingual or bilingual because all the children appeared to know at least some small amount of the other language, but they did attend different programs and were receiving different kinds of language instruction. The main grouping factor, therefore, is whether children were in mainstream (English) or transitional (Spanish) programs. The children were asked to judge whether pairs of words matched on rhyme, initial phoneme, or final phoneme. The task was given in kindergarten then repeated in grade one in both languages, irrespective of the program (and also, therefore, the child's competence in the other language). The data are weak, but they offer some evidence that performance on the initial phoneme task in kindergarten predicted performance on the same task in grade one for the opposite language. Hence, children who were more adept at isolating the initial sound of a word in kindergarten were generally better in this skill and could apply it to a different language a year later.

A more rigorous study of the same question was undertaken by Durgunoğlu, Nagy, and Hancin-Bhatt (1993). Their subjects were also learning Spanish and English, but the language proficiency in each language was more closely monitored in the study. All of the children were native speakers of Spanish and were learning to read in English, their second language. They found that children's levels of phonological awareness and word recognition in Spanish predicted levels of word recognition in English, the second language. Summarizing and extending this research, Durgunoğlu (1998) reports strong correlations between phonological awareness in English and Spanish for bilingual children as well as significant influences between phonological awareness and word recognition across languages. In other words, the phonological awareness skills developed in one language transferred to reading ability in another language. This is an important result. If children can establish basic concepts of phonological awareness in any language, then reading will be facilitated no matter what language initial literacy instruction occurs in.

There may be limits on this generalized effectiveness. In a comparison of Spanish-English bilinguals and Chinese-English bilinguals on the phonological awareness test described in Chapter 5 (Bialystok, Majumder, & Martin, in preparation), no benefits in English phonological awareness were found for children who spoke Chinese at home, although some advantages were found for children whose first language was Spanish. The reason for these differences may reside in either the degree of similarity in the sound systems of the two languages, the use of an alphabetic writing system that places a premium on individual phonemes, or both. Nonetheless, on a task requiring the children to read simple words and nonwords, there were no differences among any of the groups. The phonological awareness advantage recorded for the Spanish group did not translate into an advantage in early word reading. Further research is necessary to investigate these effects and evaluate alternative interpretations.

It's Just Easier

Part of popular wisdom includes descriptions about how difficult it is to learn certain languages. Some languages have a reputation for being "easy to spell," such as Spanish or Italian, and others are considered to be "hard to spell," such as English or French. These conceptions reflect the general level of regularity in the system of transcribing speech to symbols, and the more regular it is, the easier it is to master. But is it also easier to learn to read? And do languages that differ in this way place a different premium on phonological awareness? If it is easier to arrive at phonological insights in some languages, making feats such as segmentation more accessible, then it is possible that children speaking those languages may have an easier time as well in learning to read.

Cossu et al. (1988) review some of the literature that documents the different relations to phonological awareness that are engendered by different languages. Their own study examines the emergence of phonological awareness in young Italian children. Italian has a simpler phonological structure than English and more regular spelling. They compared the ability of English and Italian children to solve the same (as far as possible) phonological problems requiring syllable and phoneme segmentation. They found that the patterns of results were similar for the two groups, but the Italian children had higher levels of performance on all tasks. If the children in the two groups were indeed comparable, then it is plausible that the relative transparency of Italian made these concepts more accessible to young children than was the case for English. Similar results were reported by Wimmer and his colleagues in comparing the ability of (monolingual) English- and German-speaking children learning to read and spell (Frith, Wimmer, & Landerl, 1998; Wimmer & Goswami, 1994). German is the more regular language and German-speaking children performed better on all tasks. Finally, Bentin, Hammer, and Cahan (1991) examined the relation between phonological awareness and literacy for children who were learning to read Hebrew, a language in which the correspondences between sounds and symbols are very regular. Again, children appeared to progress more rapidly than did children learning to read in English. Although all these results are interesting, comparison studies are always suspect because it is strictly impossible to develop identical materials in different languages.

Caravolas and Bruck (1993) compared the development of phonological awareness in children who spoke Czech with those who spoke English. They found that Czech-speaking children were better than English-speaking children in isolating consonants in clusters appearing in nonsense words, indicating greater awareness of complex consonants. English-speaking children, in contrast, performed better on simpler consonant problems. Czech has complex consonant clusters but completely regular spelling patterns, and this may have facilitated children's ability to identify individual consonant phonemes. They conclude that both oral and written input influences the way in which children develop these difficult concepts. This interpretation assigns a central role to language-specific differences in children's development.

Rickard Liow and Poon (1998) were able to control for differences between languages by testing children in the same language, English, where children's other language was different. The study was conducted in Singapore and all children were attending school in English. Children's home language was either English, Chinese, or Bahasa Indonesia, a language written alphabetically with a regular (shallow) orthography. Children in this last group scored highest on English tests of spelling designed to measure phonological awareness.

For some researchers, the question needs to be formulated at a more specific level than simply the identity of the language. Gonzalez and Garcia (1995) explored specific phonological properties of Spanish and their relation to phonological awareness. They point out that some of the controversy that indicates different patterns of development for different languages may depend on how phonological awareness is defined, including sensitivity to any sound units of speech, such as syllables (e.g., Morais, Alegria, & Content, 1987) or restricting it only to the phonemic segments (e.g., Tunmer & Rohl, 1991). Their detailed experiments investigated phonemic sensitivity across many levels of analysis. Pitched at this level of detail, however, different studies using different languages report conflicting results. Treiman and Weatherston (1992) found a stop advantage, McBride-Chang (1995) found no differences in phoneme types, and this study found a continuant advantage. Although some measures replicated results obtained by Treiman and Weatherston (1992) in English, others did not. Language-specific differences in phonemic sensitivity seem to be pervasive. What is not known is whether bilingual children who acquire the ability to operate on specific phonemic distinctions in one language can transfer that ability to another language where the distinctions are less salient. Such transfer may have implications for children learning to read.

Fluent Reading

Fluent reading draws on many cognitive skills and incorporates knowledge from many mental domains. To read and understand a text, a reader must be able to interpret the symbols on the page, employ knowledge of the conventions and strategies for reading different kinds of texts, access knowledge of the language, particularly the grammar and vocabulary represented in the text, and incorporate prior knowledge of the subject matter. Each of these in turn entails subskills: interpreting the symbols on the page, for example, presumes visual recognition, alphabetic concepts, serial processing and blending, and so on. Sometimes these factors are classified as top-down, referring to the conceptual aspects, or bottom-up, referring to the decoding aspects. The attempts to define fluent reading inevitably produce complex models, even when reading is a well-defined activity emanating from a single linguistic base (e.g., Carr & Levy, 1990; Rieben & Perfetti, 1991). The process must be considerably more puzzling when, however, there are two languages, reading is acquired late in one of them, or it is learned in the weaker language.

The decoding skills (bottom-up processes) needed to interpret the text include the elemental processes involved in pattern recognition, letter identification, and lexical access. If a new language is written in a familiar script, then these factors should cause little problem in learning to read. Conceptual skills (top-down processes) are rarely in place in the new language to the same extent as they are in the first, even for advanced adult readers of a second language. The vast majority of the research and theorizing about the process of reading in a second language has been based on the experience of literate adults. Often these are adults learning to read in formal educational settings, where reading is a highly valued curricular goal. For example, Haynes and Carr (1990) developed a model for the acquisition of English literacy by highly proficient speakers of Chinese, specifying the significant role for both top-down and bottom-up factors and their interactions. For children, the situation is different and potentially even more complex. Preschool children who are bilingual cannot read in any language, and school-aged children who are immersed in a new language may or may not know how to read in their first language. For all these children, each of the top-down and the apparently simpler bottom-up processes may present formidable challenges to learning to read.

Factors in Second-Language Reading

For children in school, reading is the primary source of knowledge transmission and expression, and if this exchange takes place in a weak language or depends on compromised skills, the consequences for children's education are obvious. Indeed, this was the basis for the warning sounded by Macnamara (1966) against the practice of offering children instruction in their weaker language. In contrast to the enthusiasm expressed by Canadian researchers regarding French immersion programs (e.g., Peal and Lambert, 1962), Macnamara argued that Irish immersion was detrimental to children's academic progress. It is not a rare occurrence for children to enter school and be confronted with a text in a language that is poorly understood or in a script that is an arcane mystery. Whether because of parent's educational choices or life circumstances that impose conditions, children's first encounter with reading is frequently complicated by weak knowledge of the language of the text. These situations need to be understood for obvious practical reasons as well as the more abstruse theoretical interest they engender. The descriptions of how well children can learn to read under these conditions are among the crucial elements in the debate over bilingual education. Some of these issues are discussed in Chapter 8.

The potential impact of bilingualism on children's literacy may depend on the educational context. In some cases, a child may be required to develop literacy skills in a weak language, perhaps not the language of the home or even the community. Here the cognitive skills associated with literacy are being learned at the same time as the linguistic system that is encoded in writing. Alternatively, a child may already know how to read in one language but must additionally acquire literacy in a second language. On the surface, this situation appears to be considerably easier because the conceptual barriers to reading have already been conquered. Nonetheless, the new language may not be written in the same script, or with the same attention to sound-symbol correspondence as the child's first language, and these differences could easily diminish any potential advantage the child may have reaped from already knowing how to read.

Research with adults learning to read in a second language has shown that top-down conceptual factors play a strong and consistent role in determining the proficiency with which reading can be mastered. Specifically, reading fluency and comprehension can be predicted by the learner's level of proficiency in the first language (Cummins, 1991), the level of proficiency in the second language (Barnett, 1989), the difficulty of the text (Alderson, 1984), and the learner's knowledge of cultural schemata and discourse structures of the second language (Barnitz, 1986; Carrell, 1994). These factors interact to determine how readers will comprehend texts in a second language (Bernhardt, 1991; Carrell, Devine, & Eskey, 1988). Presumably, children are vulnerable to the same influences.

Both Durgunoğlu (1997) and Koda (1994) identify three sources of such conceptual knowledge that are relevant in explaining how bilinguals acquire high levels of reading comprehension in the second language. Two of the factors are common to both: linguistic knowledge of the second language and literacy knowledge from the first language. For the third, Durgunoğlu (1997) adds prior knowledge of the subject matter, while Koda (1994) lists limited linguistic knowledge. All these factors ultimately have an impact on the extent to which readers understand texts in a second language and all of them rely on strong connections between the two languages. In addition to the importance of these conceptual factors, both authors continue to attribute an explanatory role to the more straightforward and perhaps lower-level influence of limitations in second-language vocabulary. Although this research is largely based on adult learners, these factors remain relevant in explaining how children attain high levels of reading fluency in a second language.

An important theme in much of the discussion is the role that similarity between the first and second languages plays in assisting readers to access texts in the second language. The effect of similarity is obvious for the bottom-up factors such as decoding, although some specific consequences of transfer from other scripts are discussed below. The more complex role for similarity relations between the two languages is in the comparison of higher-order linguistic and conceptual structures.

There is some evidence that readers spontaneously exploit the similarity between languages. Ringbom (1992) reported that Finnish students who also spoke Swedish performed better on English reading (and listening) comprehension tests than did comparable Finnish students who did not know Swedish. Swedish offered some access to English that Finnish, a typologically unrelated language, was unable to provide. However, Nagy et al. (1993) showed that the mere existence of cognates was insufficient for such facilitation; students needed to recognize the pairs as cognates and understand their significance. This caveat regarding learner awareness can be also inferred from a study by Jiménez, Garcia, and Pearson (1995). They conducted a case study investigation of three children – a proficient

Spanish-English bilingual reader, a marginal Spanish-English bilingual reader, and a native English reader – for their ability to read and comprehend texts in English. The study assessed a variety of aspects of the reading process through measures such as think-aloud protocols. All three children were different from each other in many ways, so the interpretation of the differences is precarious because the children could hardly be said to represent groups. Nonetheless, one important dimension that distinguished the proficient from the marginal bilingual in reading comprehension was that the proficient reader made explicit use of the structural relations between Spanish and English. This explicit analysis of linguistic similarity was instrumental in the ability of the proficient reader to interpret the difficult text.

Decoding the Text

It seems clear from the literature that high-level cognitive processes easily transfer into reading in a weaker language, but the problem of orthography is not so simply solved. The issue of whether or not first-language reading skill transfers to the foreign language barely arises if the two languages are written differently. How the languages differ in their written form is also important. Following Coulmas (1989), a distinction can be made between the terms "writing system" to indicate systems based on different linguistic structures, such as morphemes (character system) or phonemes (alphabetic system), and "scripts" to describe different notational forms (for a given writing system) to encode those distinctions, such as Roman, Cyrillic, or Greek alphabets. Each of these has implications for how reading skills can transfer from one language to another.

Different kinds of writing systems are read most efficiently with different reading strategies, and comprehension is a direct result of how efficiently and skilled the reading is carried out. Henderson (1984) argues that each of the three main types of writing systems – logographic, syllabographic, and alphabetic – place different demands on readers. Even these broad classifications miss important differences among writing systems. Some syllabographic languages represent syllables and mark syllable distinctions visually (e.g., Japanese) while others represent phonemes but mark syllable distinctions (e.g., Korean). Alphabetic languages represent phonemes but may or may not mark word boundaries (e.g., English vs. Sanskrit). Writing systems that represent higher-order units, such as words, morphemes, or syllables, may require configuration cues to decode, while those that represent phonemic units likely require rule systems (Biederman & Tsao, 1979).

The most interesting case for investigating the transfer of bottom-up processes is one in which a reader must embark upon the acquisition of literacy skills in a second language that is written in a categorically different system than is the first language of literacy. Although these cases present important junctures for isolating decoding processes, Geva and Wade-Woolley (1998) point out that studies investigating these situations have found a pervasive and positive correlation between decoding ability across writing systems and scripts and between decoding ability and general cognitive processes such as memory and speed of processing. Nonetheless, systematic differences in reading attributable to experience with different writing systems are important and must play a central role in modeling reading comprehension.

Several researchers have examined the influence of strategies appropriate for reading one kind of script on the approach that learners take when learning a new script. In one study, Rickard Liow, Green, and Tam (1999) demonstrated cognitive differences in the way in which strings of letters or characters are scanned in a visual search task that corresponded with the preferred writing system. High proficiency with an alphabetic script leads to scanning strategies in which greater attention is paid to the first and final position of a string of letters but not to a string of characters. The argument is that these positions are phonologically crucial in alphabetic writing but not in character writing.

Koda (1989, 1990) has studied these situations in some detail by conducting research with Japanese, Arabic, and Spanish learners of English. Unlike the other languages in the study, Japanese is written as a morphography – the written symbols represent units of meaning and not units of sound. Decoding sounds, therefore, is not routinely part of the process of reading Japanese. Her studies show that Japanese learners of English approach English text differently from the other learner groups. When English texts are presented in which phonological information is unavailable, either because some words have been written in uninterpretable characters (Sanskrit) or because some written words are unpronounceable, Japanese learners are not impaired in their performance, but the Arabic and Spanish learners, as well as native English controls, find the task difficult. She concludes that the Japanese speakers transfer their reading strategies from their first language even though the second language uses a writing system that makes other strategies more appropriate. By not relying on phonological strategies, there is less interference in reading when phonological information is not accessible. Therefore, the Japanese readers do well on this task. In more usual reading circumstances, however, this may not be an advantage. The fact that phonological decoding plays little role in reading English, their second language, would not seem to serve these readers well in the long run since it remains the most effective strategy for reading alphabetic texts.

Even alphabetic writing systems using the same scripts differ from each other in important ways. Serbo-Croatian is phonetically regular so reading is based on phonological analysis to a degree that would be inappropriate for a language such as English (Turvey, Feldman, & Lukatela, 1984). Because the phonology can be generated directly from the print, the orthography is considered to be *shallow*. Hebrew, on the other hand, does not represent vowels and so the reader must know something about what the word is before it can be read. This orthography is *deep*. English is somewhere in between. Frost, Katz, and Bentin (1987) have demonstrated how these differences in orthographic depth translate into differences in processing. The kinds of information to which the reader must attend as well as the extent to which the text is phonologically recorded into speech varies with these orthographic correspondence patterns. For this reason, it is not necessarily sufficient to be familiar with a writing system, such as Roman script, if the new language is based on a different type of orthographic principle. Lukatela and Turvey (1998) describe how the writing system and orthographic depth interact to produce different reading strategies.

Another factor that alters the skill with which reading takes place in a second language is the cognitive processes that are deployed to interpret the written forms. Even when the writing systems are the same and basic reading skills are well established, the processes responsible for interpreting the grammatical and semantic information in the text may simply work more automatically and more efficiently when they are applied to the first language (McLeod & McLaughlin, 1986; Segalowitz, 1986). Low-level skills such as word identification and grammatical analysis are carried out more slowly and more deliberately in a weak language. This difference in speed between processing the first and second language is evident even at very high levels of proficiency in the second language. On this view, reading in a second, or weaker, language always carries a cost in efficiency because the mechanics of reading simply run more slowly. Following the interactive views in which extracting meaning from text is a result of both these and higher order conceptual skills, children will invariably have more difficulty conducting high-level processing on texts in a second language.

Segalowitz and his colleagues have studied differences in second-language reading proficiency among fluent bilinguals. Their subjects are generally adults, but the results have implications for children who are attempting to read in a weaker language. Bilinguals who otherwise appear to be equally fluent in both languages frequently find reading in the second language to be slower and more difficult than in the first language, in spite of apparent oral facility in the two languages (Favreau & Segalowitz, 1982, 1983). Segalowitz (1986) identifies a number of reasons for these differences, including less automaticity of word recognition in the second language and weaker skills in orthographic processing.

Another difference between reading in the two languages is the extent to which the second-language reader adopts the same strategies for reading in that language that are used by monolinguals. Segalowitz and Hebert (1994) studied French-English bilinguals who were completely fluent in both languages but differed in whether or not they read the two languages at the same rate. Hence, they created two groups, an equal rate group and an unequal rate reading group. In English, phonological recoding is used by native speakers when reading unfamiliar words. This means that words are accessed through the sound structure represented in the orthography. This is not the case in French where more holistic strategies are the norm. Their results showed that equal rate readers used the language-appropriate strategy when reading in each language, but the unequal rate readers transferred their strategy from the stronger language. This means that unequal rate readers made more errors. These are subtle differences that would never be detected without measures specially designed to uncover them, but the implications are not at all subtle. Reading in the second language cannot be predicted simply on the basis of oral fluency, and the bilingual who appears to be equally proficient in both languages may nonetheless be inefficient and possibly nonproficient in reading texts.

The Difference in Reading

Children who are bilingual from a preschool age may initially encounter literacy in either one or both of their two languages. This difference may be crucial in setting the stage for the competence that can be achieved in eventually mastering the literate uses of both languages. For children whose experience with literacy is in only one of the languages, it is probably the case that this experience is presented through the weaker of the two and not the language of the home. This is the language in which children might be at greatest risk for possessing inadequate grammatical knowledge and insufficient background concepts of literacy, print, and text. Under these circumstances, the weight of evidence forces the conclusion that there will be a cost to literacy. Children will find it more difficult to acquire the skills and be more restricted in the levels they can achieve. This does not condemn bilingual children to inferior literacy skills if reading is acquired through the weaker language, but it does alert us to the potential difficulty of achieving high levels of competence. As was demonstrated by research with highly fluent adults, native-like oral skills do not necessarily translate into native-like literacy skills.

In a review of research examining some factors that determine children's ability to acquire literacy in a second language, Geva and Wade-Woolley (1998) evaluate two apparently competing proposals. The first is that the acquisition of literacy is propelled by general cognitive and linguistic development, creating a consistency in acquisition across whatever languages children are learning to read. Alternatively, literacy emerges out of specific knowledge of the linguistic forms and orthographic principles of individual languages, producing an imbalance in proficiency across the child's languages. Factors such as orthographic depth, for example, determine what strategies children will need to use when learning to read the language and the success they will achieve as they acquire these skills. Their conclusion is that the dichotomy is simplistic and that the two positions are not contradictory. Both sources contribute importantly to children's developing proficiency with written text. The very fact that general cognitive factors play into the equation means that bilingualism itself will never provide a generalized description of children's success in learning to read; individual differences will always mitigate the effect of bilingualism.

Another way to examine the question is in terms of the three rough stages described in this chapter. In the first stage that prepares children for literacy, there is reason to believe that bilingual children have significant advantages in establishing relevant concepts and interpreting the symbolic function of the text. This advantage comes from both the oral experience of speaking two languages and the nature of print exposure that may or may not (depending on the two writing systems) result in these conceptual advantages. The second stage is concerned with developing the skills for decoding. To date, there is some evidence for bilingual advantages in the earliest stages, but not much to suggest a sustained difference in progress with this second phase of reading. Perhaps the individual differences in children's success in this area are more relevant than generalized group differences and mask whatever contribution to progress is explained by bilingualism. Finally, studies of fluent reading, usually with adults, indicate that in spite of the progress in learning to read, traces of differences between reading in the first or stronger and second or weaker language can inevitably be found. These are apparent even for individuals whose oral fluency in the two languages is indistinguishable from comparable native speakers. Just as phonology carries the final trace of nonnativeness in spoken language, reading betrays the individual as a nonnative in more stringent assessments of language proficiency.

But the question is whether learning to read in a second language, or being bilingual and trying to read in even one language, presents unnecessary problems for children. So far, the most damning evidence seems to be that as adults reading in the weaker language, they will probably read more slowly and may transfer strategies that a native speaker would not think of using. Not too bad a price for being able to read!

7

Beyond Language

Several years ago, newspapers screamed out headlines announcing that playing Mozart to infants was shown to improve their performance on cognitive tasks (Rauscher, Shaw, & Ky, 1993). This magic bullet was pounced on with almost the enthusiasm that would be expected to accompany such windfalls as a map leading straight to the Fountain of Youth. It was even reported that hospitals were providing Mozart tapes to new mothers, along with samples of diapers and infant formula. The subsequent debunking and advised caution were displayed less prominently in the press (Nantais & Schellenberg, 1999). The idea that a simple and relatively common activity could significantly alter the intelligence of our children tapped into something deeply motivating in our middle-class psyches.

Bilingualism has also been considered a candidate for an experience that propels children's intelligence into a new stratum. At various times and places, teaching languages to children has been touted as beneficial because it nurtured cultural grooming (French), mathematical precision (Latin), or historical and literary sensibility (Greek). These were the official explanations for imparting languages to youth, but they all contributed to the creation of what would have been called a more "intelligent" child. Ironically, the recipients of these educational dictates were children of the privileged, and no small part of the underlying motivation was to perpetuate that privilege. If any general intellectual consequence came from the simple fact of learning another language (as opposed to specific outcomes, like learning French so one could travel abroad), it was not explicitly discussed. It went largely unnoticed, therefore, that a large portion of children who were not "privileged" routinely learned other languages, not for reasons of cultural nicety, but because of immigration, oppression, or displacement. But if bilingualism has enhancing effects on intelligence, then these children should equally be recipients of its beneficence.

An answer to the question about whether bilingualism influences children's intelligence has typically been infused with political conviction, social position, and folk wisdom. Research can be recruited to support almost any position, so some selectivity is needed to assure that the research is reliable. An additional barrier to conducting decisive research on the possible effect that bilingualism has on intelligence is the lack of consensus about what either of these concepts refers to.

Bilinguals and Intelligence

The attempt to construct an equation that links bilingualism with cognitive outcomes is frustrated by the fact that neither of the substantive terms is clear. Consider first the definition of bilingualism, an issue discussed in Chapter 1. Children become bilingual for a variety of reasons: immigration, education, extended family, temporary residence. These difference contexts are associated with differences in social class, educational opportunities and expectations, access to support systems, opportunity for enriching experiences, and home language environment. Each of these factors alone can have a significant impact on cognitive and intellectual development and would easily obfuscate any universal effect that may follow simply from the fact that the child knows two languages. Contradictory outcomes of this research can often be traced to differences in definition that were used to select bilingual subjects. One factor, the child's relative fluency in both languages, is particularly critical to the equation and is discussed in more detail below.

Second, as compelling as the possibility is that bilingualism might affect the intellectual achievement of children, the hypothesis remains untestable without some specification of what is meant by "intelligence." The usual interpretation is to operationalize intelligence as the intelligence quotient (IQ). This was the outcome used to sell parents on the idea that Mozart was good for babies. However, IQ as both a construct and a test is riddled with controversy. A sobering history of the use and misuse of the term intelligence and its measurement through IQ tests, as well as the impact of that tradition on North American immigrants who did not speak English, is documented by Gould (1981) and Hakuta (1986). The assumptions that intelligence is an attribute of individuals, that it can be quantified, and that tests can reveal the relative position of one person against some hypothetical standard have been responsible for countless injustices against individuals and dangerous misconceptions about groups. The fatal flaw in the argument is in the equation of performance on an intelligence test and a statement about the intelligence of an individual. Bilingual children may or may not perform differently from comparable monolinguals on intelligence tests, but even if they do, it is not clear that differences in either direction reflect levels of intellectual capacity or are attributable to bilingualism.

What Is Intelligence?

The literature sets out various positions for defining intelligence, each of which begins with a different premise and posits different criteria for its assessment. Three such perspectives are the psychometric approach, the componential approach, and the multiple intelligence approach. Not only does each define intelligence differently, but also each leads to different predictions (or, more precisely, conjectures) about how bilingualism might affect children.

The psychometric approach is the best known in that it is the one associated with IQ testing. The assumption is that intelligence is a product that exists in varying degrees in people's minds and that its quantitative presence can be used to predict future outcomes. The various intellectual tasks in which we engage draw on this central intellectual resource, called *g*, and drive our ability to perform any cognitive task, including reasoning, analysis, and verbal proficiency. Claims about the impact of bilingualism from this perspective would need to explain how bilingualism increased intellectual capacity.

This product-oriented approach is based on a rather static conception of intelligence, and it is not apparent how an experience, in this case, bilingualism, could make a significant change to that capacity. Nonetheless, this has been the dominant model for arguing about the dangers of bilingualism. In the 1920s, researchers armed with the newly standardized Stanford Binet Intelligence Test reveled in a flurry of research in which they indulged in massive testing of bilingual children and found their scores to be lower than those of monolinguals. For example, Saer (1923) compared Welsh children who were bilingual with monolingual English children and reported the inferiority and "mental confusion" of the bilinguals. Other studies tested immigrant children and found them to be inferior to their new native-speaking peers on IQ tests, even though testing was conducted in a language they were only beginning to learn (reviewed in Hakuta, 1986). The conclusion from this type of research was that bilingualism depressed intelligence. Ironically, the sales pitch attached to the Mozart tapes is that its impact will be seen in IQ scores. You can't have it both ways: if it is implausible that learning two languages will deplete intelligence, then it must be *prima facie* just as implausible that it will increase intelligence.

Other interpretations of intelligence are less attached to a simple metric for assessment. Although this may be a theoretical virtue, it is an empirical liability, especially when the relevant hypotheses concern group comparisons. However, if the psychometric view fails to capture what is essential about intelligence and its relation to bilingualism, then other interpretations need to be considered.

The componential approach was developed by Sternberg (1985) in an effort to provide a process-oriented account of intelligence. Unlike the psychometric approach in which the nature of intelligent behavior is less important than its quantitative manifestation through standardized tests, the componential view is rooted in information-processing explanations of cognition. Sternberg attempts to identify the cognitive processes responsible for intelligence test scores by using analyses based on models of information processing. He calls his theory triarchic because it draws from three domains: componential subtheory (components of processing), experiential subtheory (role of context and novelty), and contextual subtheory (adaptation of knowledge and skills). Intelligence is the interaction of factors in all three of these domains.

This conception of intelligence can be readily adapted to investigating the role of bilingualism in children's development. Learning two languages in childhood could affect any of the three domains and alter intelligence because the interactions among the domains would be different. First, bilingual children begin with a different knowledge base and possibly different learning algorithms because they know two languages (componential subtheory). Second, the context of learning for bilingual children includes an increased range of novelty around linguistic interactions (experiential subtheory). Finally, childhood bilingualism provides a unique environment in which knowledge and experience interact in the development of mental representations (contextual subtheory). In this view, it would not be surprising that childhood bilingualism had an impact on children's intelligence. However, it would be difficult to test the idea because there are no simple measurements for any of the subtheories. Moreover, the source of the differences would be largely speculative.

A third alternative for conceptualizing intelligence, called multiple intelligences, has been proposed by Gardner (1983). The position is a hybrid of a product- and process-oriented view. Intelligence is divided into seven relatively independent domains based on a distinct set of processing operations that is implicated in each. Hence, as in product-oriented approaches, each module can be circumscribed and quantified, but following process-oriented approaches, at least some of the criteria for determining the modules are the mental processes accompanying each The seven domains, described as "culturally meaningful activities," are linguistic, logico-mathematical, musical, spatial, bodily/kinesthetic, interpersonal, and intrapersonal.

It is not clear how this conception would interface with the experience of learning two languages in childhood. It may be that the linguistic intelligence is altered in some way by the experience, but the theory minimizes interactions among the domains, so only very local effects would be expected to occur. It follows from this view, then, that any effect of bilingualism would be confined to some conception of linguistic intelligence. The broader domain of nonverbal intelligence or general problem-solving would be unaffected by an experience in language-learning, simply because the modularity of the theory prevents interactions among the designated domains.

The Processes of Intelligence

None of these views alone provides a satisfactory definition for intelligence nor for the interactions between linguistic and other processes that might underlie an account of how bilingualism influences children's developing intelligence. The psychometric view has been the most intensely researched, probably because it is easiest to measure. The assumptions inherent in the componential theory are more appealing, although the theory itself is cumbersome and difficult to investigate. The view of multiple intelligences is too restrictive – thinking must exceed the boundaries set out by any putative domain. The present approach is to dispense with an overriding notion of intelligence and consider only the specific cognitive processes that are implicated in thought.

The elimination of independent structural domains of thought in favor of a set of generalized cognitive processes has two implications for a potential effect of bilingualism. The first is that the source of intellectual differences between monolinguals and bilinguals must be pitched at some basic cognitive function that is common across forms of thought. Second, the impact of such an effect would be seen in a range of cognitive activities rather than one domain, such as verbal. Any uncovered differences in these underlying cognitive skills may or may not make children more intelligent, but they would help to trace the way that bilingualism interacts with children's developing cognitive profile.

Where would we look for such potential differences in cognition? Whether or not it turns out to be true, it is plausible that bilingual children might develop linguistic and literacy skills differently from monolingual children. Some of these effects have been discussed in Chapters 5 and 6. However, it is less transparent that bilingual children could also experience differences in cognitive development.

The watershed study in the area of the cognitive effects of bilingualism is that of Peal and Lambert (1962). Following the early negatively oriented research on this topic, their intention was to carry out a properly designed experiment (in contrast to most of the early research in this area) using a large sample of carefully selected participants and a range of testing instruments. Their study had several goals, including predictions about attitude and school achievement that are not discussed here. Regarding intelligence, their hypothesis was that monolinguals and bilinguals would score the same on measures of nonverbal intelligence, but that monolinguals would score *higher* than bilinguals on tests of verbal intelligence. It would have appeared irrationally bold to propose that bilinguals would do better than monolinguals since previous research had always recorded bilingual deficits on verbal test.

The study was largely conceived in the paradigm of psychometric conceptions of intelligence, making use as it did of intelligence tests, but the design and interpretation went beyond the standard view in several respects. Not only did they include a range of tests to assess children's performance in terms broader than usually implied by IQ, but they also sought differences in the *structure* of intelligence, that is, in the relationship among the various intellectual skills that were tested. Their results, to their own surprise, were that the bilinguals did better on virtually *all* the tests, including nonverbal intelligence. A closer examination of the tests allowed them to classify the nonverbal tests into two categories, spatial-perceptual and symbolic reorganization. The bilingual advantage was found for the second type, tests involving mental reorganization. Peal and Lambert's conclusion was that the bilingual advantage was in mental flexibility. Additionally, from an advantage recorded by bilinguals in the verb tests, they concluded that bilinguals profited from a "language asset," in contrast to the "language handicap" bemoaned by earlier researchers.

The work by Peal and Lambert changed both the standards for research design in studies of bilingual children and the expectations of researchers for the outcomes of those studies. Nonetheless, the study was not flawless (no study ever is), and there is a need to moderate some of the initial enthusiasm that erupted from their results. Socially, the groups may not have been as equivalent as the researchers believed. The participants were French-speaking schoolchildren in Montreal. The research was published in 1962 (and the manuscript was received by the journal in 1961), so the research was probably carried out in 1960 at the latest, but more likely during the late 1950s. It was a select group of francophones in Montreal who were bilingual at that time, and those who were more likely to be bilingual were also more educated or more worldly than the monolingual francophones in the control group. It is not surprising that the children of those families who also became fluent in English (a criterion for participation in the study) profited from those family characteristics. Peal and Lambert hint at this possibility themselves. They state that the social context was one in which more intelligent parents would recognize the value of knowing English, and that "parents of higher intelligence may be expected to have more intelligent children" (p. 13). They also admit that selection procedures would have biased toward including children whose English was extremely good, and that might account for their superior performance on the verbal tests.

The Peal and Lambert study is immensely important in the literature of the field but a tempered interpretation of the results is in order. There may well be specific areas of cognitive functioning in which bilingual children differ from monolinguals, but broadly based statements about intellectual superiority are probably excessive and unsupportable. However, it is important to clarify the nature and extent of the bilingual influence. Furthermore, if childhood bilingualism significantly alters cognitive functioning, that evidence is also relevant data in the controversy about the nature of linguistic knowledge and its structural relation with the mind. Recall that a critical feature in distinguishing between formal and functional theories of language and its acquisition is the autonomy of linguistic knowledge in the mind (Chapter 2). If knowledge of two languages affects the development of children's nonlinguistic cognitive competencies, then serious doubt is cast upon a strictly formal conception of language. A modular approach to language proficiency that is extreme in its isolation of language from the rest of cognition, especially in the early stages of learning language, is incompatible with evidence of strong interactions in development. These issues are discussed more fully below.

Languages and Cognition

As children learn their first language, they gradually incorporate an expanding knowledge of the world into their continually widening vocabulary, creating a system of words and meanings, concepts and symbols, that defines their intelligence. Development entails learning both concepts to structure the world and words to label and express those structures. Some views place priority on one or the other of these contributory processes. One view is that cognitive prerequisites set the stage for linguistic development (e.g., Clark, 1973, 1993). Children learn language as a means of expressing the concepts they have acquired. In contrast, some views follow more closely from Whorf (1956) and claim that the lexicon signals the occasion to create a concept. In this case, the linguistic features of words that are presumed to be universal are noticed by children and guide their conceptual constructions (e.g., Pinker, 1984). As we have seen many times now, however, polarized alternatives rarely lead to a satisfactory description. It is indisputably the case that young monolingual children learn language and concepts together and it would be astonishing if there were no interaction between them.

Evidence for these interactions is found in the way that children learning different languages build up linguistic and conceptual structures. If the influence were only in one direction, either from concepts to words or words to concepts, then whichever of those was primary would be universally acquired by children regardless of the language they were learning. Research has shown, however, that this process of building up language and concepts proceeds somewhat differently for children who are learning conceptually different languages.

The acquisition of spatial concepts provides an example of these interactions. The systems of spatial prepositions in English and Korean are based on different kinds of conceptual distinctions. In English, the choice between "in" and "on" depends on the features of containment or surface area properties of the referent. In Korean, the relevant distinction between terms is whether the relationship between the referent and the object is tight fitting or loose fitting. It makes no difference in this case if the resulting configuration between the referent and the object is containment or surface attachment. The research has shown that infants exposed to each of these languages make the perceptual distinctions that correspond to the way the words are used in that language, noticing either surface properties or tight-loose relationships (Bavin, 1990; Choi & Bowerman, 1991; Choi et al., 1999). The conceptual distinctions are evident in both the early production and comprehension of these spatial terms by children less than two years old. Thus, there are strong interactions between the heard language and the conceptual system that the child is establishing.

Bowerman (1985) makes a similar point in describing the important role for cognition in children's developing grammars. The operating principles by which we process speech require different strategies in different languages, depending, for example, on the way things such as inflectional morphology and word order are used in each. Children learning to speak various languages, therefore, recruit different cognitive operations to understand and learn that language. For example, Choi and Bowerman (1991) describe how children learning either English or Korean organize verb meanings differently because of morphological differences between the two languages. Choi (1997) elaborates this argument and defines the nature of the interacting systems. She concludes that "from the very beginning of linguistic development, there is a close interaction between [children's] cognitive capacity and the influence of language-specific input" (p. 123). In these views, cognition is an integral part of building a grammar. Therefore, we may not be surprised to learn that cognition is itself affected by the process of learning a language or, more specifically, the process of learning two languages.

But what happens when children are learning two languages? If language and cognition interact, children learning two different languages are an important test case for examining the influence of each of the linguistic and cognitive structures on the other. Unfortunately, almost no research of this type has been conducted with bilingual children. A study by Ervin (1961), however, provides some insight into this question. She tested adults who were bilingual in English and Navaho on a color-naming task and compared them with monolingual speakers of each language. Participants had to name a large set of colors drawn from the set of Munsell chips. She reported that the color boundaries for bilinguals had shifted significantly, and that the nature and degree of shift was determined by the dominant language. In short, the structure of a nonverbal conceptual domain, color names, was partly shaped by the languages spoken.

Groundwork for Interactions

If an experience in language learning is to have an impact on children's developing cognition, then there should be a plausible means for describing how language and cognition interact. Although claims about the influence of bilingualism on children's cognitive development are not *contingent* on the articulation of such a model, the account would make the investigation of bilingual influences more logical. It would seem odd, for example, to explore the ways in which cognitive development might be influenced by language learning if it were assumed that language learning unfolds in an autonomous system.

Nelson (1996) has proposed an interesting account of how these interactions might take place. Her starting point is the cognitive evolutionary model described by Donald (1991) in which he posits four stages of phylogenetic progression in the development of representation. With each stage, a new representational ability is added onto the system, but the older and more primitive ones are not lost. Thus, phylogenetic development not only entails more powerful systems for representation but also more diversity in the possibilities for representation. The four representational stages are episodic, mimetic, mythic, and theoretic. Episodic representation is the ability to encode objects and events, including perceptual and other contextual details. The transition to mimetic representation takes place with the advent of social intelligence and self-awareness. In this representational form, events or relationships can be replicated by means of a reenactment, not merely a literal imitation. The criteria for mimesis converge in many respects with the requirements for representing language: "intentionality, generativity, communicativity, reference, auto-cueing" (Donald, 1991, p. 171). The third stage is mythic representation, based essentially on the narrative form: "The mythic culture enshrines a shared vision of both past and future that does not simply reconstruct human experiences but attempts to explain them in most encompassing terms" (Nelson, 1996, p. 69). The final stage of representational evolution leads to the theoretic stage. This last development is attributed not to biological change as were the previous advances, but to cultural invention. Three cognitive achievements are responsible for the development of the-oretic representation: graphic invention, external memory (especially written language), and theory construction. Nelson's thesis is that these four stages of representation apply equally to ontogeny, and therefore describe the progression in children's conceptual development.

Central to this progression through the stages of representation is the mediating role of language in thought: language becomes part of thought as well as a tool to thought. This analysis is broadly influenced by Vygotsky's (1962, 1978) argument for the role of language in directing thought through the use of egocentric speech once language development has sufficiently advanced. Part of Nelson's evidence is from research showing how a change in semantic memory organization in young children is responsible for their ability to perform more complex cognitive tasks. The advance in cognition is attributed to changes in language organization rather than conceptual organization because, she argues, the logical "hierarchies are in the language, not in the physical or material world" (p. 250).

This conception of language as instrumental to thought points to interesting questions about children being raised with two languages during the formative years of cognitive development. Although Vygotsky (1962) mused briefly about the possible enhancing effect of two languages on children's reflections, Nelson does not. Nonetheless, her theory clearly invites comparisons of the way these four stages of representation would evolve if children were developing two languages instead of just one. In addition to the allegiance to a Vygotskian position in which language guides cognitive development, she also subscribes to a Whorfian interpretation of language: "Learning words is thus learning to think in cultural forms . . . to learn the language means learning to think culturally" (p. 150). No doubt a serious examination of the implications of this view would lead to some manner of impact of learning two languages, especially two disparate languages, on children's developing cognitive competence.

Nelson's model is an interesting framework for development but is not a well-specified theory; although it lays out developmental patterns, it does not constrain developmental processes. Hence, there is no reason to evaluate this model in terms of its acceptance or rejection; rather, it stands as one story about how language and cognition could theoretically interact and affect the course of development for both.

The Style of Cognition

One approach to the study of intelligence is to consider qualitative differences in styles of learning and thinking. These descriptions, called cognitive style, capture differences in the way that information processing is carried out and the kinds of problems that are most compatible with an individual's style. The cognitive style attributes are presumed to influence cognitive outcomes because they indicate how individuals conceptually structure their environments. Some of the cognitive style structures that have been identified include field dependence-independence (Witkin et al., 1962), reflectivity-impulsivity (Kagan, 1966), and tolerance of ambiguity (review in Furnham & Ribchester, 1995). These styles are conceptualized as dimensions and individuals are placed in some relative position toward one of the endpoints. There is usually a strong disclaimer regarding the relative value of one of the endpoints, but that claim is generally fatuous, contradicted by both empirical evidence and popular belief. The fact is that one of the positions is generally associated with more valued attributes than the other.

Field Dependence-Independence

This paradigm in which cognitive style differences are treated as causal factors in determining learning outcomes has been applied to the study of both bilingualism and second-language acquisition. The cognitive style most studied is field dependence-independence (FDI) (review in Chapelle & Green, 1992). For the former, the hypothesis is that bilingualism alters children's conceptual organization and changes their position on the dimension of FDI, usually toward the more analytic (field independence) pole. For the latter, the hypothesis is that particular configurations of these cognitive styles are most conducive to learning a second language, making success more likely for individuals with those qualitative attributes. Claims have been made both that field-dependent individuals enjoy a social advantage that translates into greater success in oral language proficiency and that field-independent individuals excel in classroom situations, achieving higher levels of linguistic competence. For example, Johnson and Rosano (1993) showed that ESL (English as a Second Language) students who scored higher on the Block Design subtest of the Wechsler Intelligence Scale (Wechsler, 1974), a task they took to be a measure of FDI, could produce fewer interpretations for ambiguous metaphors and had poorer English communication than those students who scored lower. This pattern was replicated using different measures (Johnson, Prior, & Artuso, 2000). In the second study, FDI was assessed by the more conventional Embedded Figures Test and communication skill was measured by the amount of information conveyed in a conversation. They concluded that field dependence, and not the traditional field independence, may be more adaptive for certain aspects of second-language proficiency. Other studies have reported similar effects although the results are inevitably both complex and contradictory (for overviews, see Ellis, 1990; Naiman et al., 1978; Oxford & Ehrman, 1993; Skehan, 1989).

In spite of numerous claims that there are systematic relations between the position of individuals on FDI and their success in learning a language, the issue remains controversial. For the most part, researchers who assign a significant role to this factor have based the argument on a correlation between field independence and success in foreign-language classrooms. Critics have pointed out, however, that there is also a pervasive correlation between field independence and intelligence, and that intelligence mediates all aspects of classroom learning, including foreign languages. In this sense, the tests of FDI are not qualitative measures of personal style but rather ability tests that fit into the usual constellation of factors that predict student achievement. A particularly vehement criticism of the FDI research that rests largely on this argument is articulated by Griffiths and Sheen (1992). They review the theoretical and statistical structure of FDI and the tests that measure it as well as the conceptual rationale of the studies that use it in second-language acquisition. Their conclusion is that the construct of FDI has no relevance to issues in second-language acquisition.

There is less research relating FDI to bilingualism, but the general pattern is to argue that bilingual children are more field-independent than monolinguals. Again, it is field independence that is usually considered the more desirable style. Like the research relating FDI to second-language acquisition, this research, too, is methodologically and conceptually questionable. Nonetheless, some studies have reported these effects and defended them on the grounds that bilingualism alters the way that individuals conceptually structure information.

In spite of pervasive problems with these constructs, there is a repeated theme across the research claiming that bilinguals approach certain problems differently from monolinguals and that field-independent individuals are more successful second-language learners than field-dependent types. A reason for this pattern may be found in the main test used to evaluate FDI, namely, the Embedded Figures Test. The test requires respondents to find designated simple patterns that are concealed in complex and distracting perceptual fields. The solution, therefore, requires high levels of selective attention, the ability to focus on relevant information in the context of misleading distractions. In a study testing this interpretation, performance on the Embedded Figures Test correlated significantly with other tests known to measure selective attention but not with tests that did not contain this attention requirement (Bialystok, 1992a). Selective attention, moreover, may be the primary cognitive benefit of bilingualism, a hypothesis that is examined below. Thus, it could be that cognitive style is a red herring that conceals an underlying relation between bilingualism (and second-language learning) and skill in a particular cognitive process, selective attention. The sheer quantity of data that has reported systematic relations between cognitive style, especially FDI, and both SLA and bilingualism indicate that an explanation is required. The standard view, however, that it is the cognitive style that is the causal source of the patterns, is implausible. An analysis of the constructs in terms of their underlying cognitive bases offers an alternative explanation for these effects.

The Symbol Basis of Quantity

One way of conceptualizing language and the specific mental abilities that are required to learn and use language is to consider its properties as a symbolic system. In this view, language is an abstract referential system, one of many such symbol systems defined by their formal properties. This conceptualization of language was the basis for Deacon's (1997) argument concerning the evolution of symbolic representation as the key factor in its phylogenetic emergence (discussed in Chapter 2). In a detailed analysis of symbol systems, Goodman (1968) described the criteria for classifying systems based on the structure of their forms and the properties of their notational expressions. Although language clearly has special characteristics and may require unique cognitive processes, it nonetheless shares important properties with other referential systems that have symbolic and communicative dimensions such as maps, music, and art. All these systems involve abstract mental representations, conventional notation systems, and interpretive functions. The symbolic system most closely related to language, however, is the system for expressing and representing quantity. Therefore, if any extension of bilingual effects may be found in nonlinguistic aspects of children's developing cognition, then the most likely domain may be that for quantity and number.

Equating skill in these two domains, language and quantity, has even had an institutional endorsement. For about four decades ending in the mid-1960s the high school curriculum in Ontario, Canada, officially blurred the distinction between languages and math by accepting Latin toward the curricular requirements for mathematics. Although it is most unlikely that the policy was based on any scientific evidence or reasoning, it nonetheless conformed to some sense of folk wisdom.

In addition to being similar in their symbolic and notational properties, language and number have similar developmental trajectories for young children. Children learn about the basis of language and number at about the same time, both are comprised of notational constituents that are learned by rote in the preschool years, and both become the basis for the symbolic skills that are the major goal of early schooling, namely, literacy and numeracy. There are, of course, important differences between the systems. For example, print has twenty-six elements with complex rules for combination, while numbers have only ten elements with more straightforward combinatorial rules. Nonetheless, the mechanics for both systems are similar: basic forms indicate abstract-meaning constituents that are combined according to a rule-governed set of procedures. It appears as well that children develop proficiency with the number system, especially the written number system, earlier than they do for language and print, but various factors could contribute to that sequencing. For the most part, children's development of the knowledge of these as conceptual domains (language, quantity) with corresponding notational forms (print, numbers) that are required for carrying out a computational symbolic skill (reading, arithmetic) is similar.

Is there any evidence that skills involving number and quantity are mastered differently by bilinguals than by monolinguals? Macnamara (1966, 1967) raised the possibility that bilingualism might interfere with children's competence in these areas. His analysis of that literature and his own study of it are discussed below in terms of children's mathematical abilities, but his study was equally important in terms of its educational implications. He was concerned that bilingual education programs in Ireland in which English-speaking children were being taught in Irish were handicapping children in mathematical (and other cognitive) skills. His results confirmed his view that children in these programs performed poorly in both problem arithmetic and language skills and he warned about the dire consequences of such educational experiments. This admonition reverberated strongly through the community because it came at a time when immersion education was seen as an efficient educational solution for producing bilingual children. If these programs indeed impaired children in any cognitive skills, then that was a serious judgment. The target of his study, therefore, was not so much bilingualism but a common process by which children were supposedly becoming bilingual. Most of the research on the cognitive and academic achievement of children in immersion programs was carried out in Canadian schools and essentially showed that children's development and academic success was at least as good as it was for children in English programs (Lambert & Tucker, 1972; Swain & Lapkin, 1982). Indeed, immersion education went on to attract great attention in North American schools.

Just as children gain competence with language by moving through understanding the oral forms, to learning about the notational system of print, and finally to using that system for reading, the same progression marks children's mastery of quantity and number. Does bilingualism have an impact on any of these achievements? We consider them individually.

Numbers and Numerals: The Basis of Quantity

For very young children, arithmetic remains a distant problem. The initial challenge is to understand the meaning of quantity and the relation between quantity and the numerical system that symbolizes its gradations. The insight most clearly associated with this understanding is the cardinal principle: numbers have significance because they refer to invariant and identifiable quantities. Considerable research has shown that children's grasp of this idea is gradual, although the time at which children achieve it has been placed at birth (Gelman & Gallistel, 1978), early childhood (Sophian, 1988), and much later (Fuson, 1988; Marx & Kim, 1990; Wynn, 1990, 1992). An active debate has examined factors such as task differences as a means of resolving disparities in the results about when acquisition of cardinality is complete. The point, however, is that children need to learn that numbers and quantities are intricately related and represented by a symbolic system that conveys identifiable meanings. At this level, the concept is not unlike the understanding children need to acquire regarding the meaning of words and the relation between print and those meanings. Do monolingual and bilingual children differ in their achievement of this insight?

We studied the acquisition of cardinality in monolingual and bilingual preschool children by using two different tasks (Bialystok & Codd, 1997). These tasks were constructed to test predictions made by the analysis and control framework described in Chapter 5. The research with metalinguistic tasks had indicated that there was a dissociation between tasks that depended on each of these processes and that bilingual children were advantaged relative to monolinguals in tasks that had higher demands on control. Consequently, if bilingualism had an impact on the way children understood concepts of quantity, then presumably it would be demonstrated in tasks that required control of attentional processing but not necessarily in tasks requiring analysis of representational structures.

The task created to demand a high level of analysis was the sharing task. Children divided a set of candies between two recipients, agreed that the subsets were equal, counted one of the subsets, and then had to infer the number of candies in the other subset without counting. To solve this, children needed to understand the principle of equivalence, a primary component of cardinality. The control demands in this task are marginal because there is no misleading information.

The towers task was constructed to demand a high level of control. Children were told that they were going to build apartment buildings out of blocks, and that every block was one apartment and had one family living in it. The trick was that the blocks were either standard lego blocks or duplo blocks, identical versions that are twice as large on every dimension. Children had to decide which of two buildings had more families. They were told on every trial to count the blocks to decide which apartment had more families. The critical test was when the two blocks consisted of one lego tower and one duplo tower but the duplo tower was taller even though the lego tower had more blocks. The problem presents a perceptual conflict similar to that created in Piagetian conservation problems. Nonetheless, children were reminded on each trial to count the blocks before deciding. The misleading information from the height of the tower challenges attentional control because the height is irrelevant and must be ignored.

There was no difference between the two groups in their ability to solve the sharing task but there was a significant bilingual advantage in the towers task. Both tasks require children to count a set of objects and make some judgment about that quantity. The difference is that the towers task places that judgment in the context of perceptually misleading information. The monolingual children were unable to ignore that information; the bilingual children were more able to focus on the meaning, namely, the quantity, and respond accurately by considering only the relevant information. From the sharing task it is clear that the groups do not differ in their basic level of knowledge about cardinality, but from the towers task it is apparent that they differ in how they are able to apply this knowledge in the solution to specific problems.

At around the same time as children are establishing the cardinal concepts that fix clear meanings to the counting procedures, imbuing the system with symbolic significance, they also learn the notational forms that indicate the cardinal quantities. Saxe (1988) found that bilingual children understood the arbitrary nature of number symbols better than their monolingual peers did. Monolingual and bilingual children watched scenarios in which one character counted a series of objects using numbers and another character counted using letters. The number counting character counted incorrectly and the letter counting character corrected him using letters. The child was asked to decide who counted the right way, did they both count correctly, or did they both count incorrectly. The bilingual children answered correctly more often than monolinguals and appeared more able to accept the arbitrariness of the numbers and their functional role in counting. This is analogous to their advantage in similar tasks using language notations (discussed in Chapter 6). It may be, then, that bilingual children understand the symbolic function of written notations of quantity more completely than do similar monolingual children, but no research has directly addressed this question.

Computation and Quantity

The first thorough review of studies investigating the effects of bilingualism on children's mathematical abilities was assembled and reported by Macnamara (1966). Based on the research available at the time, he concluded that there was no evidence that bilingualism handicapped children's computational ability for mechanical arithmetic but that it did impair children's ability to solve mathematical word problems. His own large-scale study of English-speaking children in Irish-language schools confirmed this pattern. He attributed the deficit to what he considered the inevitable language handicap that followed from bilingualism but did not discount the logical possibility that bilingualism itself was to blame. In fact, although the deficit in performance was confined to tests of word problems and left performance on mechanical problems unscathed, his conclusions speak strongly against the educational trend at the time to use foreign languages as a medium of educational instruction. A simpler explanation, however, is compelling: children's competence in Irish was simply inadequate to the task. The culprit in this case was not bilingualism but rather the use of a language for a complex educational purpose that exceeded the children's proficiency in that language. This limitation on performance would be found whether children spoke no other languages or twelve other languages: linguistic proficiency needs to be adequate for the conceptual demands of the task.

Although Macnamara concluded that the mechanical abilities to carry out arithmetic operations were equivalent in monolinguals and bilinguals, others have presented a different view. Some researchers have reported weak but consistent evidence that adult bilinguals take longer to solve mental arithmetic problems than monolinguals (Mägistre, 1980; Marsh & Maki, 1976; McClain & Huang, 1982). It was possible that the difference was caused by the linguistic mediation used by bilinguals to solve the problems in their weaker language, so Geary et al. (1993) pursued these differences by using a task that did not involve verbal mediation. They presented arithmetic problems together with the solution and participants needed only to judge whether the solution was correct. If verbal mediation were required, participants would conduct these computations in their stronger language, eliminating the burden of the weak language effect. They found no overall differences in reaction times to solve these problems (although the mean times favored the monolinguals but was not significant). In a more detailed follow-up study, however, they divided the reaction time between time spent encoding and retrieving and time spent computing the operations. Here they found no group difference in encoding but a significant monolingual advantage in the computing. Their interpretation is that automated access to stored information (e.g., number facts) is the same for the two groups, and likely available in some abstract code that is not tied to either language. The computation difference, however, indicates differences in working memory for the two groups.

It is not clear is why having two linguistic systems should impair the working memory resources used to solve arithmetic problems, but the result is reminiscent of a widely replicated finding in another research area. Jacoby (1991) describes memory as consisting of two different processes. The first is the use of intentional controlled processes, such as those responsible for free recall, and the second is the use of automatic processes such as those that underlie implicit memory or recognition. By designing tasks so that component processes can be isolated and measured independently, he has shown that it is the intentional processes of memory, that is, those related to working memory and resource limitations, that are disrupted during a divided attention task when participants need to solve two problems simultaneously. The automatic memory processes are relatively unharmed by the need to solve a concurrent task. In an extension of this research, Craik and Jacoby (1996) have additionally demonstrated that aging impairs the intentional processes but leaves the automatic processes intact. More generally, then, the intentional resource-dependent processes are vulnerable to decay when intervening factors add stress to the system. If this analysis is relevant to the present issue, then it may be that the need to carry out arithmetic problems when there are two linguistic systems is similar to problem solving under divided attention. Like the memory research, the bilinguals are equivalent to monolinguals for those aspects of the problem that are based on automaticity and retrieval operations. Bilinguals differ from monolinguals when the problem involves the allocation of limited resources. This conjecture is speculative but could be easily tested in an appropriately designed study.

Working memory explanations are usually presented in terms of descriptions about the speed of processing. Specifically, faster processing indicates fewer demands on working memory, leaving larger portions of working memory for computation. Although we have no direct evidence that working memory is compromised for bilinguals, the speed of processing appears to be different in the bilingual's two languages. These processing speeds might have implications for certain kinds of computations, especially in the weaker (slower) language.

In a small-scale study in our laboratory, we compared the speed with which bilingual adults could count forward and backward in their two languages. The participants were highly fluent speakers of English and Portuguese. They were first asked to recall a list of words in each language to assure some rough equivalence on a verbal task. Then they were timed as they counted in both directions in both languages. The relevant measure was the ratio of the time required to count backward over the time required to count forward in the same language. Backward counting would inevitably be slower, and the more effort required would increase its difference from forward counting. Furthermore, by computing this time as a ratio of the time needed to count forward in each language, possible differences in the time required simply to recite the number sequence in the two languages were eliminated. The results showed no difference between languages on the verbal task but significant differences in the ratios calculated for each of the languages of the bilinguals. Specifically, the ratio indicating the extra time needed to count backward was much larger in English than it was in Portuguese, their dominant language.

This pattern is similar to the one reported by Geary et al. (1993) for mental arithmetic in which differences emerged only when computation was required. It is also compatible with the general framework used by Jacoby (1991) for memory in which stress to the problem affected only the computation components of the solution. Although it is premature to locate the source of difference in any specific construct, such as working memory, it does appear that certain arithmetic operations are handled more easily by monolinguals and more easily by bilinguals in their preferred language.

Secada (1991) explored some of these issues with Hispanic children solving word problems in arithmetic. He tested children in both English and Spanish for language proficiency and then gave them a series of arithmetic word problems to solve in both languages. There were two main findings. First, children could solve the problems equally well in both languages; if they could solve a given problem in English, they could also solve it in Spanish. Second, there was a small but significant effect showing a relation between greater degree of bilingualism and enhanced problem-solving ability. He concluded that the problem-solving ability of the bilingual children was equivalent to that of their monolingual peers. Although his study did not include an explicit comparison with monolingual children solving the same problems, it showed nonetheless that lower levels of language proficiency did not interfere with the ability of these children to solve the problems in their weaker language. In general, it suggests a weak role for language proficiency in this area of problem-solving.

This conclusion is different from the one reached by Mestre (1988). He claimed that bilinguals with mathematical skills comparable to monolinguals tended to solve math word problems incorrectly because of language deficiency. His argument is based on studies with bilingual children who were studying in English but for whom English was their weaker language, a situation similar to that in which Macnamara (1966) predicted grave results for bilinguals. Mestre identified four forms of language proficiency that are required to solve these problems: (1) ability to read and comprehend a problem, (2) familiarity with technical language, (3) syntactic proficiency, and (4) comprehension of math symbols and how they are used in combination with numbers. He argued that all these are compromised for bilingual children. These results are consistent with the warning about negative outcomes predicted by Macnamara (1966) when school instruction is in a weak language. But are these deficiencies rooted in cognitive impairment or are they reflections of linguistic incompetence?

The devastating prognosis for bilingual children indicated by Mestre did not materialize for the children studied by Secada (1991). In that study, the children were in bilingual education programs with most of their instruction conducted in English. Importantly, however, English was the dominant language for most of the children at the time of the study. The children in this study were able to solve the word problems, and they could do so in both languages. The fact that English was their dominant language would prevent them from experiencing deficiencies of the kind that Mestre warned about when solving the problems in English, but these children were also equally able to solve the problems in Spanish. According to Mestre, the children should have found problems more difficult in the weaker language. This deficit did not materialize.

Morales, Shute, and Pellegrino (1985) hypothesized that if language proficiency were not an issue, then bilingual children should perform just as well as monolingual children on problem-solving tasks. In their study, there were no differences between monolingual and bilingual groups when math problems were presented to each in the dominant language. It is often difficult to disentangle the role that language plays in problem-solving, either as a mediator for computation or as the medium in which the relevant knowledge is represented. In this case at least, taking out the interference of a weak language resulted in equivalent mathematical problem-solving skills for bilingual children.

The results of these studies present a complex picture and appear in some instances to contradict each other. The most generous interpretation that is consistent with the data is that bilingualism has no effect on mathematical problem-solving, providing that language proficiency is at least adequate for understanding the problem. Even solutions in the weaker language are unhampered under certain conditions. The possible exception to this is that retrieval times for arithmetic facts may be slower for bilinguals than monolinguals. If we consider the four aspects of language proficiency identified by Mestre that are required to solve mathematical problems, there is no doubt that serious deficits in any of them will prevent children from making any progress at all. But the real issue is how language proficiency (at least reasonable levels of language proficiency) interacts with children's ability to solve these problems, and whether knowing two languages is relevant. Both answers appear to be cautiously negative. Although there may be some differences in the speed with which arithmetic calculations can proceed in a weaker language, bilingualism appears to have virtually no effect on problem-solving. One must not lose sight of the possibility that the impact of bilingualism may not be advantageous but rather detrimental to cognitive performance, so demonstrations of equivalent performance for monolinguals and bilinguals are themselves salutary.

Concepts and Creativity

There is little evidence that bilingual children acquire concepts of quantity differently from monolinguals, although they do solve certain kinds of problems differently that make use of their knowledge of quantity. One might have expected that the overlap between the representational systems for language and quantity would impart some advantage for children who know two languages, but this was not the case. If shared knowledge across domains is responsible for bilingual influences in areas beyond language, then it would be surprising if this advantage spread to domains even less similar to language than is the case for number. However, it may be that bilingualism exerts an influence not through shared structures of knowledge but through a process-related cognitive operation that is modified for children who know two languages. In other words, the effect of bilingualism may not be in the structure of knowledge but in the nature of processing. To test this possibility, we need to extend the search further from the center and explore aspects of cognition that are more at the periphery of linguistic influence.

Problem-Solving in Bilingual Children

Kessler and Quinn (1980, 1987) examined the effects of bilingualism on creativity and scientific problem-solving. They hypothesized that relevant aspects of a problem may become more salient to bilingual children because their experiences with two languages and cultures would enable them to incorporate different perspectives to the solution. In one study, children were shown a physical science problem on film and were required to write as many hypotheses as possible to solve the problem within a limited time. The bilingual children performed better than monolingual children did: their hypotheses were more structurally complex and qualitatively sophisticated than those given by the monolingual children (Kessler & Quinn, 1980). The authors' interpretation of these results is that there is a common underlying ability that governs both formulating a hypothesis and expressing it in complex linguistic structures. The results also conform to the patterns claimed by Peal and Lambert in that the primary index of bilingual advantage involves a measure of creativity.

There were other early signs that the positive effect of bilingualism into nonverbal cognitive domains was not such a bizarre idea. Although Darcy (1946) is primarily associated with the effort to expose bilingualism for the harm it does to children, she reported nonetheless that Italian-English bilingual preschoolers performed better than monolinguals on the Atkins Object Fitting test, a measure of nonverbal intelligence. Still, the bilinguals in her study performed worse on the verbal measure.

Later studies that included measures of spatial performance in the battery of tasks replicated the emerging pattern. Feldman and Shen (1971) reported better performance by bilingual five-year-olds in perceptual tasks such as object constancy. Ricciardelli (1992) compared monolingual and bilingual six-year-olds on a large number of tasks in which the nonlinguistic measures included tests of creativity and geometric design. Her bilinguals were divided into those who were fully bilingual and those whose knowledge of the second language (Italian) was limited. She found a significant advantage in all the cognitive measures for children who were proficient in both languages, but no difference between monolinguals and children who were only partially bilingual.

Lemmon and Goggin (1989) extended these ideas in a study with bilingual Spanish-English college students. Their purpose was to examine the structure of linguistic representation for bilinguals, but they included an experiment in which the participants were given cognitive tasks assessing fluency, flexibility of thinking, creativity, and concept formation. The main finding was that the monolinguals scored higher on virtually all the cognitive tasks. A more detailed analysis that subdivided the bilingual subjects into high (balanced) and low (unbalanced) bilinguals, however, showed that the deficits occurred only for the low bilingual subjects; fully bilingual participants were equivalent to monolinguals. Although the trend is compatible with the results reported by Ricciardelli (1992) in that the greatest advantage is associated with balanced bilingualism, these results are still more negative than the research with children. It is possible that the positive effects of balanced bilingualism on cognitive performance disappear with age. It is also possible, however, that methodological or subject differences are responsible for disparate results with the two populations.

Bochner (1996) took a different approach to deciding how cognitive outcomes should be measured. His measure was the child's learning style, scored on scales such as "deep motive," "surface strategy," and "deep achieving approach." The participants were academically successful fourteen-year-olds, about half of whom were fluently bilingual. Although there were some interactions with age and gender, bilinguals scored higher overall on the scales that indicate a more deeply intellectual approach to learning. The measure is hard to interpret – What does it mean to use these learning strategies? – but the study adds an interesting dimension to possible influences that a bilingual experience can have on a particular kind of cognitive or academic performance.

Whether it leads to advantages, as in the study by Ricciardelli (1992), or the absence of disadvantages, as in the study by Lemmon and Goggin (1989), the extent to which the individual is fully bilingual is instrumental in mediating the effect on cognitive performance. This difference was incorporated into the design of a study by Bialystok and Majumder (1998). The tasks assessed nonverbal problem-solving and were designed to distinguish between the representational processes of analysis and the attentional flexibility of control. Previous research had shown bilingual children to demonstrate consistent advantages over comparable monolinguals in tasks most heavily dependent on attentional control but less reliable differences on tasks that depend primarily on analysis of representational structures (reviewed in Bialystok, 1992b). Therefore, the study examined children who were fully or partially bilingual solving problems that relied more strongly on either analysis or control.

All the children were in third grade, approximately eight years old, and were either monolingual, had partial knowledge of Bengali, or were completely fluent in both English and French. The relevant findings come from the three cognitive tasks: Block Design subtest of the Wechsler intelligence scale (Wechsler, 1974), the Water Level task (Pascual-Leone, 1969), and Noelting's Juice Task (1980a, b). The first two were considered to demand high levels of control and the third to test levels of analysis. Consistent with this classification, the correlation matrix showed a significant relation between performance on the first two tasks but no correlation with the third. The fully bilingual children scored significantly higher than the other two groups on the Block Design and Water Level tasks, both of which measured control. No group differences were found on the Noelting task, an assessment of analysis. In more detailed statistical examination, a score was assigned to each child indicating degree of bilingualism, operationally defined as the difference between the language proficiency measures in each language. These degree of bilingualism scores were entered into regression analyses with each of the three tasks as the dependent variable, controlling first for age and absolute levels of language proficiency. Degree of bilingualism was a significant predictor of performance on both control tasks (Block Design and Water Level) but was unrelated to performance on the analysis task (Noelting). These results provide evidence for bilingual advantages in nonverbal problems, but only when bilingualism is at a sufficiently high level and only when the problem is one that depends primarily on selective attention.

Conceptualization in a Sorting Task

How far can this pattern extend? In the study by Bialystok and Majumder (1998), it is difficult to attribute performance on those cognitive tasks to any linguistic advantage – the tasks are beyond the reach of verbal skills. Furthermore, the bilingual advantage was restricted to problems that included the need to attend to relevant features when there is distracting information. Therefore, a study was designed to see how bilingual children would perform on a problem even more removed from the influence of verbal skills but that included the kind of conflicting information that bilingual children were adept at resolving (Bialystok, 1999). Moreover, following from the results of the Bialystok and Majumder study and previous research on the role of level of bilingual proficiency, all the children tested were, as far as possible, fully balanced bilinguals.

The task was based on one developed by Zelazo and his colleagues (Frye, Zelazo, & Palfai, 1995; Zelazo, Frye, & Rapus, 1996) as part of the evidence for the theory called cognitive complexity and control (Zelazo & Frye, 1997). The materials consisted of a set of cards, each depicting one stimulus, and two containers, each marked by a target stimulus. For example, the cards might contain red circles or blue squares and the target stimuli on the sorting compartments would be a blue circle and a red square. Children are told first to sort the cards by one dimension, say, color, and then to resort the cards by the other dimension, shape. In the second sorting, children must reclassify each card and place it in the opposite sorting bin. Zelazo and his colleagues have manipulated the stimuli on the cards and the rules that define the sorting compartments and reliably found that the problem is extremely difficult until children are about five years old. The error is always the same: children continue to sort the cards by the first criterion even after the new rules have been explained. The thrust of the explanation offered by the cognitive complexity and control theory is that the task requires children to construct complex embedded representations of rules and that they are unable to do this until they are about five years old.

The structure of the problem, however, also challenges control of selective attention. Specifically, children must resist attending to the dimensional feature that was relevant in the first phase of sorting and attend instead to a different feature of the stimulus. This is the kind of inhibition of attention in which bilingual children have been shown to excel. Consequently, we compared monolingual and bilingual children for their ability to solve this problem (Bialystok, 1999). Children in this study also solved the moving word task (see Chapter 6) because it had previously been shown to be solved better by bilingual children. The results showed a bilingual advantage in solving the card sort task, and the size of the advantage was about the same as that found for the moving word task.

Why did the bilingual children perform better than monolinguals on this sorting problem? The problem contains two kinds of demands. Children need to conceptualize the stimuli and the rules by constructing appropriate mental representations, and, as argued by Zelazo and Frye (1997), this is difficult for young children. The solution, according to Frye, Zelazo, and Palfai (1995), requires these mental representations to allow "reasoning conditions." Additionally, children need to inhibit the response tendency set up by the initial stage of sorting. This inhibition actually has two possible interpretations. At the level of motor response, children need to resist putting the card in the location specified by the first set of rules. This response was established in the first phase as an association to a particular card. Moreover, they need to inhibit mentally attending to the stimulus feature (in the mental representation) that defined the placement in the first phase. The results of the study could not isolate which of these demands was responsible for the group differences, so another study was designed to disentangle them.

Bialystok and Martin (in preparation) created four versions of the card-sorting task by manipulating the semantic complexity of the sorting rule. The tasks involved classification by (1) color (red squares, blue squares), (2) color and shape (red squares, blue circles), (3) color and object (red bunnies, blue flowers), and (4) function and location (thing to wear/play with, things that go inside/outside the house). This range permits predictions regarding the comparative performance of monolinguals and bilinguals. First, for Zelazo and his colleagues the bilingual advantage would be from a superiority in conceptualizing the rules. Therefore, bilinguals should be better able to conceptualize the rules in all the conditions and outperform monolinguals on all four tasks. Furthermore, the bilingual advantage would increase across the conditions as the rules and stimuli increased in the complexity required for their mental representation. As conceptualization became more complex, the bilingual advantage would increasingly exert its effect by increasing the distance between the ability of the monolingual and bilingual children.

Second, the bilingual advantage might be in inhibition. This could occur in one of two interpretations of inhibition: motor inhibition of the response or cognitive inhibition of attention. If the bilingual advantage were in the ability to inhibit motor responses, then the bilinguals would outperform monolingual in all four conditions because they all impose this requirement.

The prediction is different if the bilingual advantage is in the ability to inhibit attention to misleading mental representations. Attention to mental representations means that the mental representations need to be specified. If both groups are equally capable of representing the information in the rules and the difference is in their attention to those representations, then only the rules of moderate complexity will distinguish between the groups. The first condition is too easy so processing is not sufficiently challenged; the fourth condition requires more complex representations so only children who were advanced in representational abilities would solve these problems. The bilingual advantage should appear in the second and third conditions. The results supported this last pattern: bilingual children outperformed monolinguals on the second and third condition with no difference between the groups on the other two.

The relevant process needed to solve this task is inhibition to the mental representation constructed for the problem. Children code the target stimuli according to the first rule system, for example, the red thing and the blue thing. When the second rule system is explained, those descriptions become obsolete and must be revised, recoding the targets as the square thing and the round thing. Having already represented the targets in one way, however, it is difficult for children to now think of the items as a square thing and a round thing. This reinterpretation of the targets requires inhibition of their original values, and that is difficult because the colors remain perceptually present even though they are now irrelevant.

Other accounts of this problem have considered the role of inhibition but defined it differently. Jacques et al. (1999), for example, interpret inhibition as the need to suppress the physical response of placing the card in the familiar and previously correct sorting container. In a modification of the task, a puppet carried out the placements and children needed only to comment on the correctness of the puppet's actions. Therefore, children did not need to inhibit their own tendency to place the card in a previous container. Nonetheless, the results replicated previous versions of the problem and registered no improvement in children's performance.

Perner, Stummer, & Lang (1999) distinguish between two kinds of inhibition that might underlie the solution to these tasks. Their distinction is between automatic control and executive inhibition. The first is a natural outcome of different response saliencies. A dominant response will automatically inhibit its less dominant competitors without the need for the child to understand the representational competition that has taken place. Executive inhibition, in contrast, requires intervention by the child to suppress a competing response. According to these authors, the prerequisite is that the child understands the representational nature of the information. Their application of this idea to the card sorting problem is that children must inhibit the representation of the action scheme that would incorrectly place the card in the wrong box. Thus, the interpretation is partway between that of Jacques et al., who consider the inhibition needs to be applied directly to a motor response, and the explanation proposed here, namely, that the inhibition needs to be applied to a mental representation of a conceptual value. The difference is that Perner, Stummer, and Lang have made the relevant target for inhibition a mental representation of a motor response.

The present explanation, then, is that the difficulty in solving the sorting task is in the inhibition of the symbolic association that defines the box. Evidence in support of this interpretation is reported by Bialystok and Martin (in preparation), who show that the problem become easy to solve if the obsolete target (e.g., blue square) is removed from the sorting container for the second phase and replaced with a neutral value (e.g., yellow square) that makes only the new relevant dimension visible. Furthermore, there is no evidence that the physical response is problematic, even in the representation of that physical response, or that bilingual children have more control over these physical responses that monolingual children do. Indeed, if this were the case, then the bilingual advantage should have emerged in all four conditions. The inhibition of attention to the symbol includes the complexity of the symbol in the prediction.

These studies support the interpretation that the bilingual children are approaching certain nonverbal problems differently from monolinguals, and that this difference leads to better performance in some situations. Importantly, the advantages found for bilinguals are constrained and limited – there is no sense in which it could be simply, or simplistically, concluded that bilingual children are more intelligent or more adept at problem-solving than monolinguals. When advantages occur, they tend to be confined to individuals who have high proficiency in both languages. Additionally, the tasks that demonstrate this advantage are those that involve characteristic demands such as flexibility and attention. What is the processing difference that leads to the performance effects that are found? Why does bilingualism affect processing in this way?

Piecing It Together

Across the domains examined, there are specific problems in which bilingual children performed better than monolinguals, but equally problems in which there was no difference between groups. Is there a pattern to these results? If so, the pattern is not explained by categories such as metalinguistic or linguistic, because advantages and disadvantages of bilingualism were found for both. Similarly, the pattern is not explained by domains such as linguistic or nonverbal, again because each incorporates both outcomes. Therefore, the explanation is most likely to be found at the level of specific cognitive processes. Even Peal and Lambert (1962) recognized that the main factor in understanding the difference between monolinguals and bilinguals would ultimately be a detailed description of how cognitive processing was carried out and not some overall judgment of superior or inferior intelligence. "The results of this study indicate the value of shifting emphasis from looking for favorable or unfavorable effects of bilingualism on intelligence to an inquiry into the basic nature of these effects" (Peal & Lambert, 1962, p. 21).

Pattern of Results

Consider first the problems discussed in the domain of number and quantity. The sharing task and the towers task both assessed the extent to which children understood the cardinality of quantity. In both tasks, children needed to count a small set of objects and then make some judgment about the resulting quantity. In the towers task, the quantities were used to establish which of the two buildings had more blocks, and in the sharing task, the quantity was the basis for an inference about the number of items in an equivalent set. These are similar processes and tap similar levels of understanding cardinality. The difference is that the towers task requires that this counting process be carried out in a misleading context. Specifically, children need to mentally attend to the quantities that result from the counting procedure irrespective of the perceptual height of the towers. The difficulty for children is in accepting that the higher tower may have fewer blocks because the visual information leads the judgment in the other direction.

This tendency for bilingual children to outperform monolinguals when there is misleading information was found as well in metalinguistic problems. Consider again the grammaticality judgment task described in Chapter 5. Children were trained to ignore the meaning of the sentence and simply determine whether it was grammatically correct. When the sentence was meaningful but contained a grammatical error, monolingual and bilingual children were equally proficient in the task. However, when the sentence contained a semantic anomaly *(Why is the cat barking so loudly?)*, bilingual children were significantly more advanced than monolinguals in making the correct judgment. Like the pair of tasks assessing cardinality, the underlying knowledge in both cases is the same. In fact, the design of the study counterbalanced sentences so that precisely the same sentence frames with the same grammatical errors occurred equally often in each condition. What was different was that the anomalous sentence required the judgment to be made in a misleading context, and bilingual children were more able to carry out this procedure.

These pairs of tasks illustrate that the bilingual advantage comes when the knowledge required to solve a problem is embedded in a misleading context. In terms of analysis and control, the representation of knowledge to solve a given problem is constructed through the process of analysis, but the attention to aspects of that representation is guided by control. Hence, the bilingual children have an advantage in control but no necessary advantage in analysis.

This claim is consistent with other observations and empirical results. For example, the nonverbal tests in which Peal and Lambert's (1962) bilinguals excelled all required a degree of manipulation as opposed to more straightforward concept formation or computation. They described the relevant feature as "flexibility," indicating that the bilingual children were better able to switch attention and see things in different ways than were the monolinguals. This manipulation or flexibility may reflect some common process with the attention that is involved in problems that demand control of processing. Creativity tasks, such as requiring the participant to generate unusual uses for common objects, can be explained in these terms. The barrier to solving the problem is in suppressing the usual use and freeing oneself to entertain alternatives. This suppression requires inhibition of the salient and automatically associated familiar function. Again, these are the kinds of tasks that bilinguals have been reported to solve better than monolinguals.

If there is a bilingual advantage in control, it is far from absolute. Indeed, many problems that contain conflicting or misleading information are not solved any differently by the two groups. What determines which problems will reveal processing differences?

If we consider only those problems that include a misleading context, that is, problems requiring high levels of control, they vary as well in the complexity of the mental representation required for their solution. In other words, the analysis demands influence the extent to which the bilingual effect can be seen. Specifically, problems that contain higher demands for analysis are not solved better by bilinguals.

Consider pairs of problems that both involve a misleading context but differ in the complexity required for the mental representation. All four conditions of the card-sorting task described above carry the same distraction for attention, namely, that the sorting decision for the first phase becomes obsolete and interferes with the decision required for the second phase. Nonetheless, the bilingual advantage occurs only for the middle two, the color-shape and color-object tasks. The first condition involving only color is simple and solved equally by both groups, and the fourth one requiring a more complex semantic decision is the most difficult and both groups again perform at the same level. The difference among these tasks is in the complexity of the information required to make the classification judgment. Bilingual performance on the second phase exceeded that of monolinguals only when these conceptual demands on classification were moderate.

The second example involves linguistic material. Two tasks described as demonstrating children's development of concepts of print were the moving word task and the word size task (Chapter 6). In the moving word task, children were shown a card with a word printed on it and were asked three times what word was on the card. The first question occurred when the card was under a corresponding picture, the second when it was accidentally moved to be under a conflicting picture, and finally when it was returned to the corresponding picture. The important question is the one when the word and the picture were in conflict. In the word size task, children were given two words and needed to judge which one was longer. On half the trials, the longer word named the smaller object.

Both tasks assess children's knowledge of how written language signifies words, but they require understanding these principles to different levels of detail. The moving word task requires only that children realize that print stands for an invariant meaning because of the notations, but the word size task additionally requires some knowledge of how the meaning is encoded in that notation. Both tasks, however, are presented in a misleading context. For the moving word task, the misleading context is given by the conflicting picture, and for the word size task, the misleading context is created by the discrepancy between word size and object size. On this pair of tasks, there was a bilingual advantage for the moving word task but not (necessarily) for the word size task (although the additional experience of learning two writing systems helped children to master this problem). Again, there are bilingual advantages in solving problems requiring high levels of control only when the analysis demands are kept to a moderate level.

Toward an Explanation

Tasks that showed a bilingual advantage had in common a misleading context and moderate conceptual demands. Tasks that showed no difference between groups of monolinguals and bilinguals tended to make more complex conceptual demands or require more detailed mental representations. Therefore, what bilingual children are able to do is to inhibit attention to misleading information *of greater salience or complexity* than monolingual children can.

The statement attributes performance to an interaction between the levels demanded of conceptualization (analysis) and the levels demanded of attention (control) by placing the advantage for control within limits set by analysis. Neither factor alone sufficiently accounts for outcomes: statistically, there is no main effect. There is no evidence that bilinguals excel in the representation of complex information or that the simple requirement to switch attention or ignore misleading information inevitably leads to a bilingual advantage. Rather, the advantage is in the interaction between the demands for these processes. Put another way, a bilingual advantage in processing occurs as a function of an interaction between demands for representational analysis and demands for attentional control.

This interpretation can be placed in a larger developmental context by considering how these attentional abilities develop in childhood. Tipper and his colleagues (Tipper & McLaren, 1990; Tipper et al., 1989) have argued that attention is comprised of independent and independently developing components. One of these, inhibition, develops slowly in childhood in contrast to other aspects of attention, selection and habituation, that are as well-formed for children as for adults. Inhibition is the essential factor in distinguishing the performance of the bilingual children, so it may be that bilingualism exerts its effect selectively on the inhibition component of attention.

The development of inhibition of attention from infancy to early childhood has been studied in detail by Diamond and her colleagues (Diamond, 1991; Gerstad, Hong, & Diamond, 1994). They have shown systematic development over the first few years in children's ability to inhibit a prepotent response. Their explanation regarding the centrality of inhibition has been applied to the familiar A not B error in infancy and extended to performance on the day-night task in early childhood. In this task, children must respond "day" when shown a picture of a dark sky at night, and "night" when shown a picture of a bright sunny day. The ability to solve these problems is traced to developments in the prefrontal cortex, the seat of executive functioning, and presumably, inhibition of attention (Diamond et al., 1997).

Locating the source of inhibition of attention in the prefrontal cortex leads to an interesting extension of the argument. The performance profile obtained with bilingual children is the reverse of that reported for patients with frontal lobe damage (Burgess & Shallice, 1996; Kimberg, D'Esposito, & Farah, 1997; Luria, 1966; Perret, 1974). For these people, tasks that require switching attention, especially with distracting information, is difficult. Even automated tasks, such as Stroop tests, are difficult for these patients because they have inadequate control over attention. Kimberg, D'Esposito, and Farah (1997, p. 191) explain: "One way of describing what prefrontal-damaged patients cannot do is to say that they cannot select the appropriate response when there is more than one possible response at hand, or when the correct response is not the one that is readiest at hand."

Other groups also show predictable abilities (or disabilities) in attentional control. Hasher and Zacks (1988) propose a model of attention that includes both the excitatory mechanisms that are triggered by environmental stimuli and the inhibitory mechanisms that are required to suppress the activation of extraneous information. One of the cognitive consequences of aging is a decline in this inhibitory control. A lack of inhibitory control makes one more reliant on the familiar, practiced, and salient routines that characterize automatic responses and less able to carry out intentional thought. Furthermore, without adequate inhibition, working memory becomes cluttered with irrelevant information and decreases the efficiency of cognitive processing (Hasher, Zacks, & May, 1999). Dempster (1992) proposes a similar description but takes a longer approach to the rise and fall of these inhibitory processes over the lifespan. The consequence is that older adults have less control over the contents of working memory than do younger adults, a situation that is functionally similar to the difference between monolingual and bilingual children solving problems based on selective attention.

Another conceptualization that points to the same type of process but provides a more integrative account is offered by Duncan (1996). He relates the effects of frontal lobe lesions, differences in intelligence (defined by g), and divided attention as evidence of the same process that distinguish between active or passive control of attention. These processes are situated in the frontal lobes, making the frontal structures the seat of highly generalized forms of intelligence. If the transitive logic underlying these observations is valid, then a fanciful speculation may be worth considering: if bilingualism enhances activity of the frontal lobe, and the frontal lobe is responsible for g, then perhaps bilingualism also enhances g. This would place bilingualism back into an equation with an aspect of measured intelligence, in some sense the origin of all this research. Still, there is a vast leap of inference to arrive at this conclusion and many of the steps are without substantiation at this time. A carefully designed research program may ultimately add empirical plausibility to these speculations.

What may be less speculative is that the comparisons described above with the research literature on neuropathology and aging suggest that there may be an impact of bilingualism on some aspect of frontal lobe functioning. Hence, tasks that are most reliant on processing by the frontal lobe are solved differently by bilingual children.

The Source of Inhibition

Why would bilingualism affect this particular structure? Research on the organization of two languages in the mind of adult bilinguals has shown convincingly that both languages remain active during language processing in either language (Grainger, 1993; Grainger & Dijkstra, 1992; Guttentag, Haith, Goodman, & Hauch, 1984). Unlike earlier models that posited a "switch" that activated only the relevant language (e.g., Macnamara & Kushnir, 1971; Penfield & Roberts, 1959), this research demonstrates that the activation is distributed throughout both of the speaker's languages (discussion in Chapter 4). But if both languages are active, then how do speakers (or listeners, or readers) manage to maintain performance in only one of the languages without suffering from massive intrusions by the other? According to some researchers, the explanation is that there is a constant inhibition of the nonrelevant language, allowing the desired system to carry out the processing (Green, 1998; Kroll & De Groot, 1997). This inhibition is undoubtedly achieved by means of processes carried out in the frontal lobe. If this model is correct, then bilingual children experience extensive practice of these functions in the first few years of life, at least once both languages are known to a sufficient level of proficiency to offer viable processing systems. It would appear that this practice in inhibiting linguistic processing carries over to processing in highly disparate domains.

This explanation also lends itself to further speculation that is at this time wholly without evidence but logically connected to the premises. Suppose that the suggestion is correct and that the use of one language by a bilingual requires inhibition of the other language to avoid intrusions. Consider too that inhibition develops through childhood and declines with aging. This would mean that inhibition of the nonrelevant language is most fragile for young children and older adults, and evidence for that would be increased language intrusions by these two groups. We know that children routinely include pieces of one language in utterances designated for the other. These are described in Chapter 4 with some discussion about possible reasons. Evidence for greater intrusions by older adults is more anecdotal, but there is an intuitive sense from observation that elderly people have less control over the language they are speaking than do younger bilinguals. Also, several middle-aged bilinguals have reported to me that they find more words from the other language slipping into their speech than used to be the case. Perhaps it is the growth and decline of inhibition that is reflected in these patterns of speech.

The idea that a linguistic experience, learning two languages in child-hood, leads to a cognitive outcome, namely, enhanced attentional inhibition, that is reflected across a set of diverse tasks suggests that cognition cannot be strictly compartmentalized into domains of performance. What is most challenged by this conception is a formal theory of language that isolates a linguistic module from the rest of cognitive processes. Not only are the processes shared, but also the experience from one, language, can modify the processes that reside in the other, cognition.

There is, nonetheless, some degree of modularity in cognition. The domains of knowledge are different from each other, and the skill with which we carry out processing in them can be radically different. Someone with a gift for mathematics may not have a gift for language, and facility with spatial computations need not correspond to expertise with perceptual or musical discriminations. A principal difference between domains is in the representational structures that form the knowledge base. The process of analysis is responsible for building these up, but the outcome of analysis on representations in different domains can yield knowledge structures that are incommensurate in their richness and sophistication. In contrast, domains of cognitive functioning rely in some measure on a small set of general cognitive processes, and these processes are employed broadly. Similarity across domains is determined by the similarity of underlying cognitive processes recruited for individual tasks. Mathematical cognition, for example, may be similar in some respect to linguistic cognition, but if the representational form underlying the specific function is not similar, then there will be no transfer of effect across these domains. Although analysis and control both impact on domain-general and domain-specific aspects of cognition, analysis remains primarily responsible for the uniqueness of different domains, and control primarily responsible for uniting diverse domains under coherent processing.

It is difficult to reconcile the view of language functioning and the impact of bilingualism that emerges from this discussion with any of the conceptions of intelligence outlined at the beginning of this chapter. The psychometric approach carries the burden of dubious assumptions and flawed instruments of assessment. There is the possibility mentioned earlier that one aspect of *g*, namely, the control over attention and inhibition, is enhanced by bilingualism, but that in itself would still not translate into higher performance on standardized intelligence tests, nor should it. Following this approach, bilingualism does not make children smarter.

The componential definition is interesting because it is based on conceptions of processing and includes interactions among broad aspects of experience. But the theory is almost too broad to be falsified. Essentially, any experience that influences some intellectual outcome can be taken as being consistent with the theory, even though it was not predicted by it. It is not helpful to consider the influence of bilingualism on cognition in terms of a theory that simply accepts that influences occur, both from low-level cognitive processes and high-level experiences. More specification is necessary to understand the nature of that influence.

The multiple intelligences view relies too much on a modular conception of mind, one which is incompatible with the broad patterns of influence that bilingualism has with cognitive development. In a clearly demarcated and modular mind, a linguistic experience should not alter ability in another module, such as logical or spatial.

No theory of intelligence appears capable of predicting either the manner in which bilingualism might have its effect or the pattern of data that emerges from the research. In this sense, there is no reason to believe that bilingual children differ in intelligence from monolingual children, all else being equal. The primary difference between these groups is that one type of cognitive process, selective attention, matures more rapidly in the bilinguals. However, an examination of the effect of childhood bilingualism on cognition and its development has turned out to be a powerful tool for exploring the structure of cognition, and particularly the relation between linguistic and other forms of thought. Moreover, the investigation has reinforced the centrality of selective attention in cognition, not only in terms of its pervasive role in problem-solving, but also in terms of its amenability to modification through a common linguistic experience.

8

The Extent of the Bilingual Mind

Who is this bilingual child, the epistemic subject of the inquiry recounted in the preceding chapters? Who is the hypothetical child whose brain has been glared at and whose language has been subjected to the equivalent of linguistic spectroscopy? To whom do the dictums, conclusions, and generalizations of this book apply?

The two central points asserted in Chapter 1 were, first, that bilingualism and bilingual children are as variegated as are individuals themselves and, second, that proficiency is at best elusive and at worst impossible to define as a standard for describing linguistic mastery. Although these claims set daunting limits on the possibility of learning anything coherent about bilingual children as a group, a picture nonetheless emerges that has structure and, hopefully, validity. The picture was created by making simplifying assumptions about the variability and the methodological barriers to studying the most difficult of the questions. The task now is to relax those assumptions and explore the territory that is included in the canvas, especially on the periphery. What happens when we extend the arguments across the boundaries set out by social class, learning circumstances, and educational opportunities?

This chapter is about extensions. It is an attempt to see how the patterns described here can apply to new situations and to different questions. It also explores an implicit set of questions that adults have about child bilingualism. These include some of the issues discussed earlier as well as questions about specific educational approaches, an issue not dealt with thus far. Finally, it reflects on the contribution this research has made to the study of bilingual children to assess its broader potential to advance scientific thought.

A Matter of Class

An omission has woven its way through the pages of this book, molding the descriptions and manipulating the arguments. The omission is powerful because it can make the conclusions narrow and the declarations weak. It was committed with the best of intentions: an attempt to find simple patterns and discover underlying structure. The effect of the omission is to create a fiction, namely, that language is static and sterile, that everyone who learns and uses a language is the same, and that laboratory behavior is exactly like real life. But these statements are quickly rendered false by the reintroduction of the missing piece. The omission is a consideration of the social reality that embraces and defines every encounter with language by each individual.

Socioeconomics and Learning

Grosjean (1982) captures the essence of how social factors infiltrate the life of bilingual children by describing two children, similar in their linguistic profile but cast apart on every conceivable social dimension. Both are eight-year-old bilingual children living in the same American city. The similarities end there. One, a girl, was born in the United States and is the daughter of academic parents who decided at her birth to use their different native languages with her (Swedish and English) and to encourage her Swedish development through conversation, books, and travel. The other, a boy, was born in Haiti and immigrated to the United States when he was five years old. The social circumstances of his life prevented him from having much encounter with English. Both children entered school in the same year. The outcomes of their experiences were markedly different – the girl succeeded and the boy failed. Both children, in some measure, are bilingual, but are both children equally described by the discussion in this book? Does social context set some children apart, making their experience qualitatively different from others who also know two languages?

Until now, we have considered the bilingual child in a rather monochromatic context. For the sake of empirical reliability and theoretical prudence, we have narrowed the terms of reference and excised the protruding details that make all children, but especially bilingual children, different from each other. The trimming has not been carried out randomly: the product of this sculpting was deliberately meant to conform to some simple prototype of a comparable monolingual who was middle-class, educated, and literate, or at least potentially so. In fact, the exercise of creating this mythical "bilingual child" is almost an abrogation of the description presented in Chapter 1 that attempted to convey the complexity of bilingualism and the myriad circumstances and conditions that define it.

But what about all the other bilingual children, those whose bilingualism is attributed to immigration or political circumstance and not to the deliberate and calculated decisions of educated parents, a distinction not unlike that captured by the two children in Grosjean's (1982) story? Is the abstraction from one set of experiences to the other valid? Do children who enjoy less privilege respond in the same way as those who are more favored, learning their two languages according to the same principles, and profiting from the same cognitive benefits of bilingualism where they arise?

The problem is that the factors that define the social circumstances for bilingual children frequently impact on cognitive and linguistic development. For example, children's acquisition of literacy is strongly influenced by social conditions and educational expectations in the home (Bowey, 1995; Heath, 1983; White, 1982). If bilingual children suffer from a lack of environmental support on these dimensions, are they at even greater risk in learning to read? The analytic challenge here is to distill the effects of bilingualism from the effects of an unfavorable social environment. But this requires a further assumption. If the methodological problems could be met and the social variance isolated in the equation, it is still not clear what is being compared. One needs to assume that there is something common that persists across the variation in bilingual experiences and defines the fundamental nature of children who grow up with two languages. Is this assumption valid?

It is at least intuitively clear that the abstract construct of the "bilingual child" is coherent. Something essential is the same for children who learn about the world around them in different languages and are indoctrinated into the rules and protocols of social relationships through two systems of interaction. That is sufficient reason to justify the systematic study of the development of bilingual children. The problem is that empirical examination of this abstract construct, the bilingual child, requires ignoring all that variation that we understand to be important. The methodological principles of control and balance must be followed and the extraneous variance eradicated from the design. In other words, any investigation of the specific developmental profiles of bilingual children must be carried out in the context of monolingual children who are comparable in all ways except for their bilingualism. For this reason, the majority of the research investigates only one configuration: middle-class bilingual children living in communities similar to those of their monolingual classmates.

There is little empirical guidance for describing the development of bilingual children from other social contexts or even comparing that development across contexts. A detailed examination of these social context effects has been undertaken by the Miami group (Oller et al., 1997) discussed below, but that may be a special situation of a large Hispanic community within a majority English culture. There is nothing in the evidence to suggest that their generalizations about language and cognitive development do not apply to all bilingual children, but it is not certain that they do. The caveat for extending results from one context into another may be simply that the children actually have sufficient competence in the two languages, an issue that is discussed below. If they do, then the patterns should be identical.

It is known that social class changes the learning environment in ways that are often reflected in children's development, although an enumeration of these effects is beyond the scope of the present discussion. What is important is that the course and timeliness of children's language acquisition are marked by the social class in which the child resides. There is some evidence that social class alone affects children's vocabulary development, depressing the scores of children from lower social classes (Morisset et al., 1990). In the large-scale study by Fenson et al. (1994), they found a small but significant positive correlation between social class and productive vocabulary.

A Bilingual Disadvantage?

Bilingual children develop vocabulary more slowly than a comparison group, in this case, their monolingual peers. The evidence reviewed in Chapter 3 demonstrated that bilingual children frequently have a smaller vocabulary in each of their languages than monolinguals, at least in the first few years. It was also argued that the expressive powers of bilingual children were not compromised, even if they needed to incorporate words or expressions from another language. Nonetheless, formal measures, such as vocabulary counts, indicate a developmental lag. Does the combination of lower social class and bilingual acquisition conspire to further depress the vocabulary acquisition of lower-class bilingual children?

A comprehensive empirical study of Hispanic children in Miami conducted by Oller and his colleagues (Oller et al., 1997; Oller & Eilers, in press) includes an examination of how socioeconomic status (SES) affects the language and cognitive development of these children. They studied over 950 children at three grade levels, representing two socioeconomic classes, and attending two different kinds of schools, English immersion and two-way bilingual. There were predictable effects of SES in various areas of the work although very few interactions of SES with other factors. A particularly interesting result emerged from an interaction between SES and the language of assessment. In general, the high SES bilinguals did better on English measures than the low SES bilinguals, but the low SES bilinguals did better on Spanish measures than the high SES bilinguals. However, those were temporary results from the early and intermediate stages of language acquisition. By about the fifth grade, all the children had caught up to the levels enjoyed by the more advanced group in that language. As systematic as these results appear, Gathercole (in press, c) is cautious about their interpretation. She argues that the pattern is likely caused by the amount of exposure each group has to each language and not by some inherent advantage in being middle-class. Were that the case, then it would be expected that the middle-class bilingual children would score higher on tests in both languages, not just English. In Miami, high SES children are more likely to have greater exposure to English than low SES children, and low SES children may in turn have a greater proportion of their linguistic input in Spanish.

These results indicate that social class is not an insurmountable barrier to access the benefits of bilingualism. Oller et al. (1997) arrive at the same conclusion and state that "all the social, political and economic advantages of bilingualism are available to these children." Nonetheless, the penalty of poverty is in the time it takes for advances to occur. Children from more disadvantaged backgrounds progress more slowly and more effortfully. This was demonstrated as well in a study by Hakuta, Butler, and Witt (2000) described below. Classifying children by SES in two school districts showed large effects of poverty and parental level of education on children's progress in mastering both oral and academic uses of English. Yet, without denying that the experiences of middle-class and working-class children are substantively different from each other, the differences do not amount to a disenfranchisement of working-class children. Therefore, once the usual caution has been heeded, it appears that the extension of the results from research with middle-class children to those of more modest means is reasonable and valid.

Vocabulary development is one measure of language proficiency, but it is a limited one. As we have already seen, two somewhat diminished vocabularies need not impair communicative ability relative to monolinguals with a larger single vocabulary. The real departure from monolingual language acquisition emerges when one goes beyond the simple metric of vocabulary size. Some bilingual children develop high-level language abilities that are logically unavailable to monolinguals.

The prime example of a unique bilingual language ability is translation. There are almost no formal studies of the translation skills of bilingual children, although some authors report details of its occurrence (Harris & Sherwood, 1978; Leopold, 1970). Malakoff and Hakuta (1991) take a more systematic approach. They frame their research by describing the cognitive and linguistic demands of translation and identifying the requirements for metalinguistic ability, bilingual proficiency, and specific translation strategies. Translation, in short, is a complex process that requires elaborate skills. They report two studies in which they asked Spanish-English bilingual children (about ten years old) to translate texts and utterances under various conditions. Although not perfect, the quality of translation was extremely high. The important point, however, is that these children were socioeconomically disadvantaged in practically every way and yet displayed high levels of a sophisticated language skill. Bilingualism has its own rewards.

The studies of bilingual children in different social conditions do not allow us to dismiss the profound impact of reduced social circumstances on the development of these children. Poverty does put children at risk and a weak tradition in education reduces the escape routes for children born without access to other resources. What does seem apparent, however, is that bilingualism does not exacerbate the negativity of this experience. Similarly, bilingualism does not singularly depress the possibility that children will achieve at school, providing that the school program is designed to be responsive to the special needs of these children. This issue is discussed below. In the most clinical sense, the bilingual experience in both its rewarding (access to special language skills) and costly (slow vocabulary development) implications is experienced by all children in the same way.

Time, Timing, and Timeliness

Some people achieve bilingualism through an effort of will and others have it thrust upon them. Some children are presented with an array of languages in a linguistic smorgasbord and others are served their languages as courses, one at a time. Some people even arrive rather late to the dinner, quickly catching up on the appetizer and lingering only for dessert. And just like dinner, sometimes the satisfaction lasts through the day and sometimes the pleasure is short-lived and ephemeral. If bilingualism is represented by this meal, then how much difference do these dining preferences make? Does it matter whether the languages are served individually or together? Do the beneficial effects of bilingualism apply only to those who come to the table at a very young age? Do the effects persist through time into adulthood?

Most of the research has been based on the assumption that children's bilingualism begins in the home from almost the beginning of language acquisition and that children's competence in both languages is relatively equivalent. This may be the prevailing image of a bilingual child: one who learns to speak two languages from birth and who moves effortlessly between them as situations evolve and contexts change. But what about children who begin learning a second language later or have only limited proficiency in one of the languages? These factors of timing and proficiency are often related: unless children begin learning both languages at the same time, the knowledge of one will invariably be different from the knowledge of the other.

One at a Time?

Consider first the issue of timing. The order in which children learn languages is sometimes reflected in the distinction between simultaneous and sequential acquisition of the second language. However, there are only subjective guidelines and little consensus on what point marks the boundary between these. How coincident in time do these languages need to be learned? Meisel (1990) describes the process of learning two languages in childhood as bilingual first-language acquisition but does not explicitly specify a limit beyond which simultaneous acquisition no longer applies. McLaughlin (1978) somewhat arbitrarily sets the limit at three years old for languages to be considered as simultaneously acquired, but Padilla and Lindholm (1984) insist that both languages must be present from birth. De Houwer (1990) allows one week to intervene between the introduction of the two languages but then cautions that both languages need to be used regularly. These disputes are important for resolving methodological controversies regarding the designation of bilingualism and linguistic debates about potential influences across languages. They are less important, however, in understanding the cognitive and linguistic world of children who, at some point early in childhood, have learned to use two linguistic systems. It is this achievement, namely, the mastery of two languages, that is responsible for the consequent modifications to cognition. Therefore, it should not matter developmentally whether the two languages came into active use relatively earlier or later in the child's life. McLaughlin (1978) makes the same point and dismisses the distinction between simultaneous and successive acquisition as irrelevant to the study of bilingual children. A child of six or seven years old who becomes bilingual is a bilingual child. Everything follows from that. That position, however, may be too stark and, hence, inaccurate. In Chapter 7, it was argued that the source of the bilingual advantage for solving problems in selective attention might come from practice in inhibition, a frontal lobe function. It might also be, then, that the massive practice required for this effect can occur only in very early childhood, when the child is normally engaged in language acquisition. The experience later in childhood may be too diluted to exert this serendipitous effect.

Proficiency is different: it is clearly relevant for the manner and extent of influence that bilingualism will have on children's development. There are two dimensions on which proficiency is pertinent to the development of bilingual children. The first is the *absolute* level of proficiency in each language, that is, a judgment of the child's competence relative to native speakers; the second is the *relative* level of proficiency across the two languages, that is, an estimate of the command of each of the bilingual's languages with respect to the other. Both of these have been investigated, although the distinction between them has not always been made clear.

The threshold hypothesis proposed by Cummins (1979) is a formal attempt to incorporate proficiency levels into predictions about the effects of bilingualism. The hypothesis is primarily driven by absolute levels, but it is framed within a context that places some significance on relative proficiency. The dependent variable of the hypothesis is academic success. Three types of bilingualism, based on both the relative and absolute mastery of the two languages, are identified. In limited bilingualism, the child lacks age-appropriate skills in both languages. In partial bilingualism, the child has achieved age-appropriate proficiency in one of the two languages. Finally, proficient bilingualism is marked by normal levels in both languages. He argues that limited bilingualism leads to cognitive and academic deficits but that proficient bilingualism results in cognitive advantages.

Cummins claims that no consequences follow from partial bilingualism, but it is on this point that absolute and relative proficiency levels make different predictions. For the measures that Cummins examines, primarily academic achievement, the most critical element is that children have age-appropriate levels in one of their languages and that this language gives them access to the abstract concepts that are the currency of schooling. Therefore, the relevant contrast is between children who have such facility in at least one language (partial bilingualism and proficient bilingualism) and children who do not (limited bilingualism). In contrast, research into cognitive, but not necessarily academic, consequences of bilingualism have used more subtle and arguably more arcane instruments of assessment. In this research, the important question is whether bilingualism adds benefits beyond those enjoyed by comparable children, not those at risk. The relevant contrast groups here are bilingual children with age-appropriate language skills in one language (partial bilingualism) versus bilingual children with age-appropriate language skills in both languages (proficient bilingualism). None of these children is at risk of academic failure, as Cummins rightly points out. Nonetheless, their bilingualism has had different impacts on subtle aspects of their developing cognitive profiles.

Some research with bilingual children who are not balanced in their relative language proficiency but are sufficiently skilled in one of the languages (cf. partial bilinguals) has sometimes reported positive cognitive effects for these children (e.g., Bialystok, 1988; Cromdal, 1999; Hakuta & Diaz, 1985; Yelland, Pollard, & Mercuri, 1993). In fact, Hakuta and Diaz (1985) showed that the greatest gains to cognitive and metalinguistic insights came in the earliest stages of being bilingual, when proficiency in the two languages was most asymmetrical. None of this research contradicts the point made by Cummins regarding the essential need for language proficiency to minimally place children in the domain of having access to academic language skills. The important point is that children have not been found to suffer any disadvantages from learning and using two languages, even in academic settings, providing that one of their languages is established to a level appropriate for children their age. McLaughlin (1978) even claims that there may be no negative consequence if the instruction is carried out in the child's weaker language, the one that is not developed to age-appropriate levels (contradicting the warnings of Macnamara, 1966) as long as the level is *sufficient* to function in the instructional setting.

A related question is how skills developed in one language can be transferred to the other. The question is particularly important for children who have one stronger and one weaker language, and even more crucial when schooling is in the weaker language. Again, it is Cummins (1991) who has contributed significantly to this question. He reviews a large number of studies that compare the oral and academic language proficiency of children in their first language and the level of skill they acquire in each of these domains in their second language. These studies cover many language pairs and many instructional models. For academic uses of language, such as reading, there tend to be moderately strong correlations between the level of skill attained in both languages. Cummins attributes these relationships to the underlying cognitive involvement in development these skills. For oral uses of language, the correspondence between children's competence in the two languages depends more on individual child attributes, such as personality and interaction style.

Part of the explanation for the transfer of skills across languages, as well as their lack of transfer, can be found again in the threshold hypothesis. Cummins' (1979) review of the literature shows that the detrimental effect of the lower threshold (lack of adequate competence in both languages) on academic achievement is well established. The reason is that there is no language in which children are able to establish the cognitive systems that are at the base of academic functioning. Even setting up these concepts in one language would permit their transfer to the other. The principle is the same whether the child is learning one or two languages: cognitive structures require the establishment of particular concepts, and these concepts require linguistic support.

These relations may appear circular but they illustrate that both absolute and relative proficiency levels are decisive in determining how the bilingual experience will affect children's academic and cognitive development. The positive cognitive consequences of bilingualism emerge when children control a reasonably balanced and competent mastery of the two languages. Although some cognitive processes have been shown to be enhanced from asymmetrical configurations of language competence, these effects are less reliable than are those that accompany regular and equivalent use of two languages. These effects of balance between languages appear more decisive than does the effect of time, namely, whether the two languages were acquired together. Admittedly, however, no research has established this. As long as children ultimately master the two languages across the relevant contexts of use (home, school), it should not matter that they learned one before the other. Even under ideal conditions, bilingual children go through different periods of favoring one or the other of their languages. Therefore, to some extent the notion of simultaneity in the acquisition of two languages is irrelevant.

For education to either profit from children's bilingualism or escape impairment because of it, the absolute proficiency level of at least one language is crucial. Considering only educational outcomes, the balance between the two languages is less critical than is the need for one of them to be developed to a level that is sufficient for schooling. But again, the timing for achieving that proficiency does not seem to matter.

Timing and proficiency, therefore, are two dimensions that distinguish among some of the configurations in which children learn two languages. Timing, the question of whether the languages should be learned one at a time or together, is probably not very important in the long run. Proficiency, however, does matter. Therefore, we can return to the question of the likely impact on a child who is moved to a different country and begins school in a different language from that spoken in the home. The child's weaker language may be either the one spoken at home or the one used in school. It is improbable that any academic consequence would follow from having some, even minimal, competence in a language that was not the language of schooling, but it is very consequential to consider the effect of having limited competence in the language of school. In Chapters 6 and 7, the prototypical case under discussion was one in which children were bilingual by virtue of speaking two languages at home but educated in a language that was safely established. (That is not the situation for children in bilingual education programs discussed below). Although bilingual advantages were only found in specialized circumstances, there were never any disadvantages.

Consider the following situation: An educated middle-class family living in Berlin is about to move to Los Angeles because of a career opportunity for the mother. (Let's assume she was offered an important chair at a famous university and her husband has agreed to find work as a sales clerk or, better still, to stay at home and take are of the house). Their only child is four years old and speaks only German. The parents will continue to speak German at home because that is what is natural, but the child will enter school and begin to learn English. What will happen to the child and what should the parents do?

The indications are that the child will do just fine. She will learn English from the environment (because she will likely socialize with English-speaking children), from television, and from kindergarten. Kindergarten will require sufficient English to build the academic foundation for her education. By the time she starts first grade, she will probably have enough English upon which to build an academic base, although her English skills will be weaker than those of her native-speaking classmates. While her classmates are learning about letters, numbers, and the names of dinosaurs, she will additionally be learning the forms and structures of English, but the burden will not be onerous. If it is, or if she is slightly older and has not had the time to master English to levels appropriate for the grade, then some ESL training would be helpful. The parents will, of course, be worried that the child's English places her at a disadvantage and possibly consider imposing English as the language of the home. That would be unfortunate. Surrounded by her supportive environment and felicitous educational circumstances, English will develop in due course. Although there may be initial delays, there is no reason to expect any ultimate handicap in academic success.

The Learning Latency

But what does "in due course" mean? How long should it take children to acquire a level of proficiency in the school language that allows them to function and thrive in an academic environment? Many of our attitudes, expectations, and policies are based on some implicit notion of how long it is prudent to allow children to gain language proficiency before we judge them by the standards set out for the system. During that time, we make allowances and evaluate them by relative rather than absolute standards, accepting progress itself as the measure of success. This is the difference between the standards set by norm-referenced and criterion-referenced assessments discussed in Chapter 1. But school success is ultimately determined by the absolute (criterion-referenced) standards of the institution. Parents want their children to do well; they do not want them to do well *for an immigrant.*

A large-scale study by Hakuta, Butler, and Witt (2000) examined this question for immigrant children in California. They tested children in two school districts that had high proportions of nonnative English-speaking children. The two districts also differed in their socioeconomic standing, one being more middle-class (district A) than the other (district B). In district A, the more affluent of the two, the study included all the children who had been designated LEP (limited English proficiency) when they entered kindergarten and were between first and sixth grades at the time of testing. This sample included 1,872 children. In district B, a sample of 122 children in grades one, three, and five were selected according to the same criteria, namely, that they entered the school district in kindergarten and were designated LEP. Unfortunately, the testing instruments used in the two districts were not the same so direct comparison between the two districts can be made only cautiously. Still, the design had merits that are largely absent in other evaluations of this type, especially more informal ones. Notably, assuring that all children entered the school district in kindergarten controlled the age at which English was introduced. If there are any effects of age on the ability and success of learning another language, they were not influencing the results of this study. Minimally, then, the study provides a means of assessing the length of time it took children to reach levels of English that were comparable with native speakers. As a secondary issue, some insight into the role of social class could be gleaned.

The results for the two districts were comparable although the learning latencies were different. In district A, children's test scores were compared with the norm achieved by the native English-speaking students in the same district. By the end of grade four (representing five years of schooling), over 90 percent of the LEP students had achieved oral English proficiency that was comparable to their native-speaking peers. The range of time needed to arrive at this level was two to five years. Academic English proficiency took longer; the 90 percent criterion was not reached until the end of grade six and the range of time needed was four to seven years. The tests used in district B compared children's performance to native speaker norms rather than to classmates in the school district. The LEP children in this board had a more difficult time reaching criterion and the gap between their performance and native speakers actually widened throughout the period examined. In grade three, they were about one year behind the norm in various reading measures, but by grade five they were two years behind. Many differences between the districts, however, prevent a direct comparison of these achievement levels. Some of the factors are economic levels, types of programs available, and nature of the tests used. The general conclusions from this study are that children can reach both age- and peer-referenced norms for English but that it takes time. The first two or three years are a time of rapid growth, but the curve rises at a slower rate for many years after.

Hakuta (1999) states: "When strict comparisons are made that control for the background factors, children learn English at the same rate regardless of the kinds of programs they are in, i.e., instruction through the native language does not slow down student acquisition of English. It takes most students 2 to 5 years to attain a level of English that does not put them at a disadvantage in regular instruction. Their rate of acquisition of English depends on the level of development of native language – children with strong native language skills learn English rapidly. Motivation to learn English is uniformly high both among parents and the students."

Cummins (1991) reported a similar pattern by surveying a range of studies carried out in different countries. His conclusion was that it took about two years for children to reach peer-appropriate conversational skills and four years to achieve grade norms in English academic skills. All these children were in socioeconomically advantaged situations, similar in some respects to the children in district A or to the more advantaged children in both districts when the data were disaggregated by social position. Similarly, Collier (1987) proclaimed that five years were needed to achieve adequate proficiency for school success. These estimates are at the low end of those reported by Hakuta, Butler, and Witt (2000), but the criteria for academic adequacy may have been set to a lower standard.

Into the Future

Bilingualism obviously makes a difference. It changes children's lives. Children who are being educated in a weak language need to learn the subject material and the language at the same time. Raising children as bilinguals will likely delay their vocabulary growth in at least one of the languages and may set them apart from monolingual peers who speak that language. Children who live in a bilingual and bicultural world have a different perspective that may not only influence arcane cognitive and linguistic skills but also challenge their world views and social identity. These consequences of bilingualism appear to be intangible and to defy quantification and measurement. Bilingualism also alters aspects of cognitive processing, sometimes to the detriment of bilingual children. Bilinguals, for example, displayed slower retrieval processes for mental arithmetic and confusion in the early stages of literacy acquisition if the two languages were written in different ways. Still, the penalty of bilingualism in these examples is minimal: bilingual children (and adults) can presumably still do mental arithmetic at normal speeds in their stronger language, and the confusion about writing systems disappeared by the time children were five years old.

The vast majority of cognitive differences were advantageous to the bilingual children. This is easily accepted as a positive effect, and assurance of a cognitive benefit would conceivably tip the scales away from some of the potential hazards of bilingualism. The research that revealed this effect was conducted with young children, often in preschool years, solving simple contrived tasks. In this respect, the interpretation claiming a cognitive victory for bilingualism may be both lofty and hasty. It would be important to know whether the differences observed in childhood persist through adolescence and even adulthood.

The main barrier to answering this question is methodological. The tasks used to uncover differences in attention and inhibition that indicated a bilingual advantage are inappropriate even for older children. They are based on simple paradigms and simple decisions, capturing the elements of processing without demanding specialized knowledge. These are tasks that children are learning to solve in the years studied, and the empirical approach was to study the process of learning how to do these tasks. The evidence for the advantage was simply that bilingual children learned to solve them earlier, often by about one year. These tasks will detect nothing about the cognitive processes of older children because such children will not make errors – monolingual and bilingual children will solve them equally and proficiently.

The obvious adaptation for older children would be to make the tasks more difficult – create versions of these problems that would *not* be solved perfectly. That tactic may not be possible. Making the tasks more difficult would require introducing more cognitively challenging content. In that case, children's ability to solve the problems would be less clearly based on their control over attention and inhibition but additionally involve their knowledge and strategic abilities. Gaps in one could be compensated by strengths in another. Therefore, complex problems do not easily provide access to pure measures of simple cognitive processes.

In spite of these difficulties, there is evidence that the advantage found in attention and inhibition persists at least until children are eight years old (Bialystok & Majumder, 1998). That study used tasks that were more complex than those normally employed with younger children but still relatively free of the need for special knowledge. Further exploration of this question, however, will require more creative methods.

There are two possible approaches to investigating this question. The first is to continue within the same paradigm by creating more complex tasks while holding constant the basic operations underlying the solution. Although theoretically feasible, it may not be logically possible. The tasks work precisely because they are cognitively simple and isolate specific processes. Tasks that are more complex and graduated to assess performance across a larger range include traditional assessments of intelligence and standardized measures of ability, such as Ravens Progressive Matrices. These tasks are unlikely to yield bilingual differences, and, in fact, are often used in research to demonstrate intellectual equivalence between groups. Therefore, it is hard to see how test development that recapitulates the tasks used with younger populations could investigate the same processes and seek the same differences in older ones.

The second possibility is to maintain the tasks but change the methodology. Errors in children's performance are often mirrored by the need for longer latencies in older subjects. In other words, there is a negative correlation between the accuracy of a response and the time needed to make it. Reaction time data with children are notoriously unreliable because the variability in response time is so high. Very young children do not focus their attention as assiduously as older children and adults do in spite of one's best efforts to instruct them to do so. Conversely, older children and adults rarely make errors on the tasks used with young children but may require slightly more decision time for some of the more difficult items. Reaction times measured in milliseconds may be sensitive enough to reveal these differences. Therefore, it may be productive to investigate these questions with older bilinguals by adapting the research paradigms to obtain reaction time measures for the solution to similar problems.

At present, there is not sufficient empirical ground to generate sound projections about the duration of these cognitive effects, but the question resonates throughout the research. Knowing the ultimate trajectory of these developments would help us to understand the significance of the small changes in the way young children process information because they happen to be bilingual.

Educating Children

The struggle over how to best serve the school-aged population of nonnative speakers is not new and not confined to the United States, although it is in that place and time that the arguments are being expounded most vociferously. The controversies and potential solutions, however, have long precedence and the fashion for particular resolutions rotates cyclically. Some of the history of the experience in the United States is recounted by August and Hakuta (1997). Their report documents the educational policy for bilingual students in the nineteenth century, beginning with the establishment of German (and other language) medium schools in the early part of the century, their subsequent demise, and their reappearance a generation later. Throughout all these vicissitudes, the arguments, justifications, and demands that were raised by parents, educators, and politicians are strikingly familiar.

Bilingual Education

The current battle in the United States is over the types of programs that should be offered to children with limited English. The most notable of these programs is bilingual education. Bilingual education, however, is one of the great misnomers in educational parlance. Hakuta and Mostafapour (1996) point out that the term is applied primarily to programs whose goal it is to bring LEP students up to a level that will allow them to function in English classrooms. Bilingualism is neither a goal of the programs nor a valued attribute of its students. Snow and Hakuta (1992, p. 390) even claim that the effect, if not the goal, is the opposite: "What it fosters is monolingualism; bilingual classrooms are efficient revolving doors between home-language monolingualism and English monolingualism." In fact, once children achieve bilingualism, at least in terms of establishing proficiency in English, they are required to exit from the program. This policy persists in spite of the fact that research has shown that transitional bilingual education is associated with "lower levels of second language proficiency, scholastic underachievement, and psychosocial disorders" (Hakuta & Mostafapour, 1996, p. 42).

Brisk (1998) makes a similar point and describes the difference in the way the term "bilingual education" is used in different countries. In the United States, bilingual education refers to the education of children whose home language is not English; elsewhere it refers to education in two valued languages. It is common for European countries to offer bilingual education schools where children are instructed in two languages, some subjects being taught in each. Normally, one of the languages will be the national language (English, French, German) and the other will be another high-prestige language. The children attending the school either are native to the country and therefore learning the other language or one of the other languages and are learning the national language. In some cases, such as Wales, bilingual schools function in a bilingual environment: Welsh language schools serve communities in which Welsh and English are equally spoken. The intention in these European examples is to instill high proficiency levels in both instructional languages, even if one of them is not an official language of that country.

There are many options for organizing bilingual programs, some of which coexist in the same countries. Brisk distinguishes between two major types of programs and lists a number of alternatives for each. The first is called Bilingual Education Models and includes programs in which there is an effort to use two languages for instruction and (theoretically) teach children competence in both languages. The examples are dual-language schools (e.g., international schools, the United Nations School in New York City), Canadian immersion education, two-way bilingual education (which includes minority-language and English-speaking children), two-way bilingual immersion, maintenance bilingual education, transitional bilingual education, submersion with native language and ESL support, bilingual immersion education, and integrated bilingual education. The second is English-only Instruction Models, programs in which little or no attention is paid to the native language of the children entering the program. These include ESL programs and structured immersion (sheltered English).

The predominant model for programs in the United States is transitional bilingual education. Brisk places this model in the first category in which two languages are theoretically incorporated into the program, but practically it functions as an example of the second type. The purpose is to provide children with enough English to move quickly into the monolingual mainstream.

Program evaluations have consistently favored models that allow children to develop their native language to high levels of proficiency in conjunction with learning English (Hakuta, 1999; Shannon, 1999; Snow, 1990; UNESCO, 1953). Willig (1985) conducted a meta-analysis of twenty-three bilingual education programs in the United States. She found an overall advantage in both English and Spanish criterion tests for children who were in bilingual programs, although the size of the effect depended on factors such as the type of program and the academic domain of the criterion test. She tentatively endorses a model of alternate immersion, in which each language is used exclusively for a portion of the day, rather than concurrent translation, where both languages are available throughout the day.

With the range of program options that are available, why do schools in the United States continue to favor the one least supported by research? Brisk (1998) offers a conclusion that is perhaps cynical but worth considering. She claims that the real debate is not about the programs but about who is entitled to enter them: "Bilingual education is actually thriving for English speakers in public schools. That such programs grow as attacks on bilingual education for language minority students intensify reinforces the impression that for many in the educational establishment, bilingualism is a luxury best afforded by those who already speak English" (Brisk, 1998, p. 30).

Part of the problem is that the American debate on bilingual education takes place in a social context that explicitly denigrates the home language of the children. Specifically, the movement for English Only (see e.g., Shannon, 1999) is the backdrop against which children attend school with another language (usually Spanish) and are delivered programs that are influenced and shaped by that political debate. Shannon (1999, p. 179) states: "In the absence of an official language policy and in the debate for such a policy, U.S. society has shifted to an ideology of English monolingualism."

The discussion about the correct policy for immigrant children who need to learn English while they attend school often degenerates into a series of mythological stereotypes and half-truths about the past. Stories about the immigrant experience of previous generations where children entered school without knowing any English and achieved great success (the American Dream) are often laid before the proponents of bilingual education as evidence of the superfluousness of these programs. Aside from the obvious admonition about the real truth behind the "good old days" and hyperbolic claims about the number of such children who succeeded (see Snow, 1990), the situations are not comparable.

Cohen (1970) reviews a large database and confirms that many immigrants did do very well in American public schools in the early decades of the twentieth century. Several factors, however, make these success stories irrelevant to the current debate. The level of education, especially in the areas of literacy skills, that is a prerequisite for success have changed dramatically in the past two generations. Additionally, the socioeconomic status (although not necessarily the wealth) of immigrants has changed, and the effects of social background, minority ethnicity, parental education levels, and expectations for children's educational levels are all known to influence children's success in schools. These factors place the majority of Hispanic children in the United States at risk irrespective of the educational program (Padilla, 1990; Snow, 1990). Finally, as discussed above, there were in fact bilingual education programs available in the past, although not necessarily widely so. Although it is compelling to look to these "success stories" of the past, they have little bearing on the current debate. The conditions were different in terms of both school experience and future prospects, and we have no idea how many students either failed in school or achieved less than their potential because their English was insufficient for the task. Those students are not included in the grand stories of the past glory.

Other countries, too, have struggled with decisions about bilingual education, especially regarding the assimilation of immigrants into a society. Israel, for example, has always been a country of immigrants and has continually had to confront the challenge of educating children who did not speak Hebrew. There has been a modest shift in ideology over the past fifty years from expecting Hebrew to replace the child's first language to some measure of acknowledging the importance of maintaining the first language (Spolsky & Shohamy, 1999). A serious commitment to this latter outcome, however, would require bilingual education classes, and these do not exist. The main problem with establishing efficient and effective programs for immigrant children in Israel is that the system is handled in a piecemeal fashion. The immigration comes from different places, with different cultures, at different periods of time, bringing different numbers of children. Once children have been declared eligible for special programs by the Ministry of Education, the programs that are available are determined by local authorities. As in the United States, the options cover a range of models, including intensive language instruction followed by mainstreaming and language instruction on a withdrawal basis. Although the formal evaluation of these programs in terms of children's language learning and academic success is still in progress (Spolsky & Shohamy, 1999), the results do not seem promising. There is a high drop-out rate for immigrants as they struggle in classes with native speakers. As in the United States, the program deemed most effective by research is not the program most likely to be implemented.

Relationship to Achievement

How can we reconcile the alternative view to determine which educational program is the most efficacious for children whose knowledge of the community language is weak or nonexistent? Those who advocate placing children in mainstream schools as quickly as possible make the sensible point that future success in both school and beyond depends on mastery of the community language. This language, they insist, is best learned in school with all the other children who speak that language, and they may also point to examples of other immigrant groups who succeeded under these conditions. Those who advocate bilingual education programs that function in the child's home language, introducing the community language only gradually over a long period of time, point to research that indicates higher levels of achievement for these children across all school subjects, including skill in the community language. These positions are so different they are almost contradictory, yet both sides can support their arguments with evidence. How is this possible?

There is no dispute about the ultimate goals in terms of both linguistic and academic success for children who are not native speakers of the school language. The debate is about the best strategy for achieving those goals. The problem is that the formal evidence and informal anecdotes that are recruited in support of each position describe children who are rooted in different social and cultural contexts. These factors are crucial ingredients in the prognosis for children's success.

The key to understanding the impact of these educational programs may be in the assertion that success in school occurs when children "develop the native language to high levels of proficiency" (see above). For children who live in communities where education and achievement are strongly encouraged and the home is integrally involved with children's education, children can develop the required linguistic competence in the native language and a positively motivated attitude toward school at home. When these children attend school in the community language, even if that language is not spoken at home, their adaptation is relatively straightforward and often successful. For children who live in communities where these conditions are not equally present, then the school must provide a more supportive and motivating environment to encourage the children and assist them in the educational challenges they face. These children are more likely to profit from bilingual education programs because their chances of success without this support are less certain than they are for children whose families support their education. This is the same argument that was used decades ago to explain how Canadian children in French immersion programs suffered no negative consequence of being educated in a non-home language while countless immigrant children suffered from that linguistic disparity.

Another dimension in evaluating bilingual education is the long-term effect on children's competence in the native language. Again, the home environment is crucial. In a home context that supports high levels of native language use, including the literate forms of that language, children are not at risk of losing their competence with that language as English develops and eventually dominates. In families that offer a less privileged educational environment, children benefit from school support to develop and maintain the native language.

The point is that bilingual education is one possible solution for educating minority children. Although some children succeed without such intervention, others require the structure it provides. Educational policies and instructional programs cannot be pitched at a generic level that is assumed to fit all children – one size generally fits no one. The social context requires different solutions for different kinds of children. It is certainly not necessary to provide bilingual education for all children from all backgrounds, but the data clearly demonstrate its benefits for children who need the supportive environment and linguistic structure that are part of a bilingual classroom. This has been shown for both learning English and keeping their own language. Educational programs must incorporate at least some of the diversity reflected by the children they are designed to serve.

Who Am I?

It is easy to accept that language is social culture – it is intimately connected with the style and sensibility of a community, embodying the rules of social interaction and transmitting the ritual and wisdom of generations. Equally, however, it stands as the expression of the individual – I am what I speak. We believe that because speaking is so fundamental to our constructed identity. We describe people in terms of their interactive discourse styles – gregarious, taciturn, inscrutable. Do we alter our identity and modify our personality when we change our language?

We sometimes think of national characteristics but resist (or should resist) applying those descriptions to the individuals who comprise the community. To what extent, though, are those national characteristics a reflection of either the language or conventions for speech that define the group? If these features were embedded in the language and its rules of use, then it would not be surprising if speakers of that language conveyed those same characteristics. As an extension, anyone who learned to speak the language, especially (but maybe only) to a high degree of proficiency, would also reflect that image. Are personalities also language-specific and transmitted with the sounds and structures of a linguistic code? Are they even shaped by languages? And, more mischievously, do people who speak two languages command two personalities?

As we have seen before, learning a language is much more than learning syntax. A competent language learner will additionally master the social conventions and conversational styles that the language incorporates. It is these conventions for framing intentions and styles for interacting in social contexts that embody the personality of the language, the culture, and the individual speaker. Consider, then, some of the ways that language can define the individual.

Languages differ on dimensions such as rules of formality, politeness, and indirectness. A systematic description of these linguistic characteristics is one of the objectives of pragmatic analysis. Some languages have a formal (Polish) or complex (Hindu) system of address terms; some languages require requests to be couched in layers of obfuscation (Japanese) and others are brutally direct (Hebrew). Speakers who learn and comply with these rules may well feel themselves to be reacting in socially distinct ways when they use different languages.

Put this way, the illusion of personality transformations with the adoption of another language is partly a function of proficiency level in that new language. Proficient speakers will obey the nonlinguistic rules of use, including turn-taking, deference rules, and formality restrictions, just as carefully as they will the structural rules of grammar. A detailed study of some of these differences and how second-language learners gradually master the relevant forms is presented in the collection by Kasper and Blum-Kulka (1993). A very proficient speaker of a language whose rules of use differ from the native language in these ways, therefore, may *feel* like a different person.

Just as high proficiency in the second language can signal a change in the speakers' style or personality, so too can low proficiency alter the impression conveyed by the speaker. The limitations of poor command of a language restrict the speaker's ability to freely express individuality. A common example is jokes – a high level of competence is needed to use the language playfully, and bilingual speakers do not necessary achieve that in all their languages. Second-language learners frequently lament their inability to express certain ideas and opinions, but the more frustrating experience is in misrepresenting their individuality. To the extent that our social personalities are expressed through our verbal interactions (which is, of course, only part of how this takes place), limited language proficiency can interfere with presentation of the speaker's image.

These examples illustrate the way that adapting to the sociocultural conventions of each language and functioning within a specified range of proficiency (whether high or low) can give the illusion of transforming the personality of the speaker. But what is it really like for the speaker? Does the world actually look different to a bilingual speaker who knows two languages that establish different classifications and different priorities for the world? Anecdotally, bilingual adults sometimes report that they interact differently and respond differently when they are speaking one of their languages. In a sense, they see the social world differently. A bilingual Japanese-English speaker, K., described the language-specific control over human reactions such as refusal and anger. She acknowledged that she would sometimes select a language of interaction to fortify her position in a situation. Although all these styles are indeed a part of her own personality, she is able to manipulate them for social outcomes by choosing the language she will speak. Negotiation is more constrained in Japanese and anger comes more readily in English.

These examples, and indeed, most of the research, come from adults. What about children? The problem is most troubling for children because competence in the second language is low, the rules of use have not been fully mastered, and expression is restricted by incomplete knowledge of the language. How will children function in situations where they lack the proficiency to interact appropriately? These children risk being set apart from the mainstream majority not only linguistically, but also culturally and interactively, and perhaps ethnically as well. These circumstances may be a breeding ground for responses as apparently benign as social withdrawal or as aggressive and dangerous as violence.

Rampton (1995) has documented some of the sociolinguistic processes in a multiracial urban youth culture. The adolescents in his study lived in the same city in England and spoke Punjabi, Creole, and Stylized Asian English. His analysis is based on four descriptive dimensions: language, interaction structures, institutional organization, and knowledge about social groups. The primary unit of analysis is code-switching, specifically, the choices these youths make regarding which language to speak. The choices are important because these adolescents deal with limited language proficiency and individual social rules of use for each of their languages. The rules underlying language choice reveal an important dimension in the lives of these socially struggling bilinguals and provide a starting point for explaining their typically antisocial behavior. He concludes by commenting on how the "street bilingualism" of these adolescents contrasts with official educational policy: "In England, . . . there is no encouragement for cultivation of bilingualism through a child's educational career and there is no scope for bilingual education using minority community languages as media of instruction" (Rampton, 1995, p. 326). Sadly, it appears that these bilinguals are made to suffer socially because of their facility with some languages (Punjabi) and their limited proficiency in others (English). These forces are reflected in the personalities of the adolescents he studied.

Does language affect personality? It is possible (but not necessary) for truly bilingual speakers to live in different persona. It may even become possible for them to manipulate these to their advantage. However, much of the apparent different in personality is a façade that comes with the grammar of the language

Lessons for Cognition

Bilingual children are different from monolinguals. The differences are evident in the way they acquire language, their experiences in school, and their socialization with their peers. It is the fact that they are distinct on so many dimensions that makes the empirical study of their development so tangled – as Grosjean (1989) so aptly noted: "Bilinguals are not two monolinguals in one." Partly for this reason, bilinguals also provide a unique opportunity to study cognition and its development in a configuration that is normal in every respect yet set apart from the traditional in systematic ways. The presence of two language systems cascades through children's developing mental lives and highlights pieces of that development that are usually invisible. What can we learn about the fundamental questions of cognitive science by studying the development of bilingual children? We consider the potential contribution to three questions: the nature of linguistic knowledge, the organization of cognitive processes, and the functional structure of the brain.

Language

Linguists, for the most part, live in a world of abstractions. The principal debates in linguistic theory are centered on the search for the correct description, including what language properly includes, how it is represented in the mind, and how it is connected to the rest of knowledge. The major divide on all these issues is the one that separates formal (generative grammar, learnability) from functional (cognitive grammar, construction grammar) theories (described in Chapter 2).

Studies of children's language acquisition have often been used to adjudicate the debate by offering evidence of either the effortless unfolding of language in the face of poor learning models (formal) or the crucial dependencies between language learning and nonverbal environmental contingencies (functional). Nonetheless, no single piece of evidence from any perspective has silenced the legitimate objections of the other. Studying bilingual children adds a dimension to this debate that elevates the argument on both sides.

There are two insights about language that emerge from the careful study of the development of bilingual children in the preschool and early school years. The first is that the acquisition of language follows the precepts set out by both the formal descriptions of structure and the functional descriptions of communication. The second is that language is not isolated from the rest of cognition in the modular structure envisaged by formal theorists.

Consider first the contribution of bilingual children's language learning experiences to the support of both formal and functional models of language acquisition. The emphasis of formal theories of language acquisition is on the universality and inevitability of the process for young children. The template for linguistic structure is part of children's biological heritage, and in the presence of supportive linguistic input, this template will expand into an elaborated structure that constrains the language the child is learning. In support of this view, bilingual children being raised in different kinds of environments from their monolingual peers and being the recipients of qualitatively and quantitatively different exposure to that language still progress through the fabric of syntax in much the same way as monolinguals. The match is not perfect, but the analyses documented by Meisel and his colleagues (Meisel, 1990, 1994) illustrate the close fit between the progression in grammatical knowledge made by children learning both German and French and children learning just one of those languages. For this pattern to assert itself there must be some set of constraints that make language acquisition universal and assured. Additionally, the fact that bilingual children from about two years old understand that their two languages are separate systems attests to the integrity of linguistic knowledge and the certainty of its acquisition.

Acknowledgement of a biological preparedness, however, does not lead irrevocably to the acceptance of innate linguistic knowledge as the constraining mechanism. The illusion of innate structure could be created equally by limitations in cognitive processing that set the sequence by which knowledge can be acquired. Fodor (1998) points out that nativism can be separated from the Neo-Darwinian adaptation account of how the mind evolved and how the innate modules appeared that is argued by Pinker (1997). Even some connectionists, for whom nativist premises are theoretically anathema, acknowledge a role for predetermined settings and organically prepared biases. The view proposed by Elman et al. (1996), described in Chapter 2, is at the very least interactionist: "[I]nnate refers to changes that arise as a result of interactions that occur within the organism itself during ontogeny" (p. 22). Minimally, bilingual children make it clear that the acquisition of the formal components of language structure is not random but unfolds according to a plan that is largely universal. Any account of children's language acquisition must include some element of a nativist story.

Consistent with the divide that was placed between formal and functional theories in Chapter 2, the primary territory for formal theories is syntax, and it is syntax that is most subject to internal constraints. The domain in which functionalist theories offered the most satisfactory accounts was communication, including vocabulary and pragmatic rules of use. A notable difference in the language acquisition of monolingual and bilingual children is that the latter are often delayed in vocabulary for each language compared with monolinguals who speak only that language. Furthermore, the nature and extent of vocabulary that children build up in each language is sensitive to the contextual circumstances in which the language is used. What functionalist theories are able to account for is the shape of the developing language. Functional analyses identify the contingencies between interactive experiences in the child's developing cognitive life and the emergence of language. In a purely functional account of language acquisition, this developing vocabulary is also the means by which children learn syntax.

These associations between features of bilingual language development and linguistic theory underline the need for interactive accounts of language. For bilingual children, each language develops in response to social and interactive conditions in the child's environment. Questions such as the level to which each language will develop, the degree of language mixing that will occur, and the pragmatic models for selecting a language and switching between them indicate the need for the conditions described by functionalist accounts of language acquisition. The constraints on these developments are fixed by formal accounts of linguistic structure.

The grammar of bilingual children develops in much the same way as the grammar of monolinguals learning each language, but the communicative aspects of language, including vocabulary acquisition, do not. This dissociation between two domains of language acquisition reinforces the need for different kinds of explanations for these aspects of language and underlines the inadequacies of each to provide a complete account of language acquisition on its own. These dissociations could not be discovered if empirical study were based only on the course of acquisition for monolingual children.

The second point about language to be learned from the study of bilingual children is that it seems implausible that language is a functionally isolated module in the cognitive landscape. This isolation is required by formal theories to assure that the innate components of language, whatever they are defined to be, can unfold efficiently. However, evidence for the integration of linguistic representations with children's general knowledge follows from the studies showing that there is influence on cognition that comes from the experience of learning two languages. One cognitive advantage of bilingualism discussed in Chapter 7 is the enhanced ability to selectively attend to information and to inhibit misleading cues. These are cognitive procedures, and their stimulation by the experience of learning two languages indicates that the same cognitive mechanisms that monitor the learning and use of language are implicated as well in other cognitive tasks. Across the studies examining cognitive and nonverbal aspects of development, there is little evidence for modularity in language proficiency.

Cognition

The search for cognitive differences in bilingual children has occupied researchers for several decades. One of the problems with this enterprise is that the cognitive effects that were examined were not driven by any particular theory of cognitive functioning or its development. General hypotheses referring to abstractions such as the intelligence of bilingual children or the ability to think flexibly and creatively were investigated and sometimes supported. The problem is that the results could not be interpreted in any framework that explained how cognition worked or why these effects were expected.

The most consistent empirical finding about the cognition of bilingual children, reported in Chapter 7, is their advantage in selective attention and inhibition. The study of attention and inhibition has been an active area of research in adult cognition and neuropsychology. In these studies, the process of inhibition has been attributed to the prefrontal lobe and assigned a central role in cognitive functioning. Further, the decline of this attentional function is symptomatic of aging (Hasher & Zacks, 1988) and damage to the prefrontal cortex (Kimberg, D'Esposito, & Farah, 1997). Evidence from bilingual children that these same processes are enhanced by the experience of learning two languages adds a further dimension to those studies. Identifying an enhancing experience that alters this process leads to the construction of a more complete account. Virtually all the other discussions of these attention and inhibition functions are concerned with disabling factors. It is potentially significant to discover that a specific experience, namely, childhood bilingualism, accelerates its development. Such evidence will ultimately be useful in coming to understand this central cognitive function.

If practice in selective attention and inhibition of the nonrelevant language turns out to be the mechanism that gives rise to cognitive differences in bilinguals, there may be a consequent limitation of this effect. We know that attention and inhibition are most taxing for responses that are most similar and draw on overlapping representations. It may be that oral and signed languages do not compete for the same representational and response resources in this way. That would mean that bilingual individuals who know both a signed and a spoken language do not have the same need to constantly inhibit the nonrelevant language since the modality difference makes its representation less competing. In this case, bilingualism in languages that are based on different modalities may define a case in which bilingualism provides the social and experiential effects but not the cognitive ones. This is speculative because adequate evidence is unavailable. Hauser (1996), however, summarizes research indicating that there are overlapping cortical regions engaged in both signed and spoken languages and that there is impairment and aphasia in signed languages when damage occurs to these areas. Hence, the neural substrate of spoken and signed languages may be sufficiently similar to present the same conflict and need for inhibition as that accompanying two spoken languages. In that case, these bilinguals may well reap the same benefit as those who have mastered two spoken languages. Further research, as they say, is needed.

Brain

The ultimate stop for thinking about thinking is the brain. From the time that phrenologists dared to describe the talents and humors of an individual by the topological configuration of the skull, we have harbored the belief that a clear map of the brain would equip us with the key to its magic. The promise of that map is now held in the techniques of functional neuroimaging, described in Chapter 4. The research into these new worlds has expanded at an astonishing rate in concert with the continuing evolution of its technological basis. One of the limitations of this research, however, has been a lack of direction about how to integrate theoretical modeling in language and cognition with the potential insights that come from knowing where these processes take place. The research questions, however, are also in evolution and becoming increasingly sophisticated. The use of these techniques to test specific linguistic theories is now producing evidence that allows for more careful evaluation of these theories (e.g., Brown & Hagoort, 1999; Brown, personal communication, November 1999).

Research with bilinguals stands to contribute importantly to these pursuits. Using again the example of the differential development of attention in bilinguals, it would be profitable to study the functional mapping of these processes in bilingual adults. Previous functional imaging research with bilinguals has produced disappointing results. The research goal has usually been to determine how language is configured for bilinguals, that is, whether there are two areas involved in using language and whether the right hemisphere is more active for bilinguals than monolinguals. These questions may not be the most productive. To return to the attention and inhibition function of bilinguals, behavioral evidence from bilingual children suggests that functional imaging of the frontal lobe of bilingual adults may be a fruitful area of investigation in understanding the functional organization of the brain.

Finally

What do we know about bilingual children and their development? It may seem as if an inconsequential and incoherent story has been told here. For the most part, the cognitive and linguistic differences between bilingual and monolingual children who are otherwise similar turn out to be small. Some may even consider that the differences that have been established are arcane and trivial. But that would be to miss the point. The development of two languages in childhood turns out to be a profound event that ripples through the life of that individual. Some of the consequences are examined in this volume. Most notable is the possibility that an essential cognitive process that underlies much of our intellectual life, namely, the control over attention and inhibition, may develop differently and more advantageously in bilingual children.

Other potential consequences have not been discussed. For example, the world view available to someone who moves easily through languages and cultures is necessarily different from that of someone confined to a single perspective. Admittedly, the social dimensions of bilingualism have not been dealt with in any detail in this volume even though they are significant factors in describing the experience of these children. The assertion, rather, is that considering only the observable cognitive and linguistic facets of children's experiences, childhood bilingualism is an essential and significant influence on children's development.

If this attribution of importance is correct, then the research literature on the development of bilingual children is disproportionately thin. The meagerness is especially noteworthy in light of some estimates that claim more than half of the world's population to be bilingual (Padilla, 1990). Partly, the research is difficult to conduct because it requires interdisciplinary perspectives that are not common in most developmental studies. Meaningful studies of bilingual children often require intersecting skills in cognition, linguistics, sociology, and education, a combination not usually enlisted by most researchers. But as the body of knowledge expands, it should become easier to pursue the threads of the argument and extend the stakes into new areas of inquiry. Stimulating that process of searching for new insights and developing new paradigms for studying the issues would be a worthy outcome of this book.

References

Adams, M.J. (1990). *Beginning to read: Thinking and learning about print.* Cambridge, MA: MIT Press.

Aitchison, J. (1996). *The seeds of speech: Language origin and evolution.* Cambridge: Cambridge University Press.

Akhtar, N., & Tomasello, M. (1997). Young children's productivity with word order and verb morphology. *Developmental Psychology, 33,* 129–156.

Albanese, J.F. (1985). Language lateralization in English-French bilinguals. *Brain and Language, 24,* 284–296.

Albert, M.L., & Obler, L.K. (1978). *The bilingual brain: Neuropsychological and neurolinguistic aspects of bilingualism.* New York: Academic Press.

Alderson, J.C. (1984). Reading in a foreign language: A reading problem or a language problem? In J.A. Alderson & A.H. Urquhart, eds., *Reading in a foreign language,* pp. 1–24. London: Longmans.

Allen, J., & Seidenberg, M. (1999). The emergence of grammaticality in connectionist networks. In B. MacWhinney, ed., *The emergence of language,* pp. 115–151. Mahwah, NJ: Erlbaum.

Altarriba, J., & Mathis, K.M. (1997). Conceptual and lexical development in second language acquisition. *Journal of Memory and Language, 36,* 550–568.

Anglin, J.M. (1977). *Word, object, and conceptual development.* New York: Norton.

Anglin, J.M. (1993). Vocabulary development: A morphological analysis. *Monographs for the Society for Research in Child Development, 58* (10, No. 238).

Appel, R., & Muysken, P. (1987). *Language contact and bilingualism.* London: Edward Arnold.

Ardal, S., Donald, M.W., Meuter, R., Muldrew, S., & Luce, M. (1990). Brain semantic incongruity in bilinguals. *Brain and Language, 39,* 187–205.

Arnberg, L. (1979). Language strategies in mixed nationality families. *Scandinavian Journal of Psychology, 20,* 105–12.

Arnberg, L. (1987). *Raising children bilingually: The pre-school years.* Clevedon, UK: Multilingual Matters.

Atkinson, M. (1986). *Learnability.* In P. Fletcher & M. Garman, eds., *Language acquisition,* 2nd ed., pp. 90–108. Cambridge: Cambridge University Press.

Au, T.K.F., & Glusman, M. (1990). The principle of mutual exclusivity in word learning: To honor or not to honor? *Child Development, 61,* 1474–1490.

August, D., & Hakuta, K., eds. (1997). *Improving schooling for language-minority children: A research agenda.* Washington, DC: National Academy Press.

Barnett, M.A. (1989). *More than meets the eye: Foreign language reading: Theory and practice.* Englewood Cliffs, N.J.: Prentice Hall Regents.

Barnitz, J.G. (1986). Toward understanding the effects of cross-cultural schemata and discourse structure on second language reading comprehension. *Journal of Reading Behavior, 18,* 95–113.

Barrett, M.D. (1978). Lexical development and overextension in child language. *Journal of Child Language, 5,* 205–219.

Barrett, M.D. (1986). Early semantic representations and early word usage. In S.A. Kuczaj & M.D. Barrett, eds., *The development of word meaning,* pp. 39–67. New York: Springer Verlag.

Barrett, M.D. (1995). Early lexical development. In P. Fletcher & B. MacWhinney, eds., *The handbook of child language,* pp. 362–392. Oxford: Blackwell.

Bates, E. (1976). *Language and context: The acquisition of pragmatics.* New York: Academic Press.

Bates, E., & Goodman, J.C. (1997). On the inseparability of grammar and the lexicon: Evidence from acquisition, aphasia, and real-time processing. *Language and Cognitive Processes, 12,* 507–586.

Bates, E., & Goodman, J.C. (1999). On the emergence of grammar from the lexicon. In B. MacWhinney, ed., *The emergence of language,* pp. 29–79. Mahwah, NJ: Erlbaum.

Bates, E., & MacWhinney, B. (1981). Second language acquisition from a functionalist perspective: Pragmatic, semantic and perceptual strategies. In H. Winitz, ed., *Annals of the New York Academy of Sciences conference on native and foreign language acquisition,* pp. 190–214. New York: New York Academy of Sciences.

Bates, E., & MacWhinney, B. (1989). Functionalism and the competition model. In B. MacWhinney & E. Bates, eds., *The crosslinguistic study of sentence processing,* pp. 3–73. New York: Cambridge University Press.

Bates, E., Bretherton, I., & Snyder, L. (1988). *From first words to grammar: Individual differences and dissociable mechanisms.* Cambridge: Cambridge University Press.

Bates, E., Camaioni, L., & Volterra, V. (1975). The acquisition of performatives prior to speech. *Merrill-Palmer Quarterly, 21,* 205–226.

Bates, E., Dale, P.S., & Thal, D.J. (1995). Individual differences and their implications for theories of language development. In P. Fletcher & B. MacWhinney, eds., *Handbook of child language,* pp. 96–151. Oxford: Basil Blackwell.

Bavin, E. (1990). Locative terms and Warlpiri acquisition. *Journal of Child Language, 17,* 43–66.

Bentin, S., Hammer, R., & Cahan, S. (1991). The effects of aging and first-grade schooling on the development of phonological awareness. *Psychological Science, 2,* 271–274.

Ben-Zeev, S. (1977). The influence of bilingualism on cognitive strategy and cognitive development. *Child Development, 48,* 1009–1018.

Bernhardt, E.B. (1991). *Reading development in a second language: Theoretical, empirical, and classroom perspectives.* Norwood, NJ: Ablex.

Berwick, R.C. (1986). *The acquisition of syntactic knowledge.* Cambridge, MA: MIT Press.

Best, C.T. (1994). The emergence of language-specific phonemic influences in infant speech perception. In J. Goodman & H. Nusbaum, eds., *The transition from speech sounds to spoken words: The development of speech perception,* pp. 167–224. Cambridge, MA: MIT Press.

Bialystok, E. (1986a). Factors in the growth of linguistic awareness. *Child Development, 57,* 498–510.

Bialystok, E. (1986b). Children's concept of word. *Journal of Psycholinguistic Research, 15,* 13–32.

Bialystok, E. (1987). Words as things: Development of word concept by bilingual children. *Studies in Second Language Acquisition, 9,* 133–140.

Bialystok, E. (1988). Levels of bilingualism and levels of linguistic awareness. *Developmental Psychology, 24,* 560–567.

Bialystok, E. (1990). *Communication strategies: A psychological analysis of second-language use.* Oxford: Basil Blackwell.

Bialystok, E. (1991a). Metalinguistic dimensions of bilingual language proficiency. In E. Bialystok, ed., *Language processing in bilingual children,* pp: 113–140. London: Cambridge University Press.

Bialystok, E. (1991b). Letters, sounds, and symbols: Changes in children's understanding of written language. *Applied Psycholinguistics, 12,* 75–89.

Bialystok, E. (1992a). Attentional control in children's metalinguistic performance and measures of field independence. *Developmental Psychology, 28,* 654–664.

Bialystok, E. (1992b). Selective attention in cognitive processing: The bilingual edge. In R.J. Harris, ed., *Cognitive processing in bilinguals,* pp. 501–513. Amsterdam: North Holland Elsevier.

Bialystok, E. (1993). Metalinguistic awareness: The development of children's representations of language. In C. Pratt & A. Garton, eds., *Systems of representation in children: Development and use,* pp. 211–233. London: Wiley & Sons.

Bialystok, E. (1996). Preparing to read: The foundations of literacy. In H. Reese, ed., *Advances in child development and behavior,* vol. 26, pp. 1–34. New York: Academic Press.

Bialystok, E. (1997a). The structure of age: In search of barriers to second-language acquisition. *Second Language Research, 13,* 116–137.

Bialystok, E. (1997b). Effects of bilingualism and biliteracy on children's emerging concepts of print. *Developmental Psychology, 33,* 429–440.

Bialystok, E. (1998). Beyond binary options: Effects of two languages on the bilingual mind. *Studia Anglica Posnaniensia, 33,* 47–60.

Bialystok, E. (1999). Cognitive complexity and attentional control in the bilingual mind. *Child Development, 70,* 636–644.

Bialystok, E., & Codd, J. (1997). Cardinal limits: Evidence from language awareness and bilingualism for developing concepts of number. *Cognitive Development, 12,* 85–106.

Bialystok, E., & Hakuta, K. (1994). *In other words: The psychology and science of second language acquisition.* New York: Basic Books.

Bialystok, E., & Herman, J. (1999). Does bilingualism matter for early literacy? *Bilingualism: Language and Cognition, 2,* 35–44.

Bialystok, E., & Majumder, S. (1998). The relationship between bilingualism and the development of cognitive processes in problem-solving. *Applied Psycholinguistics, 19,* 69–85.

Bialystok, E., & Martin, M. (in preparation). Attention and inhibition in bilingual children.

Bialystok, E., & Miller, B. (1999). The problem of age in second language acquisition: Influences from language, task, and structure. *Bilingualism: Language and Cognition, 2,* 127–145.

Bialystok, E., & Ryan, E.B. (1985). A metacognitive framework for the development of first and second language skills. In D.L. Forrest-Pressley, G.E. Mackinnon, & T.G. Waller, eds., *Meta-cognition, cognition, and human performance,* pp. 207–252. New York: Academic Press.

Bialystok, E., Majumder, S., & Martin (in preparation). Is there a bilingual advantage in the development of phonological awareness?

Bialystok, E., Shenfield, T., & Codd, J. (2000). Languages, scripts, and the environment: Factors in developing concepts of print. *Developmental Psychology, 36,* 66–76.

Biederman, I., & Tsao, Y.C. (1979). On processing Chinese ideographs and English words: Some implications from Stroop Test results. *Cognitive Psychology, 11,* 125–132.

Bijeljac-Babic, R., Biardeau, A., & Grainger, J. (1995). Masked orthographic priming in bilingual word recognition. *Memory and Cognition, 25,* 447–457.

Binder, J.R., Swanson, S.J., Hammeke, T.A., Morris, G.L., Mueller, W.M., Fischer, M., Benbadis, S., Frost, J.A., Rao, S.M., & Haughton, V.M. (1996). Determination of language dominance using functional MRI: A comparison with the WADA test. *Neurology, 46,* 978–984.

Birdsong, D. (1989). *Metalinguistic performance in interlinguistic competence.* New York: Springer-Verlag.

Birdsong, D. (1992). Ultimate attainment in second language acquisition. *Language, 68,* 23–52.

Birdsong, D., ed. (1999). *Second language acquisition and the critical period hypothesis.* Mahwah, NJ: Erlbaum.

Bloom, L. (1973). *One word at a time.* The Hague: Mouton.

Bloomfield, L. (1933). *Language.* New York: Holt.

Blum-Kulka, S., & Sheffer, H. (1993). The metapragmatic discourse of American-Israeli families at dinner. In G. Kasper & S. Blum-Kulka, eds., *Interlanguage pragmatics,* pp. 196–223. New York: Oxford University Press.

Bochner, S. (1996). The learning strategies of bilingual versus monolingual students. *British Journal of Educational Psychology, 66,* 83–93.

Bohannon, J., & Stanowicz, L. (1988). The issue of negative evidence: Adult responses to children's language errors. *Developmental Psychology, 24,* 684–689.

Bongaerts, T., Planken, B., & Schils, E. (1995). Can late starters attain a native accent in a foreign language? A test of the critical period hypothesis. In D. Singleton & Z. Lengyel, eds., *The age factor in second language acquisition,* pp. 30–50. Clevedon: Multilingual Matters.

Bornstein, M.H. (1989). Sensitive periods in development: Structural characteristics and causal interpretations. *Psychological Bulletin, 105,* 179–197.

Bowerman, M. (1973). Structural relationships in children's utterances: Syntactic or semantic? In T. Moore, ed., *Cognitive development and the acquisition of language,* pp. 197–214. New York: Academic Press.

Bowerman, M. (1985). What shapes children's grammars? In D.I. Slobin, ed., *The crosslinguistic study of language acquisition,* vol. 2: *Theoretical issues,* pp. 1257–1319. Hillsdale, NJ: Erlbaum.

Bowey, J.A. (1988). *Metalinguistic functioning in children.* Geelong, Australia: Deakin University Press.

Bowey, J.A. (1995). Socioeconomic status differences in preschool phonological sensitivity and first-grade reading achievement. *Journal of Educational Psychology, 87,* 476–487.

Bowey, J.A., & Patel, R.K. (1988). Metalinguistic ability and early reading achievement. *Applied Psycholinguistics, 9,* 367–383.

Bradley, L. & Bryant, P.E. (1983). Categorizing sounds and learning to read: A causal connection. *Nature, 301,* 419–421.

Braine, M.D.S. (1976). Children's first word combinations. *Monographs of the Society for Research in Child Development, 41,* (Whole No. 1).

Brauer, M. (1998). Stroop interference in bilinguals: The role of similarity between the two languages. In A.F. Healy & L.E. Bourne, Jr., eds., *Foreign language learning: Psycholinguistic studies on training and retention,* pp. 317–337. Mahwah, NJ: Erlbaum.

Bresnan, J., ed. (1982). *The mental representation of grammatical relations.* Cambridge, MA: MIT Press.

Brisk, M.E. (1998). *Bilingual education: From compensatory to quality schooling.* Mahwah, NJ: Erlbaum.

Brown, C.M., & Hagoort, P., eds. (1999). *The neurocognition of language.* New York: Oxford University Press.

Brown, R. (1973). *A first language: The early stages.* Cambridge, MA: Harvard University Press.

Bruck, M., & Genesee, F. (1995). Phonological awareness in young second language learners. *Journal of Child Language, 22,* 307–324.

Bruner, J. (1983). *Child's talk: Learning to use language.* New York: W.W. Norton.

Burgess, P.W., & Shallice, T. (1996). Response suppression, initiation and strategy use following frontal lobe lesions. *Neuropsychologia, 34,* 263–272.

Byrne, B., & Fielding-Barnsley, R. (1993). Evaluation of a program to teach phonemic awareness to young children: A 1-year follow-up. *Journal of Educational Psychology, 85,* 104–111.

Byrne, B., & Fielding-Barnsley, R. (1995). Evaluation of a program to teach phonemic awareness to young children: A 2- and 3-year follow-up and a new preschool trial. *Journal of Educational Psychology, 87,* 488–503.

Cabeza, R., & Nyberg, L. (1997). Imaging cognition: An empirical review of PET studies with normal subjects. *Journal of Cognitive Neuroscience, 9,* 1–26.

Campbell, R., & Sais, E. (1995). Accelerated metalinguistic (phonological) awareness in bilingual children. *British Journal of Developmental Psychology, 13,* 61–68.

Caravolas, M., & Bruck, M. (1993). The effect of oral and written language input on children's phonological awareness: A cross-linguistic study. *Journal of Experimental Child Psychology, 55,* 1–30.

Carr, T.H., & Levy, B.A., eds. (1990). *Reading and its development: Component skills approaches.* New York: Academic Press.

Carrell, P.L. (1994). Awareness of text structure: Effects on recall. In A.H. Cumming, ed., *Bilingual performance in reading and writing,* pp. 23–41. Ann Arbor, MI: John Benjamins.

Carrell, P.L., Devine, J., & Eskey, D.E., eds. (1988). *Interactive approaches to second language reading.* New York: Cambridge University Press.

Castle, J.M., Riach, J., & Nicholson, T. (1994). Getting off to a better start in reading and spelling: The effects of phonemic awareness instruction within a whole language program. *Journal of Educational Psychology, 86,* 350–359.

Cazden, C.R. (1974). Play with language and metalinguistic awareness: One dimension of language experience. *The Urban Review, 7,* 28–39.

Chapelle, C.A., & Green, P. (1992). Field independence/dependence in second language acquisition research. *Language Learning, 42,* 47–83.

Choi, S. (1997). Language-specific input and early semantic development: Evidence from children learning Korean. In D.I. Slobin, ed., *The crosslinguistic study of language acquisition,* vol. 5: *Expanding the contexts,* pp. 41–133. Mahwah, NJ: Erlbaum.

Choi, S., & Bowerman, M. (1991). Learning to express motion events in English and Korean: The influence of language-specific lexicalization patterns. *Cognition, 41,* 83–121.

Choi, S., McDonough, L., Bowerman, M., & Mandler, J.M. (1999). Early sensitivity to language-specific spatial categories in English and Korean. *Cognitive Development, 14,* 241–268.

Chomsky, N. (1965). *Aspects of the theory of syntax.* Cambridge, MA: MIT Press.

Chomsky, N. (1981). *Lectures on government and binding.* Dordrecht: Foris.

Chomsky, N. (1995). *The minimalist program.* Cambridge, MA: MIT Press.

Churchland, P.M. (1996). *The engine of reason, the seat of the soul: A philosophical journey into the brain.* Cambridge, MA: MIT Press.

Ciscero, C.A. & Royer, J.M. (1995). The development and cross-language transfer of phonological awareness. *Contemporary Educational Psychology, 20,* 275–303.

Clark, A. (1989). *Microcognition: Philosophy, cognitive science and parallel distributed processing.* Cambridge, MA: MIT Press.

Clark, E.V. (1973). Nonlinguistic strategies and the acquisition of word meanings. *Cognition, 2,* 161–182.

Clark, E.V. (1978). Awareness of language: Some evidence from what children say and do. In A. Sinclair, R.J. Jarvella, & W.J.M. Levelt, eds., *The child's conception of language*, pp. 17–43. Berlin: Springer-Verlag.

Clark, E.V. (1987). The principle of contrast: A constraint on language acquisition. In B. MacWhinney, ed., *Mechanisms of language acquisition*, pp. 1–33. Hillsdale, NJ: Erlbaum.

Clark, E.V. (1993). *The lexicon in acquisition*. Cambridge: Cambridge University Press.

Clark, E.V. (1995). Later lexical development and word formation. In P. Fletcher & B. MacWhinney, eds., *The handbook of child language*, pp. 393–412. Oxford: Blackwells.

Coggins, T., & Carpenter, R. (1982). The communicative intention inventory: A system for observing and coding children's early intentional communication. *Applied Psycholinguistics, 3*, 235–251.

Cohen, D.K. (1970). Immigrants and the schools. *Review of Educational Research, 40*, 13–27.

Collier, V. (1987). Age and rate of acquisition of second language for academic purposes. *TESOL Quarterly, 21*, 617–641.

Colombo, J. (1982). The critical period concept: Research, methodological, and theoretical issues. *Psychological Bulletin, 91*, 260–275.

Cook, V. (1997). The consequences of bilingualism for cognitive processing. In A.M.B. de Groot & J.F. Kroll, eds., *Tutorials in bilingualism*, pp. 279–299. Mahwah, NJ: Erlbaum.

Cossu, G., Shankweiler, D., Liberman, I.Y., Katz, L., & Tola, G. (1988). Awareness of phonological segments and reading ability in Italian children. *Applied Psycholinguistics, 9*, 1–16.

Coulmas, F. (1989). *The writing systems of the world*. Oxford: Blackwell.

Craik, F.I.M., & Jacoby, L.L. (1996). Aging and memory: Implications for skilled performance. In W.A. Rogers, A.D. Fisk, & N. Walker, eds., *Aging and skilled performance*, pp. 113–137. Mahwah, NJ: Erlbaum.

Craik, F.I.M., & Jennings, J.M. (1992). Human memory. In F.I.M. Craik & T.A. Salthouse, eds., *The handbook of aging and cognition*, pp. 51–110. Hillsdale, NJ: Erlbaum.

Craik, F.I.M., & McDowd, J.M. (1987). Age differences in recall and recognition. *Journal of Experimental Psychology: Learning, Memory, and Cognition, 13*, 474–479.

Cromdal, J. (1999). Childhood bilingualism and metalinguistic skills: Analysis and control in young Swedish-English bilinguals. *Applied Psycholinguistics, 20*, 1–20.

Cummins, J. (1978). Bilingualism and the development of metalinguistic awareness. *Journal of Cross-Cultural Psychology, 9,* 131–149.

Cummins, J. (1979). Linguistic interdependence and the educational development of bilingual children. *Review of Educational Research, 49*, 222–251.

Cummins, J. (1991). Interdependence of first- and second-language proficiency in bilingual children. In E. Bialystok, ed., *Language processing in bilingual children*, pp. 70–89. Cambridge: Cambridge University Press.

Dale, P.S., Crain-Thoreson, C., & Robinson, N. (1995). Linguistic precocity and the development of reading: The role of extralinguistic factors. *Applied Psycholinguistics, 16,* 173–187.

Darcy, N. (1946). The effect of bilingualism upon the measurement of the intelligence of children of preschool age. *Journal of Educational Psychology, 37,* 21–44.

Davidson, D. (1996). The role of schemata in children's memory. In H.W. Reese, ed., *Advances in child development and behavior,* vol. 26, pp. 35–58. New York: Academic Press.

Davidson, D., Jergovic, D., Imami, Z., & Theodos, V. (1997). Monolingual and bilingual children's use of the mutual exclusivity constraint. *Journal of Child Language, 24,* 3–24.

Deacon, T. (1997). *The symbolic species: The co-evolution of language and the human brain.* London: Penguin Press.

Dechert, H.W. (1995). Some critical remarks concerning Penfield's theory of second language acquisition. In D. Singleton & Z. Lengyel, eds., *The age factor in second language acquisition,* pp. 67–94. Clevedon: Multilingual Matters.

De Groot, A.M.B. (1992). Determinants of word translation. *Journal of Experimental Psychology: Learning, Memory, and Cognition, 18,* 1001–1018.

De Groot, A.M.B. (1993). Word-type effects in bilingual processing tasks: Support for a mixed-representational system. In R. Schreuder & B. Weltens, eds., *The bilingual lexicon,* pp. 27–51. Amsterdam: John Benjamins.

De Houwer, A. (1990). *The acquisition of two languages from birth: A case study.* New York: Cambridge University Press.

De Houwer, A. (1995). Bilingual language acquisition. In P. Fletcher & B. MacWhinney, eds., *The handbook of child language,* pp. 219–250. Oxford: Blackwell.

Delis, D.C., Knight, R.T., & Simpson, G. (1983). Reversed hemispheric organization in a left-hander. *Neuropsychologia, 21,* 13–24.

DeLoache, J.S. (1987). Rapid change in the symbolic functioning of very young children. *Science, 238,* 1556–1557.

Démonet, J.F. (1998). Tomographic brain imaging of language functions: Prospects for a new brain/language model. In B. Stemmer & H. Whitaker, eds., *Handbook on neurolinguistics,* pp. 131–142. New York: Academic Press.

Dempster, F.N. (1992). The rise and fall of the inhibitory mechanism: Toward a unified theory of cognitive development and aging. *Developmental Review, 12,* 45–75.

Dennett, D.C. (1995). *Darwin's dangerous idea: Evolution and the meanings of life.* New York: Simon and Schuster.

Deuchar, M., & Quay, S. (1998). One vs. two systems in early bilingual syntax: Two versions of the question. *Bilingualism: Language and Cognition, 1,* 231–243.

Deuchar, M., & Quay, S. (2000). *Bilingual acquisition: Theoretical implications of a case study.* Oxford: Oxford University Press.

de Villiers, J.G., & de Villiers, P.A. (1972). Early judgments of semantic and syntactic acceptability by children. *Journal of Psycholinguistic Research, 1,* 299–310.

de Villiers, J.G., & de Villiers, P.A. (1974). Competence and performance in child language: Are children really competent to judge? *Journal of Child Language, 1,* 11–22.

de Villiers, J.G., & de Villiers, P.A. (1979). *Early language.* Cambridge, MA: Harvard University Press.

Diamond, A. (1991). Frontal lobe involvement in cognitive changes during the first year of life. In K.R. Gibson & A.C. Peterson, eds., *Brain maturation and cognitive development,* pp. 127–180. New York: Aldine De Gruyter.

Diamond, A., Prevor, M.B., Callender, G., & Druin, D.P. (1997). Prefrontal cortex cognitive deficits in children treated early and continuously for PKU. *Monographs of the Society for Research in Child Development, 62,* (no. 4).

Dickinson, D.K. & Tabors, P.O. (1991). Early literacy: Linkages between home, school, and literacy achievement at age five. *Journal of Research in Childhood Education, 6,* 30–46.

Dijkstra, A., & Van Heuven, W.J.B. (1998). The BIA model and bilingual word recognition. In J. Grainger & A.M. Jacobs, eds., *Localist connectionist approaches to human cognition,* pp. 189–225. Mahwah, NJ: Erlbaum.

Dijkstra, A., & Van Heuven, W.J.B., & Grainger, J. (1998). Simulating cross-language competition with the bilingual interactive activation model. *Psychologica Belgica, 38,* 177–196.

Dijkstra, A., van Jaarsveld, H., & Ten Brinke, S. (1998). Interlingual homograph recognition: Effects of task demands and language intermixing. *Bilingualism: Language and Cognition, 1,* 51–66.

Donald, M. (1991). *Origins of the modern mind: Three stages in the evolution of culture and cognition.* Cambridge, MA: Harvard University Press.

Dopke, S. (1992). *One parent one language: An interactional approach.* Amsterdam: John Benjamins.

Doyle, A., Champagne, M., & Segalowitz, N. (1978). Some issues on the assessment of linguistic consequences of early bilingualism. In M. Paradis, ed., *Aspects of bilingualism,* pp. 13–20. Columbia, SC: Hornbeam Press.

Dromi, E. (1987). *Early lexical development.* Cambridge: Cambridge University Press.

Duncan, J. (1996). Attention, intelligence, and the frontal lobes. In M. Gazzaniga, ed., *The cognitive neurosciences,* pp. 721–733. Cambridge, MA: MIT Press.

Durgunoğlu, A.Y. (1997). Bilingual reading: Its components, development, and other issues. In A.M.B. de Groot & J.F. Kroll, eds., *Tutorials in bilingualism: Psycholinguistic perspectives,* pp. 255–276. Mahwah, NJ: Erlbaum.

Durgunoglu, A.Y. (1998). Acquiring literacy in English and Spanish in the United States. In A.Y. Durgunoglu & L. Verhoeven, eds., *Literacy development in a multilingual context: Cross-cultural perspectives,* pp. 135–145. Mahwah, NJ: Erlbaum.

Durgunoglu, A.Y., & Roediger, H.L. (1987). Test differences in accessing bilingual memory. *Journal of Memory and Language, 26,* 377–391.

Durgunoglu, A.Y., & Verhoeven, L., eds. (1998). *Literacy development in a multilingual context: Cross-cultural perspectives.* Mahwah, NJ: Erlbaum.

Durgunoglu, A.Y., Nagy, W.E., & Hancin-Bhatt, B.J. (1993). Cross-language transfer of phonological awareness. *Journal of Educational Psychology, 85,* 453–465.

Eco, U. (2000). *Kant and the platypus.* New York: Harcourt Brace.

Edwards, D., & Christopherson, H. (1988). Bilingualism, literacy, and metalinguistic awareness in preschool children. *British Journal of Developmental Psychology, 6,* 235–244.

Eimas, P.D., Siqueland, E.R., Jusczyk, P., & Vigorito, J. (1971). Speech perception in infants. *Science, 171,* 303–306.

Elbert, T., Pantev, C., Wienbruch, C., Rockstroh, B., & Taub, E. (1995). Increased cortical representation of the fingers of the left hand in string players. *Science, 270,* 305–306.

Ellis, R. (1990). Individual learning styles in classroom second language development. In J.H.A.L. de Jong & D.K. Stevenson, eds., *Individualising the assessment of language abilities.* Clevedon: Multilingual Matters.

Ellis, R. (1994). *The study of second language acquisition.* Oxford: Oxford University Press.

Elman, J.L., Bates, E.A., Johnson, M.H., Karmiloff-Smith, A., Parisi, D., & Plunkett, K. (1996). *Rethinking innateness: A connectionist perspective on development.* Cambridge, MA: MIT Press.

Ervin, S.M. (1961). Semantic shift in bilingualism. *American Journal of Psychology, 74,* 233–241.

Ervin, S., & Osgood, C. (1954). Second language learning and bilingualism. *Journal of Abnormal and Social Psychology Supplement, 49,* 139–146.

Fabbro, F. (1999). *The neurolinguistics of bilingualism: An introduction.* Hove, UK: Psychology Press.

Fantini, A. (1985). *Language acquisition of a bilingual child: A sociolinguistic perspective.* San Diego: College Hill Press.

Favreau, M., & Segalowitz, N. (1982). Second language reading in fluent bilinguals. *Applied Psycholinguistics, 3,* 329–341.

Favreau, M., & Segalowitz, N. (1983). Automatic and controlled processes in reading a second language. *Memory and Cognition, 11,* 565–574.

Feldman, C., & Shen, M. (1971). Some language-related cognitive advantages of bilingual five-year-olds. *Journal of Genetic Psychology, 118,* 235–244.

Fenson, L., Dale, P.S., Reznick, J.S., Bates, E., Thal, D.J., & Pethick, S.J. (1994). Variability in early communicative development. *Monographs of the Society for Research in Child Development, 59* (5, no. 242).

Fenson, L., Dale, P.S., Reznick, J.S., Thal, D., Bates, E., Hartung, J.P., Pethick, S., & Reilly, J.S. (1993). *MacArthur Communicative Development Inventories.* San Diego, CA: Singular Publishing Group.

Ferreiro, E. (1978). What is written in a written sentence? A developmental answer. *Journal of Education, 160,* 25–39.

Ferreiro, E. (1983). The development of literacy: A complex psychological problem. In F. Coulmas & K. Ehlich, eds., *Writing in focus,* pp. 277–290. Berlin: Mouton.

Ferreiro, E. (1984). The underlying logic of literacy development. In H. Goelman, A. Oberg, & F. Smith, eds., *Awakening to literacy,* pp. 154–173. Exeter, NH: Heinemann Educational Books.

Fillmore, C. (1988). The mechanisms of construction grammar. In S. Axmaker, A. Jaisser, & H. Signmaster, eds., *Proceedings of the 14th annual meeting of the Berkeley Linguistics Society,* pp. 35–55. Berkeley: BLS.

Flege, J.E. (1992). Speech learning in a second language. In C.A. Ferguson, L. Menn, & C. Stoel-Gammon, eds., *Phonological development: Models, research, implications,* pp. 565–604. Timonium, MD: York Press.

Flege, J.E., & Fletcher, K.L. (1992). Talker and listener effects on degree of perceived foreign accent. *Journal of the Acoustical Society of America, 91,* 370–389.

Flege, J.E., & Frieda, E.M. (1997). Amount of native-language (L1) use affects the pronunciation of an L2. *Journal of Phonetics, 25,* 169–186.

Flege, J.E., Munro, M.J., & MacKay, I.R.A. (1995). Effects of age of second-language learning on the production of English consonants. *Speech Communication, 16,* 1–26.

Flege, J.E., Yeni-Komshian, G., and Liu, S. (1999). Age constraints on second language learning. *Journal of Memory and Language, 41,* 78–104.

Fodor, J. (1998). The trouble with psychological Darwinism. *London Review of Books, 20* (January 15).

Fox, B., & Routh, D.K. (1975). Analyzing spoken language into words, syllables, and phonemes: A developmental study. *Journal of Psycholinguistic Research, 4,* 331–342.

Frith, U., Wimmer, H., & Landerl, K. (1998). Differences in phonological recoding in German- and English-speaking children. *Scientific Studies of Reading, 2,* 31–54.

Frost, R. Katz, L. & Bentin, S. (1987). Strategies for visual word recognition and orthographic depth: A multilingual comparison. *Journal of Experimental Psychology: Human Perception and Performance, 13,* 104–115.

Frye, D., Zelazo, P.D., & Palfai, T. (1995). Theory of mind and rule based reasoning. *Cognitive Development, 10,* 483–527.

Furnham, A., & Ribchester, T. (1995). Tolerance of ambiguity: A review of the concept, its measurement and applications. *Current Psychology, 14,* 179–199.

Fuson, K.C. (1988). *Children's counting and concepts of number.* New York: Springer-Verlag.

Galambos, S.J., & Goldin-Meadow, S. (1990). The effects of learning two languages on levels of metalinguistic awareness. *Cognition, 34,* 1–56.

Galambos, S.J., & Hakuta, K. (1988). Subject-specific and task specific characteristics of metalinguistic awareness in bilingual children. *Applied Psycholinguistics, 9,* 141–162.

Galang, R. (1988). The language situation of Filipino Americans. In S.L. McKay & S.-L.C. Wong, eds., *Language diversity problem or resource?,* pp. 229–251. New York, NY: Newbury House Publishers.

Gardner, H. (1983). *Frames of mind: The theory of multiple intelligences.* New York: Basic Books.

Garton, A., & Pratt, C. (1989). *Learning to be literate: The development of spoken & written language.* Oxford: Basil Blackwell.

Gathercole, V.C.M. (1997). The linguistic mass/count distinction as an indicator of referent categorization in monolingual and bilingual children. *Child Development, 68,* 832–842.

Gathercole, V.C.M. (in press, a). Command of the mass/count distinction in bilingual and monolingual children: An English morphosyntactic distinction. In D.K. Oller & R. Eilers, eds., *Language and literacy in bilingual children.* Clevedon, UK: Multilingual Matters.

Gathercole, V.C.M. (in press, b). Grammatical gender in bilingual and monolingual children: A Spanish morphosyntactic distinction. In D.K. Oller & R. Eilers, eds., *Language and literacy in bilingual children.* Clevedon, UK: Multilingual Matters.

Gathercole, V.C.M. (in press, c). Monolingual and bilingual acquisition: Learning different treatments of *that*-trace phenomena in English and Spanish. In D.K. Oller & R. Eilers, eds., *Language and literacy in bilingual children.* Clevedon, UK: Multilingual Matters.

Gathercole, V.C.M., & Montes, C. (1997). *That*-trace effects in Spanish- and English-speaking monolinguals and bilinguals. In A.T. Pérez-Leroux & W.R. Glass, eds., *Contemporary perspectives on the acquisition of Spanish,* vol. 1: *Developing grammar,* pp. 75–95. Somerville, MA: Cascadilla Press.

Gazzaniga, M.S. (1992). *Nature's mind: The biological roots of thinking, emotions, sexuality, language, and intelligence.* New York: Basic Books.

Geary, D.C., Cormier, P., Goggin, J.P., Estrada, P., & Lunn, M.C.E. (1993). *International Journal of Psychology, 28,* 185–201.

Gelman, R., & Gallistel, C.R. (1978). *The child's understanding of number.* Cambridge, MA: Harvard University Press.

Genesee, F. (1989). Early bilingual development: One language or two? *Journal of Child Language, 16,* 161–179.

Genesee, F., Nicoladis, E., & Paradis, J. (1995). Language differentiation in early bilingual development. *Journal of Child Language, 22,* 611–631.

Gerstad, C.L., Hong, Y.J., & Diamond, A. (1994). The relationship between cognition and action: Performance of children 3-and-a-half to 7 years on a Stroop-like day-night task. *Cognition, 53,* 129–153.

Geva, E., & Wade-Woolley, L. (1998). Component processes in becoming English-Hebrew bilterate. In A.Y. Durgunoğlu & L. Verhoeven, eds., *Literacy development in a multilingual context: Cross-cultural perspectives,* pp. 85–110. Mahwah, NJ: Erlbaum.

Goldberg, A. (1995). *Constructions: A construction grammar approach to argument structure.* Chicago: University of Chicago Press.

Goldberg, A. (1998). Patterns of experience in patterns of language. In M. Tomasello, ed., *The new psychology of language: Cognitive and functional approaches to language structure,* pp. 203–219. Mahwah, NJ: Erlbaum.

Goldfield, B.A., & Reznick, J.S. (1990). Early lexical acquisition: Rate, content, and the vocabulary spurt. *Journal of Child Language, 17,* 171–183.

Golinkoff, R.M., Hirsh-Pasek, K., Cauley, K.M., & Gordon, L. (1987). The eyes have it: Lexical and syntactic comprehension in a new paradigm. *Journal of Child Language, 14,* 23–45.

Gombert, J.E. (1992). *Metalinguistic development.* Chicago: University of Chicago Press.

Gonzalez, J.E.J., & Garcia, C.R.H. (1995). Effects of word linguistic properties on phonological awareness in Spanish children. *Journal of Educational Psychology, 87*, 193–201.

Goodman, N. (1968). *Languages of art.* Indianapolis: Bobbs-Merrill.

Goodz, N.S. (1989). Parental language mixing in bilingual families. *Infant Mental Health Journal, 10*, 25–44.

Gopnik, A., & Meltzoff, A.N. (1986). Relations between semantic and cognitive development in the one-word stage: The specificity hypothesis. *Child Development, 57*, 1040–1053.

Gordon, D.P., & Zatorre, R.J. (1981). A right-ear advantage for dichotic listening in bilingual children. *Brain and Language, 13*, 389–396.

Gottardo, A., Stanovich, K.E., & Siegel, L.S. (1996). The relationships between phonological sensitivity, syntactic processing, and verbal working memory in the reading performance of third-grade children. *Journal of Experimental Child Psychology, 63*, 563–582.

Gould, S.J. (1981). *The mismeasure of man.* New York: Norton.

Gould, S.J. (1997, June 12). Darwinian fundamentalism. *New York Review of Books, 44*, 34–37.

Grainger, J. (1993). Visual word recognition in bilinguals. In R. Schreuder & B. Weltens, eds., *The bilingual lexicon,* pp. 11–25. Amsterdam: John Benjamins.

Grainger, J., & Dijkstra, A. (1992). On the representation and use of language information in bilinguals. In R.J. Harris, ed., *Cognitive processing in bilinguals,* pp. 207–220. Amsterdam: Elsevier Science.

Green, D.W. (1998). Mental control of the bilingual lexico-semantic system. *Bilingualism: Language and Cognition, 1*, 67–81.

Griffiths, R., & Sheen, R. (1992). Disembedded figures in the landscape: A reappraisal of L2 research on field dependence/independence. *Applied Linguistics, 13*, 133–148.

Grosjean, F. (1982). *Life with two languages.* Cambridge, MA: Harvard University Press.

Grosjean, F. (1989). Neurolinguists, beware! The bilingual is not two monolinguals in one person. *Brain and Language, 36*, 3–15.

Grosjean, F. (1991). The restructuring of a first language: The integration of contact variants in the competence of bilingual migrants. *Linguisitique, 27*, 35–60.

Grosjean, F. (1996). Living with two languages and two cultures. In I. Parasnis, ed., *Cultural and language diversity and the deaf experience,* pp. 20–37. New York: Cambridge University Press.

Grosjean, F. (1998). Studying bilinguals: Methodological and conceptual issues. Mental control of the bilingual lexico-semantic system. *Bilingualism: Language and Cognition, 1*, 131–149.

Guttentag, R.E., Haith, M.M., Goodman, G.S., & Hauch, J. (1984). Semantic processing of unattended words in bilinguals: A test of the input switch mechanism. *Journal of Verbal Learning and Verbal Behavior, 23*, 178–188.

Hakes, D. (1980). *The development of metalinguistic abilities in children.* New York: Springer-Verlag.

Hakuta, K. (1986). *Mirror of language: The debate on bilingualism*. New York: Basic Books.

Hakuta, K. (1987). Degree of bilingualism and cognitive ability in mainland Puerto Rican children. *Child Development, 58,* 1372–1388.

Hakuta, K. (1999). A critical period for second language acquisition? A status review. Paper written for the National Center for Early Development and Learning (University of North Carolina, Chapel Hill). To be published in proceedings. On-line draft available at http://www.stanford.edu/hakuta/Docs/CriticalPeriod.PDF.

Hakuta, K., & Diaz, R. (1985). The relationship between degree of bilingualism and cognitive ability: A critical discussion and some new longitudinal data. In K.E. Nelson, ed., *Children's language,* vol. 5, pp. 319–344. Hillsdale, NJ: Erlbaum.

Hakuta, K., & Mostafapour, E.F. (1996). Perspectives from the history and politics of bilingualism and bilingual education in the United States. In I. Parasnis, ed., *Cultural and language diversity and the deaf experience,* pp. 38–50. New York: Cambridge University Press.

Hakuta, K., Bialystok, E., & Wiley, E. (in preparation). A test of the critical period hypothesis for second language acquisition in Spanish- and Chinese-background immigrants to the United States.

Hakuta, K., Butler, Y.G. & Witt, D. (2000). *How long does it take English learners to attain proficiency.* The University of California Linguistic Minority Research Institute, policy report 2000-1. On-line. Available at http://www.stanford.edu/hakuta/Docs/HowLong.pdf.

Harley, B., & Wang, W. (1997). The critical period hypothesis: Where are we now? In A.M.B. de Groot & J.F. Kroll, eds., *Tutorials in bilingualism: Psycholinguistic perspectives,* pp. 19–51. Mahwah, NJ: Erlbaum.

Harris, B., & Sherwood, B. (1978). Translating as an innate skill. In D. Gerver & H. Sinaiko, eds., *Language interpretation and communication.* New York: Plenum Press.

Hasher, L., & Zacks, R.T. (1988). Working memory, comprehension, and aging: A review and a new view. In G.H. Bower, ed., *The psychology of learning and motivation,* vol. 22, pp. 193–225. San Diego: Academic Press.

Hasher, L., Zacks, R.T., & May, C.P. (1999). Inhibitory control, circadian arousal, and age. In D. Gopher & A. Koriat, eds., *Attention and performance,* vol. 17: *Cognitive regulation of performance: Interaction of theory and application,* pp. 653–675. Cambridge, MA: MIT Press.

Hauser, M. (1996). *The evolution of communication.* Cambridge, MA: MIT Press.

Haynes, M., & Carr, T.H. (1990). Writing system background and second language reading: A component skills analysis of English reading by native speaker-readers of Chinese. In T.H. Carr & B.A. Levy, eds., *Reading and its development,* pp. 375–421. New York: Academic Press.

Heath, S.B. (1982). Ethnography in education: Defining the essential. In P. Gilmore & A. Gilmore, eds., *Children in and out of school,* pp. 33–58. Washington, DC: Center for Applied Linguistics.

Heath, S.B. (1983). *Ways with words.* Cambridge: Cambridge University Press.

Henderson, L. (1984). *Orthography and word recognition in reading.* Hillsdale, NJ: Erlbaum.

Herman, J. (1996). "Grenouille, where are you?" Crosslinguistic transfer in bilingual kindergartners learning to read. Ph.D. dissertation. Harvard University.

Hermans, D., Bongaerts, T., de Bot K., & Schreuder, R. (1998). Producing words in a foreign language: Can speakers prevent interference from their first language? *Bilingualism: Language and Cognition, 1,* 213–229.

Hess, T.M. (1990). Aging and schematic influences on memory. In T.M. Hess, ed., *Aging and cognition: Knowledge organization and utilization,* pp. 93–160. Amsterdam: North-Holland.

Hirsh-Pasek, K., & Golinkoff, R.M. (1991). Language comprehension: A new look at some old themes. In N. Krasnegor, D. Rumbaugh, M. Studdert-Kennedy, & R. Schiefelbusch, eds., *Biological and behavioral aspects of language acquisition,* pp. 301–320. Hillsdale, NJ: Erlbaum.

Hirsh-Pasek, K., & Golinkoff, R.M. (1996). *The origins of grammar: Evidence from early language comprehension.* Cambridge, MA: MIT Press.

Hirsh-Pasek, K., Treiman, R., & Schneiderman, M. (1984). Brown and Hanlon revisited: Mother's sensitivity to ungrammatical forms. *Journal of Child Language, 11,* 81–88.

Hoffman, C. (1985). Language acquisition in two trilingual children. *Journal of Multilingual and Multicultural Development, 6,* 479–495.

Hultsch, D.F., & Dixon, R.A. (1990). Learning and memory in aging. In J.E. Birren & K.W. Schaie, eds., *Handbook of the psychology of aging,* 3rd ed., pp. 259–274. San Diego, CA: Academic Press.

Huttenlocher, J. (1974). The origins of language comprehension. In R.L. Solso, ed., *Theories in cognitive psychology: The Loyola symposium,* pp. 331–368. Potomac, MD: Erlbaum.

Hynd, G.W., & Scott, S.A. (1980). Propositional and appositional modes of thought and differential cerebral speech lateralization in Navaho Indian and Anglo children. *Child Development, 51,* 909–911.

Ianco-Worrall, A. (1972). Bilingualism and cognitive development, *Child Development, 43,* 1390–1400.

Jackendoff, R. (1990). *Semantic structures.* Cambridge, MA: MIT Press.

Jackendoff, R. (1997). *The architecture of the language faculty.* Cambridge, MA: MIT Press.

Jacoby, L.L. (1991). A process dissociation framework: Separating automatic from intentional uses of memory. *Journal of Memory & Language, 30,* 513–541.

Jacques, S., Zelazo, P.D., Kirkham, N.Z., & Semcesen, T.K. (1999). Rule selection and rule execution in preschoolers: An error-detection approach. *Developmental Psychology, 35,* 770–780.

Jakobsen, R. (1968). *Child language: Aphasia and phonological universals,* A.R. Keiler, Trans. The Hague: Mouton.

James, C., & Garrett, P. (1992). *Language awareness in the classroom.* London: Longmans.

Jarvis, L.H., Danks, J.H., & Merriman, W.E. (1995). The effect of bilingualism on cognitive ability: A test of the level of bilingualism hypothesis. *Applied Psycholinguistics, 16,* 293–308.

Jiménez, R.T., García, G.E., & Pearson, P.D. (1995). Three children, two languages, and strategic reading: Case studies in bilingual/monolingual reading. *American Educational Research Journal, 32,* 67–97.

Johnson, J.S., & Newport, E.L. (1989). Critical period effects in second language learning: The influence of maturational state on the acquisition of English as a second language. *Cognitive Psychology, 21,* 60–99.

Johnson, J.S., & Newport, E.L. (1991). Critical period effects on universal proper ties of language: The status of subjacency in the acquisition of a second language. *Cognition, 39,* 215–258.

Johnson, J., & Rosano, T. (1993). Relation of cognitive style to metaphor interpretation and second language proficiency. *Applied Psycholinguistics, 14,* 159–175.

Johnson, J., Prior, S., & Artuso, M. (2000). Field dependence as a factor in second language communicative production. *Language Learning, 50,* 529–567.

Johnson, J.M., Watkins, R.V., & Rice, M.L. (1992). Bimodal bilingual language development in a hearing child of deaf parents. *Applied Psycholinguistics, 13,* 31–52.

Juffs, A., & Harrington, M. (1995). Parsing effects in L2 sentence processing: Subject and object asymmetries in Wh-extraction. *Studies in Second-Language Acquisition, 17,* 483–516.

Kagan, J. (1966). Reflection-impulsivity: The generality and dynamics of conceptual tempo. *Journal of Abnormal Psychology, 71,* 17–24.

Karmiloff-Smith, A. (1992). *Beyond modularity: A developmental perspective on cognitive science.* Cambridge, MA: MIT Press.

Kasper, G. & Blum-Kulka, S. (1993). Interlanguage pragmatics: An introduction. In G. Kasper & S. Blum-Kulka, eds., *Interlanguage Pragmatics,* pp. 3–20. Oxford and New York: Oxford University Press.

Kemper, S. (1992). Language and aging. In F.I.M. Craik & T.A. Salthouse, eds., *The handbook of aging and cognition,* pp. 213–270. Hillsdale, NJ: Erlbaum.

Kent, R.D., & Miolo, G. (1995). Phonetic abilities in the first year of life. In P. Fletcher & B. MacWhinney, eds., *The handbook of child language,* pp. 303–334. Oxford: Blackwell.

Kessel, F., ed. (1988). *The development of language and language researchers: Essays in honor of Roger Brown.* Hillsdale, NJ: Erlbaum.

Kessler, C., & Quinn, M.E. (1980). Positive effects of bilingualism on science problem-solving abilities. In J.E. Alatis, ed., *Current issues in bilingual education: Proceedings of the Georgetown round table on languages and linguistics,* pp. 295–308. Washington, DC: Georgetown University Press.

Kessler, C., & Quinn, M.E. (1987). Language minority children's linguistic and cognitive creativity. *Journal of Multilingual and Multicultural Development, 8,* 173–186.

Kim, K.H.S., Relkin, N., Lee, K., & Hirsch, J. (1997). Distinct cortical areas associated with native and second languages. *Nature, 388,* 171–174.

Kimberg, D.Y., D'Esposito, M., & Farah, M.J. (1997). Effects of bromocriptine on human subjects depend on working memory capacity. *Neuroreport, 8,* 3581–3585.

Kimura, D. (1993). *Neuromotor mechanisms in human communication*. New York: Oxford University Press.

Kirsner, K., Smith, M.C., Lockhart, R.S., King, M.L., & Jain, M. (1984). The bilingual lexicon: Language specific units in an integrated network. *Journal of Verbal Learning and Verbal Behavior, 23,* 519–539.

Klein, D., Zatorre, R.J., Milner, B., Meyer, E., & Evans, A.C. (1995). The neural substrates of bilingual language processing: Evidence from positron emission tomography. In M. Paradis, ed., *Aspects of bilingual aphasia*, pp. 23–36. Oxford: Pergamon.

Klima, E., & Bellugi, U. (1979). *The signs of language*. Cambridge, MA: Harvard University Press.

Koda, K. (1989). Effects of L1 orthographic representation on L2 phonological coding strategies. *Journal of Psycholinguistic Research, 18,* 201–222.

Koda, K. (1990). The use of L1 reading strategies in L2 reading. *Studies in Second Language Acquisition, 12,* 393–410.

Koda, K. (1994). Second language reading research: Problems and possibilities. *Applied Psycholinguistics, 15,* 1–28.

Kolers, P. (1963). Interlingual word associations. *Journal of Verbal Learning and Verbal Behavior, 2,* 291–300.

Kroll, J.F. (1993). Accessing conceptual representation for words in a second language. In R. Schreuder & B. Weltens, eds., *The bilingual lexicon*, pp. 53–81. Amsterdam: John Benjamins.

Kroll, J.F. & De Groot, A.M.B. (1997). Lexical and conceptual memory in the bilingual: Mapping form to meaning in two languages. In A.M.B. de Groot & J.F. Kroll, eds., *Tutorials in bilingualism*, pp. 169–199. Mahwah, NJ: Erlbaum.

Kroll, J.F., & Stewart, E. (1994). Category interference in translation and picture naming: Evidence for asymmetric connections between bilingual memory representations. *Journal of Memory and Language, 33,* 149–174.

Kuhl, P.K., Williams, K.A., Lacerda, F., Stevens, K.N., & Lindblom, B. (1992). Linguistic experience alters phonetic perception in infants by 6 months of age. *Science, 255,* 606–608.

Lado, R. (1957). *Linguistics across cultures*. Ann Arbor: University of Michigan Press.

Lakoff, G. (1987). *Women, fire, and dangerous things: What categories reveal about the mind*. Chicago: University of Chicago Press.

Lakoff, G. (1991). Cognitive versus generative linguistics: How commitments influence results. *Language and Communication, 11,* 53–62.

Lalonde, C.E., & Werker, J.F. (1995). Cognitive influences on cross-language speech perception in infancy. *Infant Behavior and Development, 18,* 459–475.

Lambert, W.E., & Tucker, G.R. (1972). *Bilingual education of children: The St. Lambert experiment*. Rowley, MA: Newbury House.

Lambert, W.E., Havelka, J., & Crosby, C. (1958). The influence of language acquisition contexts on bilingualism. *Journal of Abnormal and Social Psychology, 56,* 239–244.

Langacker, R. (1986). An introduction to cognitive grammar. *Cognitive Science, 10,* 1–40.

Langacker, R. (1987). *Foundations of cognitive grammar,* vol. 1. Stanford: Stanford University Press.

Langacker, R. (1988). An overview of cognitive grammar. In B. Rudzka-Ostyn, ed., *Topics in cognitive linguistics,* pp. 4–48. Amsterdam: John Benjamins.

Langacker, R. (1991). *Foundations of cognitive grammar,* vol 2. Stanford: Stanford University Press.

Lanza, E. (1988). Language strategies in the home: Linguistic input and infant bilingualism. In A. Homen, E. Hansen, J. Gimbel, & J.N. Jorgensen, eds., *Bilingualism and the individual,* pp 69–84. Clevedon: Multilingual Matters.

Lanza, E. (1992). Can bilingual two-year-olds code-switch? *Journal of Child Language, 19,* 633–658.

Lazna, E. (1997). *Language mixing in infant bilingualism: A sociolinguistic perspective.* Oxford: Oxford University Press.

Lehmann, W. (1988). Review of "Foundations of cognitive grammar, vol. 1." *General Linguistics, 28,* 122–129.

Lemmon, C.R., & Goggin, J.P. (1989). The measurement of bilingualism and its relationship to cognitive ability. *Applied Psycholinguistics, 10,* 133–155.

Lenneberg, E.H. (1967). *Biological foundations of language.* New York: Wiley.

Leopold, W.F. (1939–49). *Speech development of a bilingual child: A linguist's record,* 4 vols. Evanston, IL: Northwestern University Press.

Leopold, W. (1954). A child's learning of two languages. *Fifth annual Georgetown University round table on languages and linguistics,* pp. 19–30. Washington, DC: Georgetown University Press.

Leopold, W.F. (1961). Patterning in children's language learning. In S. Sapporta, ed., *Psycholinguistics.* New York: Holt, Rinehart & Winston.

Levy, Y. (1985). Theoretical gains from the study of bilingualism: A case report. *Language Learning, 35,* 541–554.

Liberman, I.Y., & Liberman, A.M. (1990). Whole language vs. code emphasis: Underlying assumptions and their implications for reading instruction. *Annals of Dyslexia, 40,* 51–75.

Liberman, I.Y. & Shankweiler, D. (1991). Phonology and beginning to read: A tutorial. In L. Rieben & C. Perfetti, eds., *Learning to read: Basic research and its implications,* pp. 3–17. Hillsdale, NJ: Erlbaum.

Liberman, I.Y., Shankweiler, D., Liberman, A.M., Fowler, C., & Fischer, F.W. (1977). Phonetic segmentation and recoding in the beginning reader. In A.S. Reber & D. Scarborough, eds., *Toward a psychology of reading: The proceedings of the CUNY Conference,* pp. 207–225. Hillsdale: NJ: Erlbaum.

Lindholm, K.J., & Padilla, A.M. (1978). Language mixing in bilingual children. *Journal of Child Language, 5,* 327:335.

Locke, J.L. (1993). *The child's path to spoken language.* Cambridge, MA: Harvard University Press.

Locke, J.L. (1995). Development of the capacity for spoken language. In P. Fletcher & B. MacWhinney, eds., *The handbook of child language,* pp. 278–302. Oxford: Blackwell.

Long, M. (1990). Maturational constraints on language development. *Studies in second language acquisition, 12,* 251–285.

Lukatela, G., & Turvey, M.T. (1998). Reading in two alphabets. *American Psychologist, 53,* 1057–1072.

Lundberg, I., & Tornéus, M. (1978). Nonreaders' awareness of the basic relationship between spoken and written words. *Journal of Experimental Child Psychology, 25,* 404–412.

Luria, A.R. (1966). *Higher cortical functions in man.* London: Tavistock.

Macnamara, J. (1966). *Bilingualism and primary education.* Edinburgh: Edinburgh University Press.

Macnamara, J. (1967). The effect of instruction in a weaker language. *Journal of Social Issues, 23,* 121–135.

Macnamara, J., & Kushnir, S. (1971). Linguistic independence of bilinguals: The input switch. *Journal of Verbal Learning and Verbal Behavior, 10,* 480–487.

MacWhinney, B. (1991). *The CHILDES project: Tools for analyzing talk.* Hillsdale, NJ: Erlbaum.

MacWhinney, B. (1997). Second language acquisition and the competition model. In A.M.B. de Groot & J.F. Kroll, eds., *Tutorials in bilingualism,* pp. 113–142. Mahwah, NJ: Erlbaum.

MacWhinney, B., & Leinbach, A.J. (1991). Implementations are not conceptualizations: Revising the verb learning model. *Cognition, 29,* 121–157.

Mägistre, E. (1980). Arithmetical calculations in monolinguals and bilinguals. *Psychological Research, 42,* 363–373.

Malakoff, M., & Hakuta, K. (1991). Translation skill and metalinguistic awareness in bilinguals. In E. Bialystok, ed., *Language processing in bilingual children,* pp. 141–166. Cambridge: Cambridge University Press.

Mann, V.A. (1986). Phonological awareness: The role of reading experience. *Cognition, 24,* 5–92.

Marcus, G.F., Pinker, S., Ullman, M., Hollander, M., Rosen, T.J., & Xu, F. (1992). Overregularization in language acquisition. *Monographs of the Society for Research in Child Development, 57,* (no. 228, 4).

Markman, E.M. (1989). *Categorization and naming in children: Problems of induction.* Cambridge, MA: MIT Press.

Marler, P. (1984). Song learning: Innate species differences in the learning process. In P. Marler & H.S. Terrace, eds., *The biology of learning,* pp. 289–309. Berlin: Springer-Verlag.

Marler, P. (1991). The instinct to learn. In S. Carey & R. Gelman, eds., *The epigenesis of mind: Essays on biology and cognition,* pp. 37–66. Hillsdale, NJ: Erlbaum.

Marsh, L.G., & Maki, R.H. (1976). Efficiency of arithmetic operations in bilinguals as a function of language. *Memory and Cognition, 4,* 459–464.

Marx, M.H., & Kim, Y.C. (1990). Discovery of basic ordinality and cardinality by young preschoolers. *Bulletin of the Psychonomic Society, 28,* 461–463.

McBride-Chang, C. (1995). What is phonological awareness? *Journal of Educational Psychology, 87,* 179–192.

McClain, L., & Huang, J.Y.S. (1982). Speed of simple arithmetic in bilinguals. *Memory and Cognition, 10,* 591–596.

McClelland, J.L. & Rumelhart, D.E. (1986). *Parallel distributed processing: Ex-*

plorations in the microstructures of cognition, vol. 2: *Psychological and biological models.* Cambridge, MA: MIT Press.

McCune-Nicholich, L. (1981). The cognitive bases of relational words in the single-word period. *Journal of Child Language, 8,* 15–34.

McLaughlin, B. (1978). *Second language acquisition in childhood.* Hillsdale, NJ: Erlbaum.

McLeod, B., & McLaughlin, B. (1986). Restructuring or automaticity? Reading in a second language. *Language Learning, 36* (2), 109–123.

Meisel, J. (1986). Word order and case marking in early child language. Evidence from simultaneous acquisition of two first languages: French and German. *Linguistics, 24,* 123–183.

Meisel, J. (1989). Early differentiation of languages in bilingual children. In K. Hyltenstam & L. Obler, eds., *Bilingualism across the lifespan: Aspects of acquisition, maturity, and loss,* pp. 13–40. Cambridge: Cambridge University Press.

Meisel, J. (1990). Grammatical development in the simultaneous acquisition of two first languages. In J. Meisel, ed., *Two first languages: Early grammatical development in bilingual children,* pp. 5–22. Dordrecht: Foris.

Meisel, J.M. (1993). Simultaneous first language acquisition: A window on early grammatical development. *D.E.L.T.A., 9,* 353–385.

Meisel, J., ed. (1994). *Bilingual first language acquisition: French and German grammatical development.* Amsterdam: John Benjamins.

Menn, L., & Stoel-Gammon, C. (1995). Phonological development. In P. Fletcher & B. MacWhinney, eds., *The handbook of child language,* pp. 335–359. Oxford: Blackwell.

Merriman, W.F., & Bowman, L. (1989). The mutual exclusivity bias in children's word learning. *Monographs of the Society for Research in Child Development, 54* (nos. 3–4).

Merriman, W.E., & Kutlesic, V. (1993). Bilingual and monolingual children's use of two lexical acquisition heuristics. *Applied Psycholinguistics, 14,* 229–249.

Mestre, J.P. (1988). The role of language comprehension in mathematics and problem solving. In R.R. Cocking & J.P. Mestre, eds., *Linguistic and cultural influences on learning mathematics,* pp. 201–220. Hillsdale, NJ: Erlbaum.

Mikeš, M. (1990). Some issues of lexical development in early bi- and trilinguals. In G. Conti-Ramsden & C. Snow, eds., *Children's language,* vol. 7, pp. 103–120. Hillsdale, NJ: Erlbaum.

Miller, K., Zhang, H., & Zhang, D. (1999, April). How phonological awareness changes as children learn alphabetic scripts: A longitudinal study in China and the United States. In K. Miller, chair, *Learning to read in China and the United States: Identifying common and script dependent developmental processes,* symposium presented at the annual meeting of the Society for Research in Child Development, Albuquerque, NM.

Milner, B. (1975). Psychological aspects of focal epilepsy and its neurosurgical management. In D.P. Purpura, J.K. Penry, & R.D. Walters, eds., *Advances in neurology,* vol. 8: *Neurosurgical management of the epilepsies,* pp. 299–321. New York: Raven Press.

Morais, J. (1987). Phonetic awareness and reading acquisition. *Psychological Research, 49,* 147–152.

Morais, J., Alegria, J., & Content, A. (1987). The relationships between segmental analysis and alphabetic literacy: An interactive view. *Cahiers de Psychologie Cognitive, 7,* 415–438.

Morais, J., Bertelson, P., Cary, L. Alegria, J. (1986). Literacy training and speech segmentation. *Cognition, 24,* 45–64.

Morales, R.V., Shute, V.J. & Pellegrino, J.W. (1985). Developmental differences in understanding and solving simple mathematics word problems. *Cognition and Instruction, 2,* 41–57.

Morisset, C.M., Barnard, K.E., Greenberg, M.T., Booth, C.L., & Spieker, S.J. (1990). Environmental influences on early language development: The context of social risk. *Development and Psychopathology, 2,* 127–149.

Muller, N. (1990). Developing two gender assignment systems simultaneously. In J. Meisel, ed., *Two first languages: Early grammatical development in bilingual children,* pp. 193–234. Dordrecht: Foris.

Muller, N. (1998). Transfer in bilingual first language acquisition. *Bilingualism: Language and Cognition, 1,* 151–171.

Muter, V., Hulme, C., & Snowling, M. (1997). Segmentation, not rhyming, predicts early progress in learning to read. *Journal of Experimental Child Psychology, 65,* 370–396.

Myers-Scotton, C. (1997). Codeswitching. In F. Coulmas, ed., *Handbook of sociolinguistics,* pp. 217–237. Oxford: Blackwell.

Nagy, W.E., Garcia, G.E., Durgunoglu, A.Y., & Hancin-Bhatt, B. (1993). Spanish-English bilingual students' use of cognates in English reading. *Journal of Reading Behavior, 25,* 241–259.

Naiman, N., Frohlich, M., Stern, H.H., & Todesco, A. (1978). *The good language learner.* Toronto: Ontario Institute for Studies in Education.

Nantais, K.M., & Schellenberg, E.G. (1999). The Mozart effect: An artifact of preference. *Psychological Science, 10,* 370–373.

Nelson, K. (1973). Structure and strategy in learning to talk. *Monographs of the Society for Research in Child Development, 38* (1 and 2), no. 149.

Nelson, K. (1996). *Language in cognitive development: Emergence of the mediated mind.* New York: Cambridge University Press.

Neville, H.J. (1993). Neurobiology of cognitive and language processing: Effects of early experience. In M.H. Johnson, ed., *Brain development and cognition: A reader,* pp. 424–448. Oxford: Blackwell.

Neville, H.J., & Bavelier, D. (1999). Specificity and plasiticity in neurocognitive development in humans. In M.S. Gazzaniga, ed., *The new cognitive neurosciences,* 2nd ed., pp. 83–98. Cambridge, MA: MIT Press.

Neville, H.J., & Weber-Fox, C.M. (1994). Cerebral subsystems within language. In B. Albowitz, K. Albus, U. Kuhnt, H.-Ch. Northdurft, & P. Wahle, eds., *Structural and functional organization of the neocortex,* pp. 424–438. New York: Springer-Verlag.

Neville, H.J., Bavelier, D., Corina, D., Rauschecker, J., Karni, A., Lalwani, A., Braun, A., Clark, V., Jezzard, P., & Turner, R. (1998). Cerebral organization for language in deaf and hearing subjects: Biological constraints and effects of experience. *Proceedings of the National Academy of Science, 95,* 922–929.

Neville, H.J., Mills, D.L., & Lawson, D.S. (1992). Fractionating language:

Different neural subsystems with different sensitive periods. *Cerebral Cortex, 2,* 244–258.

Newport, E.L. (1991). Contrasting conceptions of the critical period for language. In S. Carey & R. Gelman, eds., *The epigenesis of mind: Essays on biology and cognition.* Hillsdale, NJ: Erlbaum.

Nicoladis, E. (1998). First clues to the existence of two input languages: Pragmatic and lexical differentiation in a bilingual child. *Bilingualism: Language and Cognition, 1,* 105–116.

Nicoladis, E., & Genesee, F. (1996). A longitudinal study of pragmatic differentiation in young bilingual children. *Language Learning, 46,* 439–464.

Nicoladis, E., & Genesee, F. (1998). Parental discourse and codemixing in bilingual children. *International Journal of Bilingualism, 2,* 85–99.

Ninio, A., & Bruner, J. (1978). The achievement and antecedents of labeling. *Journal of Child Language, 7,* 565–573.

Ninio, A., & Snow, C.E. (1996). *Pragmatic development.* Boulder, CO: Westview Press.

Noelting, G. (1980a). The development of proportional reasoning and the ratio concept: Part I – Differentiation of stages. *Educational Studies in Mathematics, 11,* 217–253.

Noelting, G. (1980b). The development of proportional reasoning and the ratio concept: Part II – Problem-structure at successive stages: Problem-solving strategies and the mechanism of adaptive restructuring. *Educational Studies in Mathematics, 11,* 331–363.

Oller, D.K., & Eilers, R., eds. (in press). *Language and literacy in bilingual children.* Clevedon, UK: Multilingual Matters.

Oller, D.K., Eilers, R.E., Pearson, B., Gathercole, V., Cobo-Lewis, A. & Umbel, V. (1997, April). Poster symposium, Language and Literacy in Bilingual Children, at the Biennial Meeting of the Society for Research in Child Development, Washington, DC.

Opoku, J.Y. (1992). The influence of semantic cues in learning among bilinguals at different levels of proficiency in English. In R.J. Harris, ed., *Cognitive processing in bilinguals,* pp. 175–189. Amsterdam: North Holland.

Oxford, R.L., & Ehrman, M. (1993). Second language research on individual differences. *Annual Review of Applied Linguistics, 13,* 188–205.

Padilla, A.M. (1990). Bilingual education: Issues and perspectives. In A.M. Padilla, H.H. Fairchild, & C.M. Valadez, eds., *Bilingual education: Issues and strategies,* pp. 15–26. Newbury Park, CA: Sage.

Padilla, A.M., & Lindholm, K. (1984). Child bilingualism: The same old issues revisited. In J.L. Martinez & R.H. Mendoza, eds., *Chicano psychology,* pp. 369–408. New York: Academic Press.

Papandropoulou, I., & Sinclair, H. (1974). What is a word? Experimental study of children's ideas on grammar. *Human Development, 17,* 241–258.

Paradis, J., & Genesee, F. (1996). Syntactic acquisition in bilingual children: Autonomous or interdependent? *Studies in Second Language Acquisition, 18,* 1–25.

Paradis, M. (1997). The cognitive neuropsychology of bilingualism. In A.M.B. De

Groot & J.F. Kroll, eds., *Tutorials in bilingualism: Psycholinguistic perspectives*, pp. 331–354. Mahwah, NJ: Erlbaum.

Paradis, M., ed. (1995). *Aspects of bilingual aphasia.* Oxford: Pergamon.

Pascual-Leone, J. (1969). *Water Level Test.* Toronto: York University.

Patkowski, M. (1994). The critical age hypothesis and interlanguage phonology. In M. Yavas, ed., *First and second language phonology*, pp. 205–221. San Diego: Singular Publishing Group.

Peal, E. & Lambert, W. (1962). The relation of bilingualism to intelligence. *Psychological Monographs, 76,* (Whole No. 546), 1–23.

Pearson, B.Z., & Fernández, S.C. (1994). Patterns of interaction in the lexical growth in two languages of bilingual infants and toddlers. *Language Learning, 44,* 617–653.

Pearson, B.Z., Fernández, S.C., Lewedeg, V., & Oller, D.K. (1997). The relation of input factors to lexical learning by bilingual infants. *Applied Psycholinguistics, 18,* 41–58.

Pearson, B.Z., Fernández, S.C., & Oller, D.K. (1993). Lexical development in bilingual infants and toddlers: Comparison to monolingual norms. *Language Learning, 43,* 93–120.

Pearson, B.Z., Fernández, S., & Oller, D.K. (1995). Cross-language synonyms in the lexicons of bilingual infants: One language or two? *Journal of Child Language, 22,* 345–368.

Penfield, W., & Roberts, L. (1959). *Speech and brain mechanisms.* Princeton, NJ: Princeton University Press.

Perani, D., Dehaene, S., Grassi, F., Cohen, L, Cappa, S.F., Dupoux, E., Fazio, F., & Mehler, J. (1996). Brain processing of native and foreign languages. *NeuroReport, 7,* 2439–2444.

Perfetti, C.A., Beck, I., Bell, L.C., & Hughes, C. (1987). Phonemic knowledge and learning to read are reciprocal: A longitudinal study of first grade children. *Merrill-Palmer Quarterly, 33,* 283–319.

Perfetti, C.A., Beck, I., Bell, L.C., & Hughes, C. (1988). Phonemic knowledge and learning to read are reciprocal: A longitudinal study of first grade children. In K.E. Stanovich, ed., *Children's reading and the development of phonological awareness*, pp. 39–75. Detroit: Wayne State University Press.

Perner, J., Stummer, S., & Lang, B. (1999). Executive functions and theory of mind: Cognitive complexity or functional dependence? In P.D. Zelazo, J.W. Astington, & D.R. Olson, eds., *Developing theories of intention: Social understanding and self-control*, pp. 133–152. Mahwah, N.J.: Erlbaum.

Perret, E. (1974). The left frontal lobe of man and the suppression of habitual responses in verbal categorical behavior. *Neuropsychologia, 12,* 323–330.

Petersen, J. (1988). Word-internal code-switching constraints in a bilingual child's grammar. *Linguistics, 26,* 479–493.

Petitto, L.A. (1997). In the beginning: On the genetic and environmental factors that make early language acquisition possible. In M. Gopnik, ed., *The inheritance and innateness of grammars*, pp. 45–69. New York: Oxford University Press.

Piaget, J. (1929). *The child's conception of the world.* New York: Harcourt, Brace, Jovanovich.

Pinker, S. (1984). *Language learnability and language development.* Cambridge, MA: Harvard University Press.

Pinker, S. (1989). Language acquisition. In M.I. Posner, ed., *Foundations of cognitive science,* pp. 359–399. Cambridge, MA: MIT Press.

Pinker, S. (1994). *The language instinct.* New York: W. Morrow.

Pinker, S. (1995). Language acquisition. In L.R. Gleitman & M. Liberman, eds., *Language: An invitation to cognitive science,* 2nd ed., vol. 1, pp. 135–182. Cambridge, MA: MIT Press.

Pinker, S. (1997). *How the mind works.* New York: Norton.

Pinker, S. & Prince, A. (1988). On language and connectionism: Analysis of a parallel distributed processing model of language acquisition. *Cognition, 28,* 73–193.

Plunkett, K. (1995). Connectionist approaches to language acquisition. In P. Fletcher & B. MacWhinney, eds., *The handbook of child language,* pp. 36–72. Oxford: Blackwell.

Plunkett, K., & Marchman, V. (1991). U-shaped learning and frequency effects in a multi-layered perceptron: Implications for child language acquisition. *Cognition, 38,* 1–60.

Poeppel, D. (1996). A critical review of PET studies of phonological processing. *Brain and Language, 55,* 317–351.

Pratt, C., & Nesdale, A.R. (1984). Pragmatic awareness in children. In W.E. Tunmer, C. Pratt, & M.L. Herriman, eds., *Metalinguistic awareness in children: Theory, research, and implications,* pp. 105–125. Berlin: Springer-Verlag.

Priestly, T.M.S. (1977). One idiosyncratic strategy in the acquisition of phonology. *Journal of Child Language, 4,* 45–66.

Prior, S.M. (1996). Contingencies in conversations: Sequential analysis of parent-child versus adult discourse. Ph.D. dissertation, York University.

Purcell-Gates, V. (1988). Lexical and syntactic knowledge of written narrative held by well-read-to kindergartners and second graders. *Research in the Teaching of English, 22,* 128–160.

Purcell-Gates, V. (1989). Written language knowledge held by low-SES, inner city children entering kindergarten. In S. McCormick & J. Zutell, eds., *Cognitive and social perspectives for literacy research and acquisition,* pp. 95–106. Chicago: National Reading Conference.

Pye, C. (1986). One lexicon or two? An alternative interpretation of early bilingual speech. *Journal of Child Language, 13,* 591–593.

Quay, S. (1995). The bilingual lexicon: Implications for studies of language choice. *Journal of Child Language, 22,* 369–387.

Rabinowitz, J.C. & Craik, F.I.M. (1986). Specific enhancement effects associated with word generation. *Journal of Memory and Language, 25,* 226–237.

Rampton, B. (1995). *Crossing: Language and ethnicity among adolescents.* New York: Longmans.

Rauscher, F.H., Shaw, G.L., & Ky, K.N. (1993). Music and spatial task performance. *Nature, 365,* 611.

Read, C., Zhang, Y., Nie, H., & Ding, B. (1986). The ability of manipulate speech sounds depends on knowing alphabetic writing. *Cognition, 24,* 31–44.

Redlinger, W.E., & Park, T.Z. (1980). Language mixing in young bilinguals. *Journal of Child Language, 3*, 449–455.

Ricciardelli, L.A. (1992). Bilingualism and cognitive development in relation to threshold theory. *Journal of Psycholinguistic Research, 21*, 301–316.

Ricciardelli, L.A. (1993). Two components of metalinguistic awareness: Control of linguistic processing and analysis of linguistic knowledge. *Applied Psycholinguistics, 14*, 349–367.

Rickard Liow, S.J., & Poon, K.K.L. (1998). Phonological awareness in multilingual Chinese children. *Applied Psycholinguistics, 19*, 339–362.

Rickard Liow, S.J., Green, D., & Tam, M.M.L-J. (1999). The development of visual search strategies in biscriptal readers. *International Journal of Bilingualism, 3*, 333–349.

Rieben, L., & Perfetti, C.A., eds., (1991). *Learning to read: Basic research and its implications.* Hillsdale, NJ: Erlbaum.

Ringbom, H. (1992). On L1 transfer in L2 comprehension and L2 production. *Language Learning, 42*, 85–112.

Roberts, M.H. (1939). The problem of the hybrid language. *Journal of English and Germanic Philology, 38*, 23–41.

Robertson, D.A., & Gernsbacher, M.A. (1998, November). fMRI Exploration of the cognitive process of mapping. Paper presented at the meeting of the Psychonomic Society, Dallas, Texas.

Romaine, S. (1995). *Bilingualism,* 2nd ed. Oxford: Blackwell.

Romaine, S. (1999). Bilingual language development. In M. Barrett, ed., *The development of language,* pp. 251–275. Hove, UK: Psychology Press.

Ronjat, J. (1913). *Le developpement du langage observe chez un enfant bilingue.* Paris: Champion.

Rosenblum, T., & Pinker, S.A. (1983). Word magic revisited: Monolingual and bilingual children's understanding of the word-object relationship. *Child Development, 54*, 773–780.

Rubin, H., & Turner, A. (1989). Linguistic awareness skills in grade one children in a French immersion setting. *Reading and Writing: An Interdisciplinary Journal, 1*, 73–86.

Rugg, M.D. (1999). Functional neuroimaging in cognitive neuroscience. In C.M. Brown & P. Hagoort, eds., *The neurocognition of language,* pp. 15–36. New York: Oxford University Press.

Rumelhart, D., & McClelland, J. (1986). *Parallel distributed processing: Explorations in the microstructure of cognition.* Cambridge, MA: Bradford Books.

Russell, James. (1996). *Agency: Its role in mental development.* East Sussex: Erlbaum.

Saer, D.J. (1923). The effects of bilingualism on intelligence. *British Journal of Psychology, 14*, 25–38.

Satz, P. (1979). A test of some models of hemispheric speech organization in the left- and right-handed. *Science, 203*, 1131–1133.

Saunders, G. (1982). *Bilingual children: Guidance for the family.* Clevedon, UK: Multilingual Matters.

Saxe, G.B. (1988). Linking language with mathematics achievement: Problems and prospects. In R.R. Cocking & J.P. Mestre, eds., *Linguistic and cultural influences on learning mathematics*, pp. 47–62. Hillsdale, NJ: Erlbaum.

Schneiderman, E., & Wesche, M. (1983). Right hemisphere participation in second language acquisition. In K. Bailey, M. Long, & S. Peck, eds., *Issues in second language acquisition: Selected papers of the Los Angeles second language research forum*. Rowley, MA: Newbury House.

Schnitzer, M.L., & Krasinski, E. (1994). The development of segmental phonological production in a bilingual child. *Journal of Child Language, 21*, 585–622.

Scovel, T. (1988). *A time to speak: A psycholinguistic inquiry into the critical period for human speech*. New York: Newbury House.

Scribner, S., & Cole, M. (1981). *The psychology of literacy*. Cambridge, MA: Harvard University Press.

Searle, J. (1992). *The rediscovery of the mind*. Cambridge, MA: MIT Press.

Secada, W.G. (1991). Degree of bilingualism and arithmetic problem solving in Hispanic first graders. *Elementary School Journal, 92*, 213–231.

Segalowitz, N. (1986). Second language reading. In J. Vaid, ed., *Language processing in bilinguals: Psycholinguistic and neuropsychological perspectives*, pp. 3–19. Hillsdale, NJ: Erlbaum.

Segalowitz, N. (1997). Individual differences in second language acquisition. In A.M.B. De Groot & J.F. Kroll, eds., *Tutorials in bilingualism*, pp. 85–112. Mahwah, NJ: Erlbaum.

Segalowitz, N., & Hebert, M. (1994). Phonological recoding in the first- and second-language reading of skilled bilinguals. In A.H. Cumming, ed., *Bilingual performance in reading and writing*, pp. 103–135. Ann Arbor, MI: John Benjamins.

Shannon, S.M. (1999). The debate on bilingual education in the U.S.: Language ideology as reflected in the practice of bilingual teachers. In J. Blommaert, ed., *Language ideological debates*, pp. 171–199. Berlin: Mouton de Gruyter.

Singleton, D. (1998). Age and the second language lexicon. *Studia Anglica Posnaniensia, 33*, 365–376.

Singleton, D. & Lengyel, Z., eds. (1995). *The age factor in second language acquisition: A critical look at the critical period hypothesis*. Clevedon: Multilingual Matters.

Skehan, P. (1989). *Individual differences in second-language learning*. London: Edward Arnold.

Skutnabb-Kangas, T. (1981). *Bilingualism or not*, L. Malmberg & D. Crane, trans. Clevendon and Avon, England: Multilingual Matters.

Slobin, D.I. (1982). Universal and particular in the acquisition of language. In L.R. Gleitman & H.E. Wanner, eds., *Language acquisition: The state of the art*, pp. 128–170. Cambridge: Cambridge University Press.

Slobin, D.I. (1985). *The crosslinguistic study of language acquisition*, vol. 1: *The data*. Hillsdale, NJ: Erlbaum.

Smith, C.L., & Tager-Flusberg, H. (1982). Metalinguistic awareness and language development. *Journal of Experimental Child Psychology, 34*, 449–468.

Smith, M.C. (1997). How do bilinguals access lexical information? In A.M.B. De

Groot & J.F. Kroll, eds., *Tutorials in bilingualism,* pp. 145–168. Mahwah, NJ: Erlbaum.

Snow, C.E. (1977). Mothers' speech research: From input to interaction. In C.E. Snow & C.A. Ferguson, eds., *Talking to children: Language input and acquisition,* pp. 31–49. Cambridge: Cambridge University Press.

Snow, C.E. (1983). Language and literacy: Relationships during the preschool years. *Harvard Educational Review, 53,* 165–189.

Snow, C.E. (1987). Relevance of the notion of a critical period to language acquisition. In M. Bornstein, ed., *Sensitive periods in development: Interdisciplinary perspectives,* pp. 183–209. Hillsdale, NJ: Erlbaum.

Snow, C.E. (1990). Rationales for native language instruction: Evidence from research. In A.M. Padilla, H.H. Fairchild, & C.M. Valadez, eds., *Bilingual education: Issues and strategies,* pp. 60–74. Newbury Park, CA: Sage.

Snow, C.E., & Ferguson, C.A., eds. (1977). *Talking to children: Language input and acquisition.* Cambridge: Cambridge University Press.

Snow, C.E., & Goldfield, B.A. (1983). Turn the page please: Situation-specific language acquisition. *Journal of Child Language, 10,* 551–569.

Snow, C.E., & Hakuta, K. (1992). The costs of monolingualism. In J. Crawford, ed., *Language loyalties: A source book on the Office English controversy,* pp. 384–394. Chicago: University of Chicago Press.

Snow, C.E., & Ninio, A. (1986). The contracts of literacy: What children learn from learning to read books. In W.H. Teale & E. Sulzby, eds., *Emergent literacy: Understanding reading and writing,* pp. 116–138. Norwood, NJ: Ablex.

Snow, C., & Tabors, P. (1993). Language skills that relate to literacy development. In B. Spodek & O.N. Saracho, eds., *Yearbook in early childhood education,* vol. 4: *Language and literacy in early childhood education,* pp. 1–20. New York: Teachers College Press.

Soares, C. (1982). Converging evidence for left hemisphere language lateralization: Monaural study. *Neuropsychologia, 20,* 653–659.

Sokolov, J.L. (1993). A local contingency analysis of the fine-tuning hypothesis. *Developmental Psychology, 29,* 1008–1023.

Sokolov, J., & Snow, C. (1994). *Handbook of research in language development using CHILDES.* Hillsdale, NJ: Erlbaum.

Sophian, C. (1988). Early developments in children's understanding of number: Inferences about numerosity and one-to-one correspondence. *Child Development, 59,* 1397–1414.

Spolsky, B. (1998). *Sociolinguistics.* Oxford: Oxford University Press.

Spolsky, B., & Shohamy, E. (1999). *The languages of Israel: Policy, ideology and practice.* Clevedon, UK: Multilingual Matters.

Stahl, S.A., & Murray, B.A. (1994). Defining phonological awareness and its relationship to early reading. *Journal of Educational Psychology, 86,* 221–234.

Stanovich, K.E., Cunningham, A.E., & Cramer, B.B. (1984). Assessing phonological awareness of kindergarten children: Issues of task comparability. *Journal of Experimental Child Psychology, 38,* 175–190.

Sternberg, R.J. (1985). *Beyond IQ: A triarchic theory of human intelligence.* New York: Cambridge University Press.

Stoel-Gammon C. (1985). Phonetic inventories, 15–24 months: A longitudinal study. *Journal of Speech Hearing Research, 28,* 505–512.

Stroop, J.R. (1935). Studies in interference in serial verbal reactions. *Journal of Experimental Psychology, 18,* 643–662.

Sulzby, E. (1986). Writing and reading: Signs of oral and written language organization in the young child. In W.H. Teale & E. Sulzby, eds., *Emergent literacy: Understanding reading and writing,* pp. 50–89. Norwood, NJ: Ablex.

Swain, M., & Lapkin, S. (1982). Evaluating bilingual education: A Canadian case study. Clevedon, England: Multilingual Matters.

Swain, M., & Wesche, M. (1975). Linguistic interaction: Case study of a bilingual child. *Language Sciences, 37,* 17–22.

Taeschner, T. (1983). *The sun is feminine: A study on language acquisition in bilingual children.* Berlin: Springer.

Teale, W.H. (1986). Home background and young children's literacy development. In W.H. Teale & E. Sulzby, eds., *Emergent literacy: Writing and reading,* pp. 173–206. Norwood, NJ: Ablex.

Teale, W.H., & Sulzby, E. (1986). Emergent literacy as a perspective for examining how young children become writers and readers. In W.H. Teale & E. Sulzby, eds., *Emergent literacy: Writing and reading,* pp. vii–xxv. Norwood, NJ: Ablex Publishing.

Tipper, S.P., & McLaren, J. (1990). Evidence for efficient visual selectivity in children. In J.T. Enns, ed., *The development of attention: Research and theory,* pp. 197–210. Elsevier Science Publishers.

Tipper, S.P., Bourque, T.A., Anderson, S.H., & Brehaut, J.C. (1989). Mechanisms of attention: A developmental study. *Journal of Experimental Child Psychology, 48,* 353–378.

Tolchinsky, L. (1998). Early writing acquisition in Catalan and Israeli communities. In A.Y. Durgunoğlu & L. Verhoeven, eds., *Literacy development in a multiligual context: Cross-cultural perspectives,* pp. 267–288. Mahwah, NJ: Erlbaum.

Tomasello, M. (1992). *First verbs: A case study of early grammatical development.* Cambridge: Cambridge University Press.

Tomasello, M., & Brooks, P.J. (1999). Early syntactic development: A construction grammar approach. In M. Barrett, ed., *The development of language,* pp. 161–190. Hove, UK: Psychology Press.

Tomasello, M., & Farrar, M.J. (1984). Cognitive bases of lexical development: Object permanence and relational words. *Journal of Child Language, 11,* 477–493.

Tomasello, M., Akhtar, N., Dodson, K., & Rekau, L. (1997). Differential productivity in young children's use of nouns and verbs. *Journal of Child Language, 24,* 373–388.

Trehub, S.E. (1976). The discrimination of foreign speech contrasts by infants and adults. *Child Development, 47,* 466–472.

Treiman, R., & Weatherston, S. (1992). Effects of linguistic structure on children's ability to isolate initial consonants. *Journal of Educational Psychology, 84,* 174–181.

Tunmer, W.E., & Herriman, M.L. (1984). The development of metalinguistic awareness: A conceptual overview. In W.E. Tunmer, C. Pratt, & M.L. Herriman, eds., *Metalinguistic awareness in children*, pp. 12–35. Berlin: Springer-Verlag.

Tunmer, W.E., & Myhill, M.E. (1984). Metalinguistic awareness and bilingualism. In W.E. Tunmer, C. Pratt, & M.L. Merriman, eds., *Metalinguistic awareness in children*, pp. 169–187. Berlin: Springer-Verlag.

Tunmer, W.E., & Rohl, M. (1991). Phonological awareness and reading acquisition. In D.J. Sawyer & J. Fox, eds., *Language and communication*, vol. 1: *Phonological awareness in reading*, pp. 2–30. New York: Springer-Verlag.

Turvey, M.T., Feldman, L.B., & Lukatela, G. (1984). The Serbo-Croatian orthography constrains the reader to a phonologically analytic strategy. In L. Henderson, ed., *Orthographies and reading*, pp. 81–89. London: Erlbaum.

Umbel, V.M., Pearson, B.Z., Fernandez, M.C., & Oller, D.K. (1992). Measuring bilingual children's receptive vocabularies. *Child Development, 63*, 1012–1020.

UNESCO. (1953). *The use of vernacular language in education*. Paris: UNESCO.

Uylings, H.B.M., Malofeeva, L.I., Bogolepova, I.N., Amunts, K., & Zilles, K. (1999). Broca's language areas from a neuroanatomical and developmental perspective. In C.M. Brown & P. Hagoort, eds., *The neurocognition of language*, pp. 319–336. New York: Oxford University Press.

Van Hell, J.G., & De Groot, A.M.B. (1998). Conceptual representation in bilingual memory: Effects of concreteness and cognate status in word association. *Bilingualism: Language and Cognition, 1*, 193–211.

Van Heuven, W.J.B., Dijkstra, T., & Grainger, J. (1998). Orthographic neighborhood effects in bilingual word production. *Journal of Memory and Language, 39*, 458–483.

Van Valin, R.D. (1991). Functionalist linguistic theory and language acquisition. *First Language, 11*, 7–40.

Vihman, M.M. (1985). Language differentiation by the bilingual infant. *Journal of Child Language, 12*, 297–324.

Vihman, M.M. (1992). Early syllables and the construction of phonology. In C.A. Ferguson, L. Menn, & C. Stoel-Gammon, eds., *Phonological development: Models, research, implications*, pp. 393–422. Timonium, MD: York Press.

Vocate, D.R. (1984). Differential cerebral speech lateralization in Crow Indian and Anglo children. *Neuropsychologia, 22*, 487–494.

Volterra, V., & Taeschner, T. (1978). The acquisition and development of language by bilingual children. *Journal of Child Language, 5*, 311–326.

Vygotsky, L.S. (1962). *Thought and language*. Cambridge, MA: MIT Press.

Vygotsky, L.S. (1978). *Mind in society*. Cambridge, MA: Harvard University Press.

Wagner, R.K., Torgesen, J.K., Laughon, P., Simmons, K., & Rashotte, C.A. (1993). Development of young readers' phonological processing abilities. *Journal of Educational Psychology, 85*, 83–103.

Wagner, R.K., Torgesen, J.K., & Rashotte, C.A. (1994). Development of reading-related phonological processing ability: New evidence of bidirectional causality from a latent variable longitudinal study. *Developmental Psychology, 30*, 73–87.

Wagner, R.K., Torgesen, J.K., Rashotte, C.A., Hecht, S.A., Barker, T.A., Burgess, S.R., Donahue, J., & Garon, T. (1997). Changing relations between phonological processing abilities and word-level reading as children develop from beginning to skilled readers: A 5-year longitudinal study. *Developmental Psychology, 33*, 468–479.

Wasow, T. (1989). Grammatical theory. In M.I. Posner, ed., *Foundations of cognitive science*, pp. 161–205. Cambridge, MA: MIT Press.

Weber-Fox, C.M., & Neville, H.J. (1996). Maturational constraints on functional specializations for language processing: ERP and behavioral evidence in bilingual speakers. *Journal of Cognitive Neuroscience, 8*, 231–256.

Wechsler, D. (1974). *Wechsler Intelligence Scale for Children, revised*. New York: Psychological Corporation.

Weinreich, U. (1968). *Languages in contact*, rev. ed. The Hague: Mouton, and New York: Linguistic Circle of New York, publication no. 2.

Wellman, H.M. (1990). *Child's theory of mind*. Cambridge, MA: MIT Press.

Wells, G. (1985). Preschool literacy-related activities and success in school. In D.R. Olson, N. Torrance, & A. Hildyard, eds., *Literacy, language and learning*, pp. 229–255. Cambridge, MA: Cambridge University Press.

Werker, J.F. (1995). Exploring developmental changes in cross-language speech perception. In L.R. Gleitman & M. Liberman, eds., *An invitation to cognitive science*, vol. 1: *Language*, pp. 87–106. Cambridge, MA: MIT Press.

Werker, J.F., & Tees, R.C. (1983). Developmental change across childhood in the perception of non-native speech sounds. *Canadian Journal of Psychology, 37*, 278–286.

Werker, J.F., & Tees, R.C. (1984). Cross-language speech perception: Evidence for perceptual reorganization during the first year of life. *Infant Behavior and Development, 7*, 49–63.

Werker, J.F., Gilbert, J.H.V., Humphrey, K., & Tees, R.C. (1981). Developmental aspects of cross-language speech perception. *Child Development, 52*, 349–353.

Werker, J.F., Pegg, J.E., & McLeod, P.F. (1994). A cross-language comparison of infant preference for infant-directed speech: English and Cantonese. *Infant Behavior and Development, 17*, 321–331.

Wexler, K., & Culicover, P. (1980). *Formal principles of language acquisition*. Cambridge, MA: MIT Press.

White, K.R. (1982). The relationship between socioeconomic status and academic achievement. *Psychological Bulletin, 91*, 461–481.

White, L. (1989). *Universal grammar and second language acquisition*. Amsterdam: John Benjamins.

Whorf, B. (1956). *Language, thought, and reality*. Cambridge, MA: MIT Press.

Willig, A.C. (1985). A meta-analysis of selected studies on the effectiveness of bilingual education. *Review of Educational Research, 55*, 269–317.

Wimmer, H., & Goswami, U. (1994). The influence of orthographic consistency on reading development: Word recognition in English and German children. *Cognition, 51*, 91–103.

Witkin, H.A., Dyk, R.B., Faterson, H.F., Goodenough, D.R., & Karp, S.A. (1962). *Psychological differentiation*. New York: Wiley.

Wong, S.-L.C. (1988). The language situation of the Chinese Americans. In S.L. McKay & S.-L.C. Wong, eds., *Language diversity problem or resource?*, pp. 193–228. New York: Newbury House Publishers.

Wuillemin, D., Richardson, B., & Lynch, J. (1994). Right hemisphere involvement in processing later-learned languages in multilinguals. *Brain and Language, 46,* 620–636.

Wynn, K. (1990). Children's understanding of counting. *Cognition, 36,* 155–193.

Wynn, K. (1992). Children's acquisition of the number of words and the counting system. *Cognitive Psychology, 24,* 220–251.

Yaden, D.B., & Templeton, S., eds. (1986). *Metalinguistic awareness and beginning literacy.* Portsmouth, NH: Heinemann.

Yelland, G.W., Pollard, J., & Mercuri, A. (1993). The metalinguistic benefits of limited contact with a second language. *Applied Psycholinguistics, 14,* 423–444.

Yopp, H.K. (1988). The validity and reliability of phonemic awareness tests. *Reading Research Quarterly, 23,* 159–177.

Zatorre, R.J. (1989). On the representation of multiple languages in the brain: Old problems and new directions. *Brain and Language, 36,* 127–147.

Zelazo, P.D., & Frye, D. (1997). Cognitive complexity and control: A theory of the development of deliberate reasoning and intentional action. In M. Stamenov, ed., *Language structure, discourse, and the access to consciousness,* pp. 113–153. Amsterdam & Philadelphia: John Benjamins.

Zelazo, P.D., Frye, D., & Rapus, T. (1996). An age-related dissociation between knowing rules and using them. *Cognitive Development, 11,* 37–63.

Index

WITHDRAWN

GUILDFORD **college**

Learning Resource Centre

Please return on or before the last date shown.
No further issues or renewals if any items are overdue.

2 9 NOV 2006   1 5 APR 2013

3 1 JAN 2007

1 9 MAY 2007

1 0 JUN 2008

1 5 OCT 2008
2 5 FEB 2009

_ 6 MAY 2009

_ 4 NOV 2009
2 1 OCT 2010

2 2 JAN 2013

Class: 404.2 BLA

Title: BILINGUALISM IN DEVELOPMENT

Author: BIALYSTOK, ELLEN

150197